IOWA

© Mapping Specialists

mobiltravelguide.com

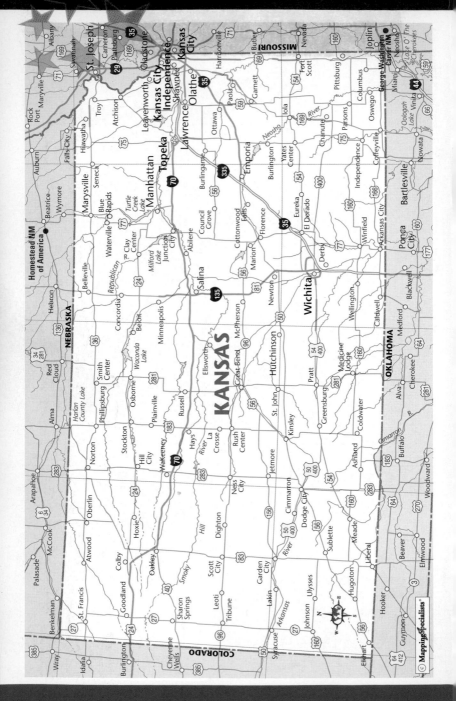

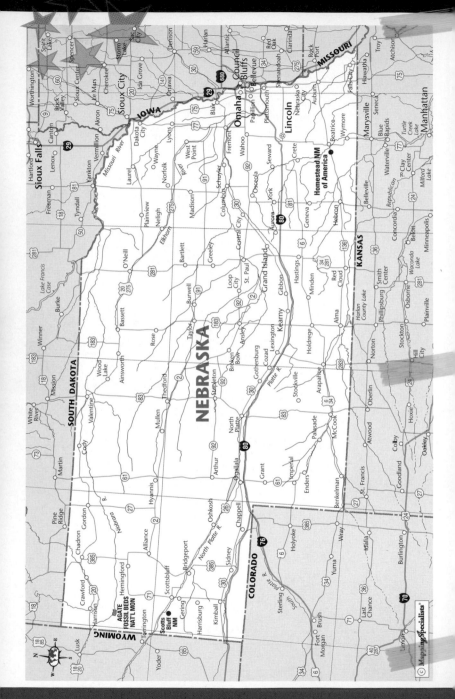

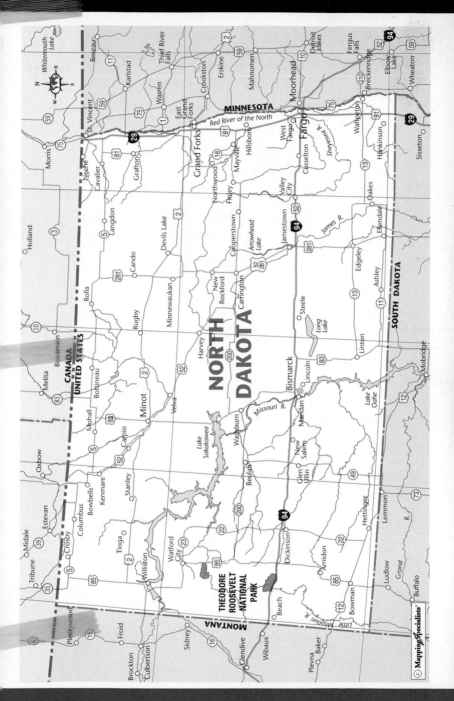

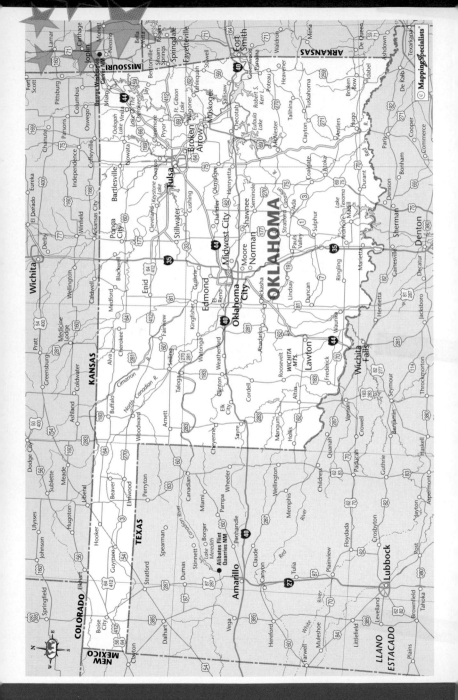

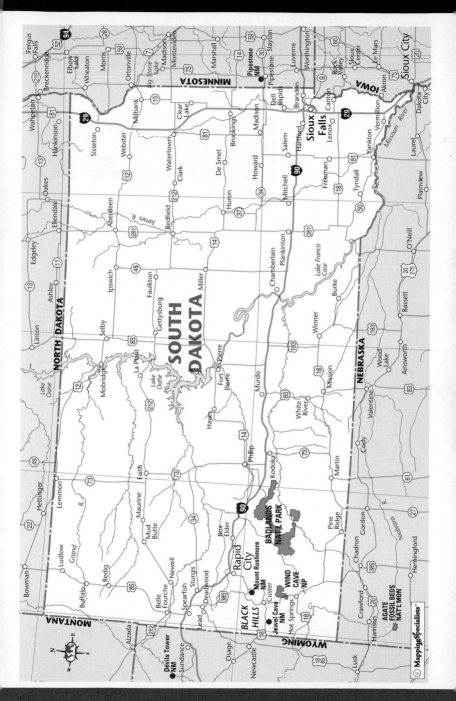

# *The* Center for Hospitality Research
Hospitality Leadership Through Learning

The Cornell School of Hotel Administration's
world-class faculty explores new ways
to refine the practice of hospitality
management.

Our research drives better results.
Better strategy.
Better management.
Better operations.

See our work at:
www.chr.cornell.edu

537 Statler Hall • hosp_research@cornell.edu • 607.255.9780

Cornell University
School of Hotel Administration

# GREAT PLAINS

# ACKNOWLEDGMENTS

We gratefully acknowledge the help of our representatives for their efficient and perceptive inspections of the lodging and dining establishments listed, the establishments' proprietors for their cooperation in showing their facilities and providing information about them, and the many users of previous editions who have taken the time to share their experiences. Mobil Travel Guide is also grateful to all the talented writers who contributed entries to this book.

Front and back cover images: ©iStockPhoto.com

All maps: created by Mapping Specialists

ISBN: 9-780841-60858-0          Manufactured in Canada

10 9 8 7 6 5 4 3 2 1

# TABLE OF CONTENTS

# WRITTEN IN THE STARS

Because time is precious and the travel industry is ever-changing, having accurate, reliable travel information at your fingertips has never been more important. With this in mind, Mobil Travel Guide has provided invaluable insight to travelers through its Star Rating system for more than 50 years.

The Mobil Corporation (known as Exxon Mobil Corporation since a 1999 merger) began producing the Mobil Travel Guide books in 1958 following the introduction of the U.S.-interstate highway system in 1956. The first edition covered only five Southwestern states. Since then, our books have become the premier travel guides in North America, covering all 50 states and Canada, and beginning in 2008, international destinations such as Hong Kong and Beijing.

Today, the concept of a "five-star" experience is one that permeates the collective conciousness, but few people realize it's one that originated with Mobil. We created our star rating system to give travelers an easy-to-recognize quality scale for choosing where to stay, dine and spa. Based on an objective process, we make recommendations to our readers that we believe will enhance the quality and value of their travel experiences. Our trusted Mobil One- to Five-Star rating system is the oldest and most respected lodging and restaurant inspection and rating program in North America. Most hoteliers, restaurateurs and industry observers favorably regard the rigor of our inspection program and understand the prestige and benefits that come with receiving a Mobil Star rating.

The Mobil Travel Guide process of rating each establishment includes unannounced inspections, incognito evaluations and a review of unsolicted comments from the general public. We inspect more than 500 attributes at each property we visit, from cleanliness to the condition of the rooms and public spaces, to employee attitude and courtesy. It's a system that rewards those properties that strive for and achieve excellence each year. And the very best properties raise the bar for those that wish to compete with them.

Only facilities that meet Mobil Travel Guide's standards earn the privilege of being listed in the guide. Properties are continuously updated, and deteriorating, poorly managed establishments are removed. We wouldn't recommend that you visit a hotel, restaurant or spa that we wouldn't want to visit ourselves.

★★★★★The Mobil Five-Star Award indicates that a property is one of the very best in the country and consistently provides gracious and courteous service, superlative quality in its facility and a unique ambience. The lodgings and restaurants at the Mobil Five-Star level consistently continue their commitment to excellence, doing so with grace and perseverance.

★★★★The Mobil Four-Star Award honors properties for outstanding achievement in overall facility and for providing very strong service levels in all areas. These award winners provide a distinctive experience for the ever-demanding and sophisticated consumer.

★★★The Mobil Three-Star Award recognizes an excellent property that provides full services and amenities. This category ranges from exceptional hotels with limited services to elegant restaurants with a less formal atmosphere.

★★The Mobil Two-Star property is a clean and comfortable establishment that has expanded amenities or a distinctive environment. These properties are an excellent place to stay or dine.

★The Mobil One-Star property is limited in its amenities and services but provides a value experience while meeting travelers' expectations. The properties should be clean, comfortable and convenient.

We do not charge establishments for inclusion in our guides. We have no relationship with any of the businesses and attractions we list and act only as a consumer advocate. We do the investigative legwork so that you won't have to.

Restaurants and hotels—particularly small chains and stand-alone establishments—change management or even go out of business with surprising quickness. Although we make every effort to continuously update information, we recommend that you call ahead to make sure the place you've selected is still open.

# STAR RATINGS

## MOBIL RATED HOTELS

Whether you're looking for the ultimate in luxury or the best bang for your travel buck, we have a hotel recommendation for you. To help you pinpoint properties that meet your needs, Mobil Travel Guide classifies each lodging by type according to the following characteristics.

★★★★★The Mobil Five-Star hotel provides consistently superlative service in an exceptionally distinctive luxury environment. Attention to detail is evident throughout the hotel, resort or inn, from bed linens to staff uniforms.

★★★★The Mobil Four-Star hotel provides a luxury experience with expanded amenities in a distinctive environment. Services may include automatic turndown service, 24-hour room service and valet parking.

★★★The Mobil Three-Star hotel is well appointed, with a full-service restaurant and expanded amenities, such as a fitness center, golf course, tennis courts, 24-hour room service and optional turndown service.

★★The Mobil Two-Star hotel is considered a clean, comfortable and reliable establishment that has expanded amenities, such as a full-service restaurant.

★The Mobil One-Star lodging is a limited-service hotel, motel or inn that is considered a clean, comfortable and reliable establishment.

For every property, we also provide pricing information. The pricing categories break down as follows:

$$\mathbf{\$} = \text{Up to } \$150$$

$$\mathbf{\$\$} = \$151\text{-}\$250$$

$$\mathbf{\$\$\$} = \$251\text{-}\$350$$

$$\mathbf{\$\$\$\$} = \$351 \text{ and up}$$

All prices quoted are accurate at the time of publication; however, prices cannot be guaranteed.

# MOBIL RATED RESTAURANTS

Every restaurant in this book has been visited by Mobil Travel Guide's team of experts and comes highly recommended as an outstanding dining experience.

★★★★★The Mobil Five-Star restaurant offers one of few flawless dining experiences in the country. These establishments consistently provide their guests with exceptional food, superlative service, elegant décor and exquisite presentations of each detail surrounding a meal.

★★★★The Mobil Four-Star restaurant provides professional service, distinctive presentations and wonderful food.

★★★The Mobil Three-Star restaurant has good food, warm and skillful service and enjoyable décor.

★★The Mobil Two-Star restaurant serves fresh food in a clean setting with efficient service. Value is considered in this category, as is family friendliness.

★The Mobil One-Star restaurant provides a distinctive experience through culinary specialty, local flair or individual atmosphere.

Because menu prices can fluctuate, we list a pricing category rather than specific prices. The pricing categories are defined as follows, per diner, and assume that you order an appetizer or dessert, an entrée and one drink:

$ = $15 and under

$$ = $16-$35

$$$ = $36-$85

$$$$ = $86 and up

# MOBIL RATED SPAS

Mobil Travel Guide's spa ratings are based on objective evaluations of hundreds of attributes. About half of these criteria assess basic expectations, such as staff courtesy, the technical proficiency and skill of the employees and whether the facility is clean and maintained properly. Several standards address issues that impact a guest's physical comfort and convenience, as well as the staff's ability to impart a sense of personalized service. Additional criteria measure the spa's ability to create a completely calming ambience.

★★★★★The Mobil Five-Star spa provides consistently superlative service in an exceptionally distinctive luxury environment with extensive amenities. The staff at a Mobil Five-Star spa provides extraordinary service beyond the traditional spa experience, allowing guests to achieve the highest level of relaxation and pampering. These spas offer an extensive array of treatments, often incorporating international themes and products. Attention to detail is evident throughout the spa, from arrival to departure.

★★★★The Mobil Four-Star spa provides a luxurious experience with expanded amenities in an elegant and serene environment. Throughout the spa facility, guests experience personalized service. Amenities might include, but are not limited to, single-sex relaxation rooms where guests wait for their treatments, plunge pools and whirlpools in both men's and women's locker rooms, and an array of treatments, including a selection of massages, body therapies, facials and a variety of salon services.

★★★The Mobil Three-Star spa is physically well appointed and has a full complement of staff.

# INTRODUCTION

If you've been a reader of Mobil Travel Guides, you may have noticed a new look and style in our guidebooks. Since 1958, Mobil Travel Guide has assisted travelers in making smart decisions about where to stay and dine. Fifty-one years later, our mission has not changed: We are committed to our rigorous inspections of hotels, restaurants and, now, spas, to help you cut through all the clutter, and make easy and informed decisions on where you should spend your time and budget. Our team of anonymous inspectors are constantly on the road, sleeping in hotels, eating in restaurants and making spa appointments, evaluating hundreds of standards to determine a property's star rating.

As you read these pages, we hope you get a flavor of the places included in the guides and that you will feel even more inspired to visit and take it all in. We hope you'll experience what it's like to stay in a guest room in the hotels we've rated, taste the food in a restaurant or feel the excitement at an outdoor music venue. We understand the importance of finding the best value when you travel, and making the most of your time. That's why for more than 50 years, Mobil Travel Guide has been the most trusted name in travel.

If any aspect of your accommodation, dining, spa or sightseeing experience motivates you to comment, please contact us at Mobil Travel Guide, 200 W. Madison St., Suite 3950, Chicago, IL 60606, or send an email to info@mobiltravelguide.com Happy travels.

# IOWA

PROBABLY MORE THAN ANY OTHER HEARTLAND STATE, IOWA CONJURES UP IMAGES OF table-top-flat cornfields dotted with silos and farmhouses. And while in some parts of the state you will indeed find yourself driving through a sea of corn that stretches to the horizon (Iowa grows more of it than any state but Illinois), with a bit of exploring, you'll find ski slopes, towering bluffs above the Mississippi River, six wildlife refuges—one harboring wetlands and fields that teem with birds during migration season, another that showcases Iowa's prairie heritage, with native grasses and wild flowers and the chance to encounter buffalo and elk, and another where you can climb up and down hills left untouched by the glaciers that chiseled and flattened the land elsewhere thousands of years ago.

The Sioux called Iowa the "Beautiful Land" and it's a name that fits. Every region of the state has a loop of Scenic Byways, well-marked routes that reveal the beauty of the countryside. Iowa has miles of bike trails, many built on the gentle grades of old railroad lines. Hikers can retreat into the tranquility of nature preserve trails that retrace historical journeys such as those of Louis and Clark or the Mormons as they moved west.

History abounds in Iowa. This is the birthplace of Buffalo Bill Cody, John Wayne and Herbert Hoover. In Des Moines, visitors to the State Historical Museum are greeted by a 16,000-year-old Hebior mammoth, while airplanes "buzz" overhead in the atrium. To the northeast, in Dubuque, freshwater creatures and habitats get their due, in the recently opened National River Museum and Aquarium. Down the road, in Eldon, see the house that inspired the background for Iowa native Grant Wood's most famous painting, "American Gothic." And in the southeast, the Amana colonies—seven historic villages formed by German immigrants as a religious communal society—offer attractions than can easily fill a day, or even a week.

You won't need a guidebook to discover Iowa's essential charm, the friendly character of people who are by heritage tied to the land and the value of work. To find this, sit down in a local café in a small town at lunchtime. Or, in the summer, make your way to one of the fairs held in each of the 99 counties. Buy yourself a corn dog and head to the agricultural barn where kids display their meticulously groomed cows, pigs and sheep. From the dedication and pride you'll see in these young people's faces, you'll learn what Iowa is about. www.iowa.gov/state/main/index.html.

**FUN FACTS**

Iowa's nickname, the Hawkeye state, is said to be a tribute to Chief Black Hawk, a Native American warrior in the War of 1812.

Iowa holds the first presidential caucus in January every election year, making it the benchmark for presidential races.

The state produces more ethanol that any other in the country.

Famous Iowans include John Wayne, Ashton Kutcher, Elijah Wood and Herbert Hoover.

## FROM THE BRIDGES OF MADISON COUNTY
## TO THE LOESS HILLS

Surrounded by wooded hills, Winterset, originally a Quaker settlement, is the hub of several short-side trips to the six covered bridges made famous by the Robert Waller's novel *The Bridges of Madison County*. If you want to make the full circuit, pick up a free brochure and map to all the bridges from local businesses (most are on remote county roads). If you don't have time for the full tour, one of the bridges is now preserved in Winterset's city park. The Madison County Historical Complex is an 18-acre park with a number of historic buildings, including a limestone barn and the old Winterset train depot.

Quaker-founded Winterset was a station along the Underground Railroad. A painted brick house, now in the Winterset Art Center, served as a temporary home for hundreds of displaced slaves during the 1850s and 1860s, including scholar George Washington Carver, who lived here after experiencing discrimination elsewhere in the Midwest. Winterset is also the birthplace of actor John Wayne, who was born Marion Robert Morrison. His family home is open to visitors.

Drive south on Highway 169 and turn west on Highway 34 to Creston, an old railroading center with an impressive core of late Victorian homes and storefronts. The town's McKinley Park houses the Union County Historical Museum, with remnants of Creston's heyday in the 1880s. Continue on Highway 34 to the village of Corning, once home to the Icarian Colony, the longest operating nonreligious utopian community in the United States. Founded in 1850, the 80-member community disbanded in 1900 after establishing vineyards, lilac hedges and stands of rhubarb in the area. (Rhubarb pie is still a favorite in local cafés.)

Follow Highway 34 across the prairies to Red Oak and then go south on Highway 59 to Shenandoah, originally a Mormon settlement. From Shenandoah, turn west on Highway 2 toward Sidney, a village in Iowa's famous Loess Hills. These green, heavily eroded hills were formed at the end of the last ice age. The Missouri River brought silt-rich waters from the north, where massive glaciers were busy grinding rock into till. As the silt deposits dried, winds blew the fine sand into dunes hundreds of feet high. Now covered with virgin prairie grasslands and upland forests, the Loess Hills are home to wildlife such as coyotes, deer, bald eagles and prairie dogs, and were considered for national park status during the Clinton administration.

While in Sidney, be sure to stop at the Penn Drug Store. Built in 1865, the store is still operated by the Penn family; it is the oldest family-owned business in the state and features an old-fashioned soda fountain. From Sidney, two scenic back roads, the Pleasant Overview Loop and the Spring Valley Loop, wind into the Loess Hills. *Approximately 205 miles.*

# ALGONA

Originally known as Call's Grove, this town later chose its present name, a shortened form of Algonquin. In its early days, a fort enclosed the town hall. After frontier hostilities subsided, this fort was torn down and the wood was used for a plank road.

*Information: Chamber of Commerce, 123 E. State St., 515-295-7201; www.algona.org*

## WHAT TO SEE AND DO
### AMBROSE A. CALL STATE PARK
*2007 Call Park Drive, Algona, 515-295-3669;*
*www.state.ia.us*
These 130 acres of rolling, timbered hills include hiking trails, a Frisbee golf course, picnic areas, a playground, 16 campsites and a log cabin lodge. Daily 4 a.m.-10:30 p.m. Camping.

### SMITH LAKE PARK
*1010 250th St., Algona, 515-295-2138;*
*www.co.kossuth.ia.us*
The 124 acres of this park include Smith Lake. Swimming, fishing, boating (electric motors only), picnicking, playgrounds, a hiking trail, camping and tree garden. Daily during daylight hours.

## HOTEL
### ★BURR OAK MOTEL
*Highway 169 S., Algona, 515-295-7213; 877-745-6315; www.burroakmotel.com*
40 rooms. Pets accepted; fee. Complimentary continental breakfast. $

## RESTAURANT
### ★★SISTER SARAH'S
*1515 N. McCoy St., 515-295-7757*
American menu. Lunch, dinner. Closed Sunday-Monday, holidays. Bar. Children's menu. Outdoor seating. $

★
★
★
★

# AMANA COLONIES
The history of this religious community goes back to the 1714 founding in Germany of the Inspirationists, a Lutheran separatist group. Members migrated to America and settled near Buffalo, New York. Later they bought 25,000 acres of prairie land in Iowa and moved west. Their first Iowa village was called Amana, a Biblical name meaning "remain faithful." Five more villages were built (West, High, Middle, East and South Amana). The village of Homestead was purchased outright so that the towns could use its railroad terminal.

At first, the members of the Amana Colonies lived a simple, communal life. Families were assigned living quarters with common kitchen and dining facilities and everything was shared equally. Farming was (and still is) a mainstay of the group. In 1932, common property was dissolved and redistributed on a stock basis. The new corporation, encouraging individual skills and vigor, prospered mostly because of the quality work of its artisans. Today, nearly every family owns its own house.
*Information: Amana Colonies Convention and Visitors Bureau, 622 46th Ave.,*
*Amana, 319-622-7622, 800-579-2294; www.amanacolonies.com*

## WHAT TO SEE AND DO
### AMANA HERITAGE SITES
*Highways 151 and 220, Amana, 319-622-3567; www.amanaheritage.org*
This community has a furniture factory that offers tours of the production area; a woolen mill with salesroom; woodworking shops, meat shop, general store, brewery,

wineries, restaurants and shops. The residence of the late Christian Metz, former leader of Amana Colonies, is here.

### AMANA HERITAGE MUSEUM

*4310 220th Trail, Amana, 319-622-3567*

Exhibits include a schoolhouse, crafts, lithographs and documents. An audiovisual presentation explains the history of the Amanas. April-November, Monday-Friday, 9 a.m.-4 p.m.

### OLD CREAMERY THEATRE COMPANY

*Price Creek Stage, 39 38th Ave., Amana, 319-622-6194,*
*800-352-6262, 319-622-6034; www.oldcreamery.com*

Professional theater company performs a variety of productions. April-mid-December, Wednesday-Sunday. Show and dinner.

## HOTELS

### ★★HOLIDAY INN

*2211 U. Ave., Williamsburg, 319-668-1175, 800-633-9244;*
*www.holiday-inn.com*

155 rooms. Pets accepted. Restaurant, bar. Fitness room. Indoor pool, children's pool, whirlpool. Little Amana complex is adjacent with an old-time general store and winery. **$**

### ★SUPER 8

*1708 N. Highland St., Williamsburg, 319-668-9718; www.super8.com*

33 rooms. Pets accepted, some restrictions; fee. Complimentary continental breakfast. Fitness room. Indoor pool, outdoor pool, whirlpool. **$**

## RESTAURANTS

### ★★BRICK HAUS

*728 47th Ave., Amana, 319-622-3278*

German, American menu. Breakfast, lunch, dinner. Closed holidays. Children's menu. Valet parking. Photos on the wall detail the history of village. **$$**

### ★★OX YOKE INN

*4420 220th Trail, Amana, 319-622-3441;*
*www.oxyokeinn.com*

German, American menu. Lunch, dinner, Sunday brunch. Bar. Children's menu. **$$**

### ★★RONNEBURG

*4408 220th Trail, Amana, 319-622-3641;*
*www.ronneburgrestaurant.com*

German, American menu. Breakfast, lunch, dinner, brunch. Bar. **$$**

### ★★ZUBER'S

*2206 45th Ave., Amana Colonies, 319-622-3911*

American menu. Lunch, dinner, Sunday brunch. Children's menu. Restored century-old inn. Baseball memorabilia. Accommodation. **$$**

**IOWA**

★
★
★
★
★

# AMES

Located near the geographical center of the state, Ames beats to the pulse of Iowa State University. The town is named in honor of a Massachusetts congressman, Oakes Ames, who was financially interested in a local railroad project.
*Information: Convention and Visitors Bureau, 1601 Golden Aspen Drive,*
*515-232-4032, 800-288-7470; www.visitames.com*

## WHAT TO SEE AND DO
### IOWA ARBORETUM
*1875 Peach Ave., Madrid, 515-795-3216; www.iowaarboretum.org*
This arboretum includes 340 acres of trees, shrubs and gardens. Trails, horticultural plantings, scenic overlooks, ravines, streams. Guided and self-guided tours; educational programs. Daily. 8:30 a.m.-4:30 p.m.

### IOWA STATE UNIVERSITY
*117 Beardshear Hall, Ames, 515-294-4777, 515-294-4111;*
*www.iastate.edu*
One of the oldest land-grant universities in the United States, founded in 1858, ISU is known for its spacious, green central campus with sculptures and fountains by artist Christian Petersen and for its many historic buildings. The school is also the birthplace of the electronic digital computer, built by John V. Atanasoff in the basement of the Physics Building in the late 1930s.

### FARM HOUSE
*290 Farm House Lane, Ames, 515-294-3342; www.museums.iastate.edu*
This 1860 house is a restored original residence on the Iowa State Agricultural College farm; period furnishings. September-May.

### GRANT WOOD MURALS
*Parks Library, Morrill Road, Ames*
Considered among the best works of this Iowa artist, the nine murals began as a Works Projects Administration project during the Great Depression. They depict various academic divisions of the school as well as the breaking of sod by pioneer farmers.

### MAMIE DOUD EISENHOWER BIRTHPLACE
*709 Carroll St., Boone, 515-432-1907; www.lmamiesbirthplace.homestead.com*
This one-story frame house includes period furnishings such as the bed in which Mamie Eisenhower was born. Summer kitchen, library, museum. June-October, daily; April-May, Tuesday-Sunday afternoons; also by appointment.

## HOTELS
### BAYMONT INN & SUITES
*1745 S.E. Marshall St., Boone, 515-296-2500, 866-999-1111;*
*www.baymontinns.com*
89 rooms. Pets accepted. Complimentary continental breakfast. Indoor pool, whirlpool. $

### ★★THE HOTEL AT GATEWAY CENTER

*2100 Green Hills Drive, Ames, 515-292-8600, 800-367-2637;*
*www.gatewayames.com*

188 rooms. Pets accepted. Restaurant, bar. Fitness room. Indoor pool, whirlpool. Airport transportation available. Business center. **$**

## RESTAURANTS
### ★HICKORY PARK

*1404 S. Duff, Ames, 515-232-8940; www.hickorypark-bbq.com*
American menu. Lunch, dinner. Children's menu. **$$**

### ★LUCULLANS

*400 Main St., Ames, 515-232-8484; www.lucullans.com*
Italian menu. Lunch, dinner. Bar. Children's menu. **$$**

# ATLANTIC

This small Southwestern Iowa town has several preserved buildings, including the historic Rock Island Depot, which houses the Chamber of Commerce.
*Information: Chamber of Commerce, 614 Chestnut St.,*
*712-243-3017, 877-283-2124; www.atlanticiowa.com*

## WHAT TO SEE AND DO
### DANISH WINDMILL

*4038 Main St., Elk Horn, 712-764-7472; www.danishwindmill.com*
Built in Denmark in 1848, this 60-foot-high working windmill was dismantled and shipped to Elk Horn where it was reassembled by community volunteers. Daily.

## HOTEL
### ★SUPER 8

*1902 E. Seventh St., Atlantic, 712-243-4723, 888-243-2378; www.super8.com*
59 rooms. Complimentary continental breakfast. Pets allowed. High-speed Internet access. Pool. Fitness center. **$**

## SPECIALTY LODGING
### CHESTNUT CHARM BED AND BREAKFAST

*1409 Chestnut St., Atlantic, 712-243-5652; www.chestnutcharm.org*
At this Victorian inn, built in 1898, there are guest rooms as well as cozy carriage houses. Nine rooms. No children allowed. Complimentary full breakfast. No pets accepted. **$**

# BETTENDORF

Bettendorf began as a quiet rural village called Gilbert. In 1903, the town's future changed with the arrival of the Bettendorf Axle and Wagon Company, which became the largest manufacturer of railroad cars west of the Mississippi. The growing city changed its name in honor of the company. Today Bettendorf, on the Mississippi River, is part of the Quad Cities metropolitan area.
*Information: Quad Cities Convention and Visitors Bureau,*
*102 S. Harrison St., Davenport, 563-322-3911, 800-747-7800;*
*www.quadcities.com*

**15**

**IOWA**

## WHAT TO SEE AND DO

### BUFFALO BILL CODY HOMESTEAD

*28050 230th Ave., Princeton, 563-225-2981; www.scottcountyiowa.com*

Restored boyhood home of Buffalo Bill Cody, built by his father in 1847. Buffalo are on the grounds. April-October, daily 9 a.m.-5 p.m.

### FAMILY MUSEUM OF ARTS & SCIENCE

*2900 Learning Campus Drive, Bettendorf, 563-344-4106; www.familymuseum.org*

This museum features hands-on exhibits as well as a traveling exhibit gallery. Daily. Monday-Thursday 9 a.m.-8 p.m.; Friday-Saturday 9 a.m.-5 p.m.; Sunday noon-5 p.m.

### ISLE OF CAPRI CASINO

*1777 Isle Parkway, Bettendorf, 563-359-7280, 800-724-5825; www.isleofcapricasino.com*

Casino gambling, restaurant, gift shop, lodging. Valet parking.

## HOTELS

### ★★HOLIDAY INN

*909 Middle Road, Bettendorf, 563-355-4761, 800-626-0780; www.holiday-inn.com*

150 rooms. Restaurant, bar. Fitness room. Indoor pool. Airport transportation available. Kids eat free. **$**

### ★★THE LODGE

*900 Spruce Hills Drive, Bettendorf, 563-359-7141, 800-285-8637; www.lodgehotel.com*

210 rooms. Restaurant, bar. High-speed Internet access. Fitness room. Indoor pool, outdoor pool, whirlpool. Spa. Airport transportation available. Pets accepted, some restrictions; fee. **$**

### ★RAMADA BETTENDORF/DAVENPORT

*3020 Utica Ridge Road, Bettendorf, 563-355-7575; www.ramada.com*

119 rooms. Complimentary full breakfast. High speed Internet access. Fitness room. Outdoor pool. Airport transportation available. Business center. Pets accepted. **$**

## SPECIALTY LODGING

### ABBEY HOTEL

*1401 Central Ave., Bettendorf, 563-355-0291, 800-438-7535; www.theabbeyhotel.com*

This Romanesque hotel, once a monastery, overlooks the Mississippi River and is surrounded by gardens and landscaping. 19 rooms. Complimentary full breakfast. Bar. High-speed Internet access. Fitness room. Outdoor pool. Airport transportation available. **$**

## RESTAURANTS

### ★★★THE FAITHFUL PILOT CAFÉ

*117 N. Cody Road, Le Claire, 563-289-4156; www.faithfulpilotcafe.com*

This restaurant features progressive American cuisine served in an elegant, modern dining room. Menu highlights include rack of lamb over minted wild rice and grilled beef tenderloin with rosemary potatoes. Monday-Thursday 5-9 p.m.; Friday and Saturday 5-10 p.m.; Sunday brunch 9:30 a.m.-1:30 p.m. American menu. Dinner. **$$**

### ★★★THE LODGE RESTAURANT
*900 Spruce Hills Drive, Bettendorf, 563-359-1607; www.lodgehotel.com*
This restaurant features an American and German menu. Specialties include Regensburg goulash, chicken von jumer and rack of lamb. American, German menu. Lunch, dinner. Bar. Children's menu. **$$**

### ★★STUBBS EDDY RESTAURANT/PUB
*1716 State St., Bettendorf, 563-355-0073*
American menu. Breakfast, lunch, dinner, late-night. Bar. Children's menu. **$$$**

# BURLINGTON

Burlington, a river port, is a shopping, industrial and farm center. It traces its history back to the days when it was called Flint Hills by Native Americans and served as neutral ground where tribes hunted flint for implements. Zebulon Pike raised the Stars and Stripes here in 1805, and a trading post was built in 1808. The city became capital of the Wisconsin Territory in 1837, then capital of the Iowa Territory from 1838 to 1840.

*Information: Convention and Tourism Bureau, 807 Jefferson St.,*
*319-752-6365, 800-827-4837; www.visit.burlington.ia.us*

## WHAT TO SEE AND DO
### APPLE TREES HISTORICAL MUSEUM
*501 N. Fourth St., Burlington, 319-753-2449; www.dmchs.org*
The museum, a remaining wing of railroad magnate Charles E. Perkins's mansion, contains Victorian furnishings, antique tools, costumes, dolls, toys, buttons, glass and china. The museum is maintained by the Des Moines County Historical Society. Guided tours, May-October: weekends 1:30-4:30 p.m.; by appointment Monday-Friday.

### HAWKEYE LOG CABIN
*501 N. Fourth St., Burlington, 319-753-2449; www.dmchs.org*
Replica of a pioneer cabin with antique furnishings and tools. Guided tours, May-September, by appointment Monday-Friday; Saturday-Sunday 1:30-4:30 p.m.

### HERITAGE HILL NATIONAL HISTORIC DISTRICT
*Washington and High streets, Burlington*
This 29-square-block area contains churches, mansions and houses in a wide variety of architectural styles, including a full range of Victorian buildings from the 1870s to the turn of the century. Walking tours and brochures available. Contact the Convention & Tourism Bureau.

### PHELPS HOUSE
*501 N. Fourth St., Burlington, 319-753-2449; www.dmchs.org*
This mansard-roofed, Italianate Victorian mansion has original furnishings used by three generations of the Phelps family. Also inside is an extensive collection of rare china and family portraits. Guided tours, May-October, by appointment Monday-Friday; Saturday-Sunday 1:30-4:30 p.m.

### SNAKE ALLEY

*Sixth Street, Burlington; www.snakealley.com*

The zigzagging brick-paved street, built in 1894, is, according to *Ripley's Believe It or Not*, the "crookedest street in the world."

## SPECIAL EVENT
### BURLINGTON STEAMBOAT DAYS AND THE AMERICAN MUSIC FESTIVAL

*200 N. Front St., Burlington, 319-754-4334;*
*www.steamboatdays.com*

Athletic competitions, fireworks, midway, parade, name entertainment. Mid-June. Carnivals. Golf.

## HOTELS
### ★★BEST WESTERN PZAZZ MOTOR INN

*3001 Winegard Drive, Burlington, 319-753-2223, 800-373-1223;*
*www.bestwestern.com*

151 rooms. Pets accepted. Restaurant, bar. Fitness room. Indoor pool, whirlpool. Airport transportation available. $

### ★QUALITY INN

*3051 Kirkwood, Burlington, 319-753-0000; www.choicehotels.com*

52 rooms. Pets accepted, some restrictions; fee. Complimentary continental breakfast. Outdoor pool. $

# CARROLL

This town is named for Charles Carroll, a signer of the Declaration of Independence.
*Information: Chamber of Commerce, 223 W. Fifth St.,*
*712-792-4383, 866-586-4383; www.carrolliowa.com*

## WHAT TO SEE AND DO
### BLACK HAWK STATE PARK

*228 S. Blossom St., Lake View, 712-657-8712; www.iowadnr.gov/parks*

This park consists of 86 acres along 925-acre Black Hawk Lake. Swimming, fishing, boating, snowmobiling, picnicking, camping. Standard hours, fees.

### WAR MEMORIAL MONUMENTS

*E. First Street, Carroll*

Located here is a monument for each war beginning with the Civil War and ending with Desert Storm.

## HOTEL
### ★★CARROLLTON INN

*1730 N. U.S. Highway 71, Carroll, 712-792-5600, 877-798-3535;*
*www.carrolltoninn.com*

86 rooms. Restaurant, bar. Indoor pool, whirlpool. Pets not allowed. $

# CEDAR FALLS

Once one of the most important milling centers in the state, today Cedar Falls is a university town, home to the University of Northern Iowa.

*Information: Tourism and Visitors Bureau, 10 Main St.,*
*319-268-4266, 800-845-1955; www.cedarfallstourism.org*

## WHAT TO SEE AND DO
### CEDAR FALLS HISTORICAL SOCIETY VICTORIAN HOME MUSEUM
*308 W. Third St., Cedar Falls, 319-266-5149; www.cedarfallshistorical.org*
This Victorian house is furnished in period style. The Carriage House Museum contains a library, archives, fashions, Lenoir train exhibit and memorabilia of the first permanent settlement in Black Hawk County. Wednesday-Saturday 10 a.m.-4 p.m., Sunday 1-4 p.m.

### GEORGE WYTH HOUSE
*303 Franklin St., Cedar Falls, 319-266-5149;*
*www.cedarfallshistorical.org*
The residence of George Wyth, founder of the Viking Pump Company, was built in 1907. It's now furnished in the Art Deco style of the 1920s and includes pieces by Gilbert Rhode. The Viking Pump Company museum is housed on the third floor. Tours, May-September, Sunday afternoons; also by appointment.

### LITTLE RED SCHOOL
*First and Clay streets, Cedar Falls, 319-266-5149;*
*www.cedarfallshistorical.org/little_Red.htm*
This country school has been authentically furnished to reflect turn-of-the-century education. May-October, Wednesday and Saturday-Sunday afternoons.

### UNIVERSITY OF NORTHERN IOWA
*1222 W. 27th St., Cedar Falls, 319-273-2311, 319-273-2838; www.uni.edu*
This campus of 14,000 students, founded in 1876, features a campanile built in Italian Renaissance style that chimes daily. Also on campus is a museum with exhibits on geology and natural history.

## SPECIAL EVENT
### CEDAR FALLS MUNICIPAL BAND
*Overman Park, Second and Franklin streets, Cedar Falls, 319-266-1253;*
*www.cedarnet.org/cfband*
The Cedar Falls Municipal Band, the oldest concert band in the state, entertains crowds each summer outdoors at a modern band shell. Bring a lawn chair or blanket and relax as these 45 musicians perform. Tuesday evenings, June-August.

## HOTEL
### ★★HOLIDAY INN
*5826 University Ave., Cedar Falls, 319-277-2230; www.holiday-inn.com*
181 rooms. High-speed Internet access. Restaurant, bar. Fitness room. Indoor pool, outdoor pool, whirlpool. Airport transportation available. Kids eat free. **$**

**19**

**IOWA**

★
★
★
★
★

## RESTAURANT

### ★★OLDE BROOM FACTORY

*125 W. First St., Cedar Falls, 319-268-0877; www.thebroomfactory.com*
American menu. Lunch, dinner, Sunday brunch. Bar. Children's menu. Structure built in 1862. Valet parking. $$

# CEDAR RAPIDS

Cedar Rapids, located at the rapids of the Cedar River, is the industrial leader of the state.

*Information: Cedar Rapids Area Convention and Visitors Bureau,*
*119 First Ave. S.E., 319-398-5009, 800-735-5557;*
*www.cedar-rapids.com, www.carrolliowa.com*

## WHAT TO SEE AND DO

### BRUCEMORE

*2160 Linden Drive S.E., Cedar Rapids, 319-362-7375; www.brucemore.org*
A Queen Anne-style 21-room mansion built in 1886, this house includes a visitor center, gift and flower shops, formal gardens, lawns, orchard and pond. The sunroom was decorated by native artist Grant Wood. The estate serves as a community cultural center. February-December, Tuesday-Saturday 10 a.m.-3 p.m.; Sunday noon-3 p.m.

### CEDAR RAPIDS MUSEUM OF ART

*410 Third Ave. S.E., Cedar Rapids, 319-366-7503; www.crma.org*
Housed here is an extensive collection of works by Grant Wood, Marvin Cone and Mauricio Lasansky. Children 7 and under free. Tuesday-Saturday 10 a.m.-4 p.m., Thursday 10 a.m.-8 p.m., Sunday noon-4 p.m.; closed Monday and holidays.

### CZECH VILLAGE

*48 16th Ave. S.W., Cedar Rapids, 319-362-2846; www.czechvillageiowa.com*
A bakery, meat market, gift shops, restaurants and historic structures preserving Czech heritage are featured here.

### INDIAN CREEK NATURE CENTER

*6665 Otis Road S.E., Cedar Rapids, 319-362-0664;*
*www.indiancreeknaturecenter.org*
On this 210-acre nature preserve is an observatory and museum offering changing exhibits in a remodeled dairy barn. Hiking trails. Monday-Friday; closed holidays.

### MASONIC LIBRARY

*813 First Ave. S.E., Cedar Rapids, 319-365-1438; www.gl-iowa.org*
This library houses the most complete Masonic collection in the United States. The building is a Vermont-marble structure with bas-relief decoration and stained-glass windows. Tours. Monday-Friday.

### NATIONAL CZECH AND SLOVAK MUSEUM AND LIBRARY

*30 16th Ave. S.W., Cedar Rapids, 319-362-8500; www.ncsml.org*
This museum houses a large collection of folk costumes. Permanent and changing exhibits; museum grounds include restored immigrant home. Tours. Daily.

## PALISADES-KEPLER STATE PARK

*700 Kepler Drive, Mount Vernon, 319-895-6039; www.iowadnr.gov/parks*

This 970-acre park includes limestone palisades that rise 75 feet above the Cedar River; timbered valleys, wildflowers. Fishing, boating; nature and hiking trails, snowmobiling; picnicking, lodge, camping, cabins. Standard hours.

## PARAMOUNT THEATRE

*123 Third Ave. S.E., Cedar Rapids, 319-398-5211; www.uscellularcenter.com*

A restored theater built in the 1920s, the Paramount hosts stage productions, films, Broadway series and is the home of the Cedar Rapids Symphony.

## SCIENCE STATION

*427 First St. S.E., Cedar Rapids, 319-363-4629;*
*www.sciencestation.org*

Science and technology museum features unusual hands-on exhibits including a working hot air balloon and giant kaleidoscope. Tuesday-Sunday.

## US CELLULAR CENTER

*370 First Ave. N.E., Cedar Rapids, 319-398-5211;*
*www.uscellularcenter.com*

This 10,000-seat entertainment center features sports events, concerts, exhibits, rodeos, ice shows and more.

# SPECIAL EVENTS
### FREEDOM FESTIVAL

*Cedar Rapids Freedom Festival, 1857 Second Ave. S.E., Cedar Rapids,*
*319-365-8313; www.freedomfestival.com*

Eighty events for all ages are held citywide, topped off by a large fireworks display. Two weeks preceding and including July 4.

**IOWA**

### HOUBY DAYS

*30 16th Ave. S.W., Czech Village, Cedar Rapids, 319-362-8500*

Features Czech fine arts, folk arts and customs, music, dancing, food; mushroom hunt contests, races. Weekend after Mother's Day.

★
★
★
★
★

# HOTELS
### ★★BEST WESTERN COOPER'S MILL HOTEL

*100 F Ave. N.W., Cedar Rapids, 319-366-5323, 800-858-5511;*
*www.bestwestern.com*

86 rooms. Pets accepted; fee. Restaurant, bar. High-speed Internet access. Complimentary break fast. Pool. **$**

### ★COMFORT INN

*5055 Rockwell Drive, Cedar Rapids, 319-393-8247, 800-228-5150;*
*www.comfortinn.com*

59 rooms. Pets accepted, some restrictions. Complimentary continental breakfast. High-speed Internet access. Free local calls. **$**

### ★COMFORT INN

*390 33rd Ave. S.W., Cedar Rapids, 319-363-7934, 800-228-5150;*
*www.comfortinn.com*
60 rooms. Pets accepted, some restrictions. Complimentary continental breakfast. High-speed Internet access. Fitness room. **$**

### ★★★CROWNE PLAZA

*350 First Ave. N.E., Cedar Rapids, 319-363-8161, 800-227-6963;*
*www.crowneplaza.com*
Located in downtown Cedar Rapids, this hotel is near shopping, restaurants, and entertainment 275 rooms. Restaurant, bar. Fitness room. Indoor pool, whirlpool. Airport transportation available. Business center. **$**

### ★HAMPTON INN

*3265 Sixth St. S.W., Cedar Rapids, 319-364-8144, 800-426-7866;*
*www.hamptoninn.com*
106 rooms. Complimentary continental breakfast. Bar. Fitness room. Indoor pool, whirlpool. Restaurant. **$**

### ★★MARRIOTT CEDAR RAPIDS

*1200 Collins Road N.E., Cedar Rapids, 319-393-6600; www.marriott.com*
221 rooms. Restaurant, bar. Fitness room. Indoor pool, whirlpool. Airport transportation available. Business center. High-speed Internet access. Unlimited local calls. **$**

# CHEROKEE

Center of one of the heaviest cattle feeding and hog-raising areas of Iowa, Cherokee is home to many processing and manufacturing plants. The Cherokee Community Center houses a symphony orchestra and an active community theater.
*Information: Chamber of Commerce, 228 W. Main St.,*
*712-225-6414; www.cherokeeiowa.net*

## WHAT TO SEE AND DO
### SANFORD MUSEUM AND PLANETARIUM

*117 E. Willow St., Cherokee, 712-225-3922; www.sanfordmuseum.org*
Natural history, science and changing exhibits. Classes (by appointment); planetarium programs (last Sunday of month; also by appointment). Daily.

## SPECIAL EVENTS
### CHEROKEE COUNTY FAIR

*416 W. Main St., Cherokee, 712-225-6414; www.cherokeechamber.com*
Features a demolition derby and team dance competition. Early July.

### CHEROKEE RODEO

*Cherokee Chamber of Commerce, 416 W. Main St.,Cherokee,*
*721-225-6414; www.cherokeeiowachamber.com*
Professional Rodeo Cowboys Association sanctioned. Weekend after Memorial Day weekend.

## HOTEL
### ★★BEST WESTERN LA GRANDE HACIENDA
*1401 N. Second St., Cherokee, 712-225-5701, 800-924-3765;*
*www.bestwestern.com*
55 rooms. Complimentary full breakfast. Restaurant. Indoor pool, whirlpool. High-speed Internet access. Pets accepted. **$**

# CLARINDA
Clarinda is the birthplace of Big Band-era legend Glenn Miller. It's also where, at the turn of the century, rural school teacher Jessie Field Shambaugh started the Boys' Corn Clubs and Girls' Home Clubs, which later became the 4-H movement.
*Information: Chamber of Commerce, 200 S. 15th St., 712-542-2166;*
*www.clarinda.org*

## WHAT TO SEE AND DO
### LAKE OF THREE FIRES STATE PARK
*2303 Highway 49, Bedford, 712-523-2700;*
*www.iowadnr.gov/parks*
This park has 691 acres with a 97-acre lake. Swimming, fishing, electric boating; hiking, bridle trails, snowmobiling; picnicking, camping, cabins.

### NODAWAY VALLEY HISTORICAL MUSEUM
*1600 S. 16th St., Clarinda, 712-542-3073; www.clarinda.org/museum.htm*
Featured here are exhibits on the history of the Nodaway River area including agricultural displays, artifacts from the early days of the 4-H movement and Glenn Miller memorabilia. Visits to the nearby Glenn Miller Birthplace Home (by appointment only; additional fee) can be arranged through the museum. May-October, Tuesday-Sunday afternoons 1-4 p.m. November-April 2-4 p.m.; closed Monday and holidays.

## SPECIAL EVENT
### GLENN MILLER FESTIVAL
*122 W. Garfield, Clarinda, 712-542-2461*
This event honor's Glen Miller and his music. Second weekend in June.

## RESTAURANT
### ★★J BRUNER'S
*1120 E. Washington St., Clarinda, 712-542-3364; www.jbruners.net/contact.htm*
Steak menu. Dinner. Closed Sunday-Monday. Bar. Children's menu. **$$$**

# CLEAR LAKE
Scene of a Native American uprising in 1854, Clear Lake challenged Mason City for honors as the county seat, but lost out because it was not in the geographic center of the area. Taking its name from the nearby lake, this is an ancient Native American fishing and hunting ground and a popular resort town.
*Information: Chamber of Commerce, 205 Main Ave.,*
*641-357-2159, 800-285-5338; www.clearlakeiowa.com*

**IOWA**

★
★
★
★
★

## WHAT TO SEE AND DO
### CLEAR LAKE STATE PARK
*2730 S. Lakeview Drive, Clear Lake, 641-357-4212; www.iowadnr.gov/parks*
Swimming, fishing, boating, snowmobiling, picnicking, camping are all available at this park.

### SURF BALLROOM
*460 North Shore Drive, Clear Lake, 641-357-6151;*
*www.surfballroom.com/contact.html*
This was the site of Buddy Holly's last concert before Holly, Ritchie Valens and J. P. Richardson (the Big Bopper) died in a plane crash nearby on February 2, 1959. The ballroom features entertainment on weekends and a museum of musical history. Tours available.

## SPECIAL EVENT
### BUDDY HOLLY TRIBUTE
*Surf Ballroom, 460 North Shore Drive, Clear Lake, 641-357-6151;*
*www.surfballroom.com*
An event to commemorate Holly's last concert, this tribute features local and national entertainers. First weekend in February.

## HOTEL
### ★★BEST WESTERN HOLIDAY LODGE
*2023 Seventh Ave. N., Clear Lake, 641-357-5253, 800-606-3552;*
*www.bestwestern.com*
138 rooms. Pets accepted, some restrictions; fee. Complimentary full breakfast. Restaurant. Indoor pool, whirlpool. Airport transportation available. High-speed Internet access. $

★
★★
★★★
★★★★
★

# CLINTON
Agriculture, industry and business are blended in this city of wide streets and modern buildings on the Mississippi River. First called New York, it was later renamed after DeWitt Clinton, former governor of New York. Once the largest lumber-producing city in the world, Clinton today is famous for its prime beef production.
*Information: Clinton Area Chamber of Commerce, 333 Fourth*
*Ave. S., 563-242-5702, 800-828-5702; www.clintonia.com*

## WHAT TO SEE AND DO
### EAGLE POINT PARK
*Highway 67 N., 563-242-0622; www.clintonia.com*
This park features flower gardens, picnicking shelters, a lodge, playground, observation tower, children's nature center and petting zoo. Mid-April-late October, daily.

### LILLIAN RUSSELL THEATRE
*311 Riverview Drive, Clinton, 563-242-6760; www.clintonia.com*
This theater is located aboard the paddle wheel showboat the *City of Clinton*. Musicals and comedies. June-August.

**MISSISSIPPI BELLE II**

*Showboat Landing, 311 Riverview Drive, Clinton, 563-243-9000,*
*800-457-9975; www.clintonia.com*

Year-round gambling along the Mississippi River is available at this casino boat.

## SPECIAL EVENTS
### CIVIL WAR REENACTMENT

*Eagle Point Park, 1401 11th Ave. N., Clinton, 563-243-5368*

See actors in period costume reenact the battle for Burnside Bridge. May.

### RIVERBOAT DAYS

*115 Fourth Ave. S., Clinton, 800-395-7277; www.riverboatdays.org*

Pageant, events, tractor pulls, entertainment, shows, carnival. July Fourth weekend.

## HOTELS
### ★★BEST WESTERN FRONTIER MOTOR INN

*2300 Lincoln Way St., Clinton, 563-242-7112, 800-728-7112; www.bestwestern.com*

113 rooms. Complimentary full breakfast. High-speed Internet access. Restaurant, bar. Fitness room. Indoor pool, whirlpool. Airport transportation available. Pets accepted, some restrictions; fee. $$

### ★COUNTRY INN & SUITES

*2224 Lincoln Way, Clinton, 563-244-9922, 888-201-1746; www.countryinns.com*

63 rooms. Complimentary continental breakfast. High-speed Internet access. Indoor pool, whirlpool. Airport transportation available. Pets accepted; fee. $

# COUNCIL BLUFFS

The Lewis and Clark expedition stopped in Council Bluffs in 1804 to rest and hold their first "council bluff" with local Native American tribes. Council Bluffs was settled in 1846 by Mormons fleeing religious persecution. They called the town Kanesville, but the city officially took the name Council Bluffs in 1853. The town subsequently became a booming hub of commerce as the nation's fifth-largest rail center. Today the Loess Hills Scenic Byway passes through the area.

*Information: Convention and Visitors Bureau, 7 N. Sixth St.,*
*712-325-1000, 800-228-6878; www.councilbluffsiowa.com*

## WHAT TO SEE AND DO
### GOLDEN SPIKE MONUMENT

*S. 21st Street and Ninth Avenue, Council Bluffs; www.cbparksandrec.org*

Erected in 1939, this 56-foot golden concrete spike commemorates the junction of the Union Pacific and Central Pacific railroads in Council Bluffs.

### HISTORIC GENERAL DODGE HOUSE

*605 Third St., Council Bluffs, 712-322-2406; www.dodgehouse.org*

Guided tours are given of this restored Victorian house built by Grenville M. Dodge, chief construction engineer for the Union Pacific Railroad and a general in the Civil War. Tuesday-Saturday 10 a.m.-5 p.m., Sunday 1-5 p.m.; closed Monday, holidays and January.

### HISTORIC POTTAWATTAMIE COUNTY JAIL

*226 Pearl St., Council Bluffs, 712-323-2509; www.thehistoricalsociety.org*

This unique three-story rotary jail is sometimes referred to as the "human squirrel cage" or "lazy Susan jail." May and September: weekends; June-August: Wednesday-Sunday or by appointment.

### LEWIS AND CLARK MONUMENT

*19962 Monument Road, Council Bluffs, 712-328-4650*

A shaft of native stone on the bluffs depicts Lewis and Clark holding council with the Oto and Missouri tribes.

### LINCOLN MONUMENT

*323 Lafayette Ave., Council Bluffs; www.parksandrec.councilbluffs-ia.gov*

This granite shaft marks the spot from which Lincoln designated the town as the eastern terminus of the Union Pacific Railroad. Erected in 1911.

### MORMON TRAIL MEMORIAL

*Bayliss Park, Council Bluffs*

A huge boulder marks the passage of Mormons out of the city on the trek to Utah.

### RAILSWEST RAILROAD MUSEUM

*16th Avenue and S. Main Street, Council Bluffs, 712-323-5182*

The historic Rock Island depot was built in 1899. Displayed here are railroad memorabilia and HO gauge model trains. March-December, Wednesday-Monday.

### WESTERN HISTORIC TRAILS CENTER

*3434 Richard Downing Ave., Council Bluffs, 712-366-4900;*
*www.iowahistory.org*

Explore preserved and restored sites along the Lewis and Clark, Mormon Pioneer, California and Oregon trails. Discover the history of Native American tribes and trails heritage in the region. Guided group tours. Daily; closed holidays.

## HOTELS

### ★★AMERISTAR CASINO

*2200 River Road, Council Bluffs, 712-328-8888, 877-462-7827;*
*www.ameristarcasinos.com*

160 rooms. Restaurant, bar. Fitness room. Indoor pool, whirlpool. Gaming. **$**

### ★FAIRFIELD INN

*520 30th Ave., Council Bluffs, 712-366-1330, 800-228-2800; www.fairfieldinn.com*

62 rooms. Complimentary continental breakfast. Indoor pool, whirlpool. High-speed Internet access. Fitness room. **$**

### ★HEARTLAND INN COUNCIL BLUFFS

*1000 Woodbury Ave., Council Bluffs, 712-322-8400, 800-334-3277;*
*www.heartlandinns.com*

87 rooms. Complimentary continental breakfast. High-speed Internet access. Indoor pool. Business center. Fitness room. **$**

## RESTAURANTS
### ★CHRISTY CRÉME
*2853 N. Broadway, Council Bluffs, 712-322-2778; www.christycreme.com*
American menu. Lunch, dinner. Closed December-January. Children's menu. Outdoor seating. $

### ★PINK POODLE STEAKHOUSE
*633 N. Old Lincoln Highway, Crescent, 712-545-3744;*
*www.pinkpoodlesteakhouse.com*
American menu. Dinner. Closed Monday. $

# DAVENPORT
Stretching five miles along the Mississippi River, Davenport is part of the Quad Cities metropolitan area. Davenport's Palmer College of Chiropractic is the fountainhead of that practice in the United States. The city is named for its founder, a former U.S. Army officer who explored this bank of the river while stationed on Rock Island. The state's first railroad came here when tracks were put across the Mississippi at this point in 1854. In pre-Civil War days, Dred Scott claimed the town as his home, and John Brown camped here before his attack on Harpers Ferry.

*Information: Quad Cities Convention and Visitors Bureau,*
*102 S. Harrison St., 563-322-3911, 800-747-7800; www.quadcities.com*

## WHAT TO SEE AND DO
### DAN NAGLE WALNUT GROVE PIONEER VILLAGE
*18817 290th St., Long Grove, 563-328-3283; www.scottcountyiowa.com*
This 3-acre walk-through site contains 18 historic buildings moved from various locations in the county. Visitors can explore a blacksmith shop, schoolhouse, pioneer family home; also St. Anne's Church. April-October, daily 9 a.m.-6 p.m.

### FIGGE ART MUSEUM
*1737 W. 12th St., Davenport, 563-326-7804; www.figgeartmuseum.org*
Rotating displays from a permanent collection of 19th- and 20th-century paintings, Mexican Colonial, Asian and native Haitian art are displayed here, as well as works by regional artists Grant Wood and Thomas Hart Benton. Tuesday-Sunday.

### PUTNAM MUSEUM OF HISTORY & NATURAL SCIENCE
*1717 W. 12th St., Davenport, 563-324-1933; www.putnam.org*
Permanent and changing exhibits of regional history, natural science and world cultures. Daily. Exhibit Hall hours: Monday-Saturday 10 a.m.-5 p.m.; Sunday noon-5 p.m.

### SCOTT COUNTY PARK
*19251 290th St., Long Grove, 563-285-9656*
More than 1,000 acres with a pioneer village and nature center. Swimming, fishing, ball fields, 18-hole golf, skiing, tobogganing, ice-skating, picnicking, camping and trailer sites. Daily.

IOWA

★
★
★
★
★

# A WALK THROUGH DAVENPORT

Davenport is one of the Quad Cities, a four-city metropolitan area that straddles the Mississippi and includes Moline and Rock Island in Illinois, plus Bettendorf, just upriver from Davenport. Begin this walk on Credit Island Park, the site of a turn-of-the-century amusement park. Scenic trails loop around the island, and number of public art pieces are found here, part of the Quad Cities Art in the Park project.

Cross over to the Iowa mainland from the east end of Credit Island Park and walk along the Mississippi through two more riverside parks. Centennial Park features riverside walkways past sports fields and stadiums. Atop the bluff on Division Street is Museum Hill, home of the **Putnam Museum of Science and Natural History** (*1717 W. 12th St.*) and the **Davenport Museum of Art** (*1737 W. 12th St.*). The Putnam houses two permanent exhibits about the Mississippi River. The art museum's permanent collection includes works by Midwestern painters, including Thomas Hart Benton and Grant Wood, an Iowa native famous for his painting *American Gothic*. Just to the east is LeClaire Park, home to summer outdoor events and concerts.

The Davenport Downtown Levee includes a riverboat casino, restaurants, nightclubs and the renovated Union Station railroad depot, which houses the Quad Cities Convention and Visitors Center. A local Farmers' Market is also held here on Wednesday and Saturday mornings from May through October.

Just downstream from the historic Government Bridge, Dam 15 provides a navigational pool for commercial shipping on the Mississippi. Lock 15 allows boats to transfer between the rivers pools. Cross Government Bridge to Arsenal Island, which was acquired by the U.S. Government in 1804 under a treaty with the Sauk and Fox Indians. Fort Armstrong was established in 1816 on the tip of the island, where a replica now stands. Manufacturing began on the island in 1840, and in 1869 it became home to the Rock Island Arsenal, a major military manufacturing facility. The island contains a number of historic homes and structures, including the Rock Island Arsenal Museum; the restored Colonel George Davenport Mansion, filled with furnishings from the mid-1800s; and the Mississippi River Visitors Center, with exhibits about the history of navigation on the river. A Confederate Soldiers Cemetery and National Military Cemetery date back to the 1800s. Hikers and bikers can enjoy a five-mile trail around the island.

## SPECIAL EVENT
### BIX BEIDERBECKE MEMORIAL JAZZ FESTIVAL
*LeClaire Park, 311 N. Ripley St., Davenport, 563-324-7170; www.bixsociety.org*
Join the crowd at a jazz festival to honor the Davenport-born musician. Mid-July.

## HOTELS
### ★LA QUINTA INN
*3330 E. Kimberly Road, Davenport, 563-359-3921; www.lq.com*
129 rooms. Pets accepted, some restrictions; fee. Complimentary continental breakfast. Fitness room. Free High-speed Internet access. Free local calls. Free parking. Indoor pool. Airport transportation available. **$**

### ★SUPER 8

*410 E. 65th St., Davenport, 563-388-9810, 800-800-8000; www.super8.com*

61 rooms. Pets accepted; fee. Complimentary continental breakfast. High-speed Internet access. **$**

## RESTAURANTS

### ★IOWA MACHINE SHED

*7250 N.W. Blvd., Davenport, 563-391-2427; www.machineshed.com*

American menu. Breakfast, lunch, dinner. Bar. Children's menu. **$$**

### ★★THUNDER BAY GRILLE

*6511 Brady St., Davenport, 563-386-2722; www.thunderbaygrille.com*

American menu. Lunch, dinner, Sunday brunch. Bar. Children's menu. Bi-level dining.

# DECORAH

A center of Norwegian culture in the United States, Decorah is the seat of Winneshiek County and located in one of the state's most picturesque areas. Within a short distance are Siewers and Twin Springs and towering spires of limestone along the Upper Iowa River. The town is named for a Native American chief who aided settlers during the Black Hawk War.

*Information: Decorah Area Chamber of Commerce, 300 W. Water,*
*563-382-3990, 800-463-4692; www.decorahia.org*

## WHAT TO SEE AND DO

### BILY CLOCKS

*323 N. Main St., Spillville, 563-562-3569; www.bilyclocks.org*

March and November, Saturday 10 a.m.-4 p.m., Sunday noon-4 p.m.; April, Monday-Saturday 10 a.m.-4 p.m., Sunday noon-4 p.m.; May-October, Monday-Saturday 9 a.m.-5 p.m., Sunday noon-4 p.m.; closed December-February.

### FORT ATKINSON STATE PRESERVE

*10225 Ivy Road, Decorah, 563-425-4161;*
*www.iowadnr.com/parks/state_park_list/fort_atkinson.html*

Fort was built in 1840 as federal protection for the Winnebago from the Sac, Fox and Sioux. Restored buildings include barracks, a blockhouse and magazine. Museum exhibits Native American and pioneer relics. Mid-May-mid-October, daily.

### SEED SAVERS HERITAGE FARM

*3094 N. Winn Road, Decorah, 563-382-5990; www.seedsavers.org*

This 173-acre farm features displays of endangered vegetables, apples, grapes and ancient White Park cattle. Preservation Gardens house 15,000 rare vegetable varieties; Cultural History Garden displays old-time flowers and vegetables. Historic Orchard has 650 19th-century apples and 160 hardy grapes. Daily.

**IOWA**

### VESTERHEIM NORWEGIAN-AMERICAN MUSEUM

*523 W. Water St., Decorah, 563-382-9681; www.vesterheim.org*

Extensive exhibits relate history of Norwegians in America and Norway. Pioneer objects, handicrafts, ship gallery, arts displayed in a complex of 13 historic buildings with a restored mill. Daily.

## SPECIAL EVENT
### NORDIC FEST

*507 W. Water St., Decorah, 563-382-3990, 800-382-3378; www.nordicfest.com*

Parades, dancing, pioneer tool display; demonstrations of cooking, needlework and rosemaling. Last full weekend in July.

## HOTELS
### ★★★HOTEL WINNESHIEK

*104 E. Water St., Decorah, 563-382-4164; www.hotelwinn.com*

The Hotel Winneshiek is a gem: an elegantly restored 1905 hotel in the heart of downtown. Guests are greeted at a concierge desk in an entryway decorated with fresh flowers and displays of antique glassware and porcelain figurines. The lobby has an octagonal three-story atrium, set under a large stained-glass skylight. Rooms are simple but decorated with antique reproductions. 31 rooms. Complimentary continental breakfast. Restaurant, bar. $

### ★SUPER 8

*810 Highway 9 E., Decorah, 563-382-8771, 800-800-8000; www.super8.com*

60 rooms. Pets accepted. Complimentary continental breakfast. Fitness room. Whirlpool. High-speed Internet access. $

## SPECIALTY LODGING
### THORNTON HOUSE

*371 Diagonal St., Lansing, 563-538-3373; www.thorntonhouse.net*

This brick mansion has more than 3,300 square feet of living space with a two-story enclosed deck. Five rooms. $$$$

## RESTAURANTS
### ★MILTY'S

*200 Main St., Lansing, 563-538-4585; www.miltys.net*

American menu. Lunch, dinner. Closed Monday. $

### ★★STONE HEARTH INN

*811 Commerce Drive, Decorah, 563-382-4614*

American menu. Lunch, dinner. Closed Sunday. Bar. Children's menu. $$

# DENISON

J. W. Denison, an agent for the Providence Western Land Company and a Baptist minister, came to this area in 1855 and gave the new town its name. In 1933, Denison farmers nearly rioted during land foreclosures triggered by the Great Depression. Denison is the seat of Crawford County.

*Information: Chamber of Commerce, 109 N. 14th St.,*
*712-263-5621; www.denisonia.com*

## WHAT TO SEE AND DO
### YELLOW SMOKE PARK

*2237 Yellow Smoke Road, Denison, 712-263-2070;*
*www.crawfordcountyconservationboard.com/cabins.html*

A 320-acre recreation area with a swimming beach, this park offers fishing, boating, hiking and camping.

## SPECIAL EVENT
### DONNA REED FESTIVAL FOR THE PERFORMING ARTS

*1305 Broadway, Denison, 712-263-3334; www.donnareed.org*

Special workshops in the performing arts conducted by professionals from around the nation. Parade. Golf tourney. 10K run. Saturday night gala. Street fair. Third full week in June.

## HOTEL
### ★SUPER 8

*502 Boyer Valley Road, Denison, 712-263-5081, 800-800-8000;*
*www.super8.com*

40 rooms. Pets accepted, some restrictions; fee. Complimentary continental breakfast, High-speed Internet access. $

## RESTAURANT
### ★ERICK CRONK'S RESTAURANT & LOUNGE

*812 Fourth Ave. S., Denison, 712-263-4191*

Steak menu. Breakfast, lunch, dinner, late-night, Sunday brunch. Bar. $

# DES MOINES

Des Moines is the capital of Iowa and largest city in the state. This city is the industrial, retail, financial and political hub of Iowa. A military garrison established Fort Des Moines at a point on the Raccoon and Des Moines rivers in 1843. Two years later the territory was opened to settlers and the town of Fort Des Moines was chosen as the county seat. The word "fort" was abandoned when the community became a city in 1857; the next year it became the state capital. Today more than 60 insurance companies have their home offices here, as does media giant Meredith Corporation, publishers of *Better Homes & Gardens* and *Ladies' Home Journal*.

*Information: Greater Des Moines Convention and Visitors Bureau,*
*405 Sixth Ave., 515-286-4960, 800-451-2625; www.ci.des-moines.ia.us*

★
★
★
★
☆

## WHAT TO SEE AND DO
### ADVENTURELAND PARK

*305 34th Ave. N.W., Altoona, 515-266-2121,*
*800-532-1286; www.adventurelandpark.com*

This amusement park has more than 100 rides, shows and attractions. June-late August, daily; May and September, weekends.

## BLANK PARK ZOO

*7401 S.W. Ninth St., Des Moines, 515-285-4722, 515-323-8383;*
*www.blankparkzoo.com*
The animal and bird habitats at this zoo are designed for close viewing. It includes Australian and African walk-through displays, a farm animal contact area, camel rides and an Old West train ride. Daily.

## DES MOINES ART CENTER

*4700 Grand Ave., Des Moines, 515-277-4405; www.desmoinesartcenter.org*
Exhibits of 19th- and 20th-century paintings and sculptures are displayed in a contemporary building designed by Eliel Saarinen, with additions by Richard Meier and I.M. Pei. Tuesday-Sunday.

## DES MOINES BOTANICAL CENTER

*909 Robert D. Ray Drive, Des Moines, 515-323-6290; www.botanicalcenter.com*
Displays of nearly 1,500 species from around the world; seasonal floral displays. Daily 10 a.m.-5 p.m.

## DRAKE UNIVERSITY

*2507 University Ave., Des Moines, 515-271-2011; www.drake.edu*
This small private university has many buildings designed by distinguished architects, including Eliel and Eero Saarinen, Harry Weese and Associates, Borg and Skiles and Ludwig Mies van der Rohe.

**32**

**IOWA**

★
★★
★★
★★
★

## HERITAGE VILLAGE

*State Fairgrounds, East 30th Street and University Avenue, Des Moines,*
*515-262-3111; www.iowastatefair.org*
Featured here are a century-old barn, exposition hall with displays of early farm machinery, an authentically furnished country school and replicas of an 1834 church. Tours mid-April-mid-October, by appointment.

## HOYT SHERMAN PLACE

*1501 Woodland Ave., Des Moines, 515-244-0507; www.hoytsherman.org*
This 1877 house was once the home of General William Tecumseh Sherman's brother. It now features the city's oldest art gallery, including artifacts, antique furniture and art collection. Tours by appointment. Theater (1,200 seats) added in 1922. Monday-Friday open 9 a.m.-4 p.m.

## IOWA HISTORICAL BUILDING

*Capitol Complex, 600 E. Locust, Des Moines, 515-281-5111;*
*www.iowahistory.org*
Modern cultural center houses state historical museum. Displays portray Iowa history and heritage. Library contains county, state and family history materials; rare books and manuscripts about Iowa; census records and newspapers. Monday-Saturday 9 a.m.-4:30 p.m., Sunday noon-4:30 p.m.; closed Thanksgiving and Christmas.

**LIVING HISTORY FARMS**

*11121 Hickman Road, Urbandale, 515-278-5286; www.lhf.org*

This complex has four farms and a town set on 600 acres. A Native American settlement includes gardens, shelters and crafts of the Ioway tribe. The pioneer farm of 1850 features a log cabin and outbuildings. The horse-powered farm of 1900 depicts farm and household chores typical of period. The 1875 town of Walnut Hill includes a Victorian mansion, schoolhouse, pottery, blacksmith and carpentry shops, veterinary infirmary, church, bank, newspaper, doctor's offices and a general store. May-mid-October, daily.

## THE DES MOINES RIVER VALLEY

This route travels through picture-perfect farming communities founded by European settlers, then along the lower Des Moines River, where historic towns have changed little since the riverboat era. From Des Moines, drive east on Highway 163 toward Pella. Founded in 1847 by Dutch settlers who came to this valley to escape religious persecution in Holland, Pella retains a sense of Dutch orderliness and is filled with trim historic homes and tulip-filled public parks.

East on Highway 163 through rolling hills is Oskaloosa, a farming town settled by Quakers. The town's past is retold at Nelson Pioneer Farm and Craft Museum, which preserves a farm community from the 1850s. From Oskaloosa, follow Highway 163 to Ottumwa, a busy industrial center.

Continuing on, turn east on Highway 34, and then turn south on Highway 16, which closely follows the Des Moines River. One of the earliest settled regions of Iowa, this section of the Des Moines valley is lined with tiny towns founded in the 1830s when the river was the only avenue for travel. Bypassed by the rail lines and the freeway system, these towns were forgotten by the forward rush of time. Today, they have handsome period architecture, newly refurbished small hotels and inns, historical museums and antique stores.

The town of Eldon contains one of the most archetypal structures in the Midwest: At the corner of Gothic and Burton streets is the house painted by Grant Wood as the backdrop to his famous portrait *American Gothic*. The rustic couple in the painting were the painter's sister and his dentist. Keosauqua is home to the oldest courthouse in the state, as well as the imposing Manning Hotel, 150 years old and still in operation. Farther downstream, the entire village of Bentonsport, once a sizable river port, is a National Historic District. The Mason House Hotel, built by Mormon craftsmen in the 1840s, is open for tours and for paying guests. At the town of Bonaparte, the original grist and woolen mills have been preserved.

From Bonaparte, follow Highway 81 south to Farmington, with the oldest Congregational Church west of the Mississippi River and a stone carriage factory. Continue east to Highway 218 and turn south to Keokuk, at the confluence of the Des Moines and Mississippi rivers. Keokuk was head of steamboat navigation on the Mississippi before Lock Number 19, the largest on the river system, was built in 1913. The lock is part of Keokuk Dam, which was the world's largest hydroelectric dam until the 1930s. *Approximately 185 miles*. www.desmoinesriver.org

33

IOWA

★
★
★
★
★

### PRAIRIE MEADOWS RACETRACK AND CASINO

*1 Prairie Meadows Drive, Altoona, 800-325-9015;*
*www.prairiemeadows.com*

Live Thoroughbred, quarter horse and harness racing (late April-October); simulcasts of Thoroughbred and greyhound racing; 24-hour casino with more than 1,500 slots, poker room and video poker machines. Daily.

### SCIENCE CENTER OF IOWA

*Science Center of Iowa, 401 W. Martin Luther King Jr. Parkway, Des Moines,*
*515-274-6868, 515-274-4138; www.sciowa.org*

Natural and physical science exhibits are the draw at this center, as are live demonstrations, Digistar planetarium shows and laser shows. Daily.

### STATE CAPITOL

*1005 Grand Ave., Des Moines, 515-281-5591; www.legis.state.ia.us*

The towering central dome of this 1871 building is covered with 23-karat gold leaf; four smaller domes have golden seam marks. State offices, Supreme Court, House and Senate chamber, law library. Paintings, mosaics, collection of war flags. Daily.

### TERRACE HILL

*2300 Grand Ave., Des Moines, 515-281-3604; www.terracehill.org*

This extravagant Italianate/Second Empire mansion, now the residence of Iowa governors, is situated on a commanding knoll above downtown. The restored house is an outstanding example of Victorian residential architecture. Tours include first and second floors, carriage house and gardens. March-December, Tuesday-Saturday 10 a.m.-1:30 p.m.

## SPECIAL EVENTS

### DRAKE RELAYS

*Drake University, 2507 University Ave., Des Moines, 515-271-3647;*
*www.godrakebulldogs.com*

One of the most prestigious intercollegiate track and field events in the country; more than 5,000 athletes compete. Last week in April.

### IOWA STATE FAIR

*Fairgrounds, East 30th Street and University Avenue, Des Moines,*
*515-262-3111; www.iowastatefair.com*

One of the oldest and largest fairs in the country, it includes 20 acres of farm machinery, fine arts, a giant midway, grandstand stage and track events, free entertainment and contests. August.

## HOTELS

### ★★ADVENTURELAND INN

*3200 Adventureland Drive, Altoona, 515-265-7321, 800-910-5382;*
*www.adventurelandpark.com*

187 rooms. Restaurant, bar. Indoor pool. $

### ★BEST INN

*5050 Merle Hay Road, Johnston, 515-270-1111, 800-237-8466;*
*www.americasbestinn.com*

91 rooms. Pets accepted; fee. Complimentary continental breakfast. Indoor pool, whirlpool. $

### ★★★DES MOINES MARRIOTT DOWNTOWN

*700 Grand Ave., Des Moines, 515-245-5500, 800-228-9290; www.marriott.com*

Connected to the Iowa Events Center by skywalk, this downtown hotel is close to the city's top shopping and restaurants. Rooms have been updated with the chain's luxury bedding, including down duvets and pillow-top mattresses. 415 rooms. Restaurant. Pools. High-speed Internet access. Pets accepted, some restrictions.

### ★★EMBASSY SUITES

*101 E. Locust St., Des Moines, 515-244-1700, 800-362-2779;*
*www.embassysuitesdesmoines.com*

234 rooms, all suites. Complimentary full breakfast. Restaurant, bar. Fitness room. Indoor pool, whirlpool. High-speed Internet access. Business center. Airport transportation available. $$

### ★★FOUR POINTS BY SHERATON

*1810 Army Post Road, Des Moines, 515-287-6464, 800-368-7764;*
*www.bestwestern.com*

140 rooms. Complimentary continental breakfast. Complimentary High-speed Internet access. Business center. Restaurant, bar. Spa. Indoor pool. Complimentary newspaper. Airport transportation available. Pets accepted. $

### ★HAMPTON INN

*5001 Fleur Drive, Des Moines, 515-287-7300, 800-426-7866; www.hampton-inn.com*

122 rooms. Complimentary continental breakfast. Fitness room. Outdoor pool. Airport transportation available. $

### ★HEARTLAND INN DES MOINES WEST

*11414 Forest Ave., Clive, 515-226-0414, 800-334-3277; www.heartlandinns.com*

85 rooms. Pets not accepted, some restrictions; fee. Complimentary continental breakfast. High-speed Internet access. Whirlpool. Business center. $

### ★★HOLIDAY INN

*6111 Fleur Drive, Des Moines, 515-287-2400, 800-248-4013; www.holiday-inn.com*

227 rooms. Restaurant, bar. Fitness room. Indoor pool, whirlpool. Airport transportation available. Business center. Complimentary breakfast; kids eat free. $

### ★★HOTEL FORT DES MOINES

*1000 Walnut St., Des Moines, 515-243-1161, 800-532-1466;*
*www.hotelfortdesmoines.com*

242 rooms. Pets accepted. Restaurant, bar. Fitness room. Indoor pool, whirlpool. Airport transportation available. Smoke free. $

**★WILDWOOD LODGE**

*11431 Forest Ave., Clive, 515-222-9876, 800-728-1223;*
*www.thewildwoodlodge.com*

100 rooms. Complimentary continental breakfast. Bar. Fitness room. Indoor pool, whirlpool. Free High-speed Internet access. $

## RESTAURANTS
### ★★★CHRISTOPHER'S

*2816 Beaver Ave., Des Moines, 515-274-3694*

Italian-American food, including pastas, steaks and seafood, and a casual atmosphere have made this dining room a local favorite for many years. American, Italian menu. Dinner. Closed Sunday. Bar. Children's menu. $$

### ★★★GREENBRIAR

*5810 Merle Hay Road, Johnston, 515-253-0124;*
*www.greenbriartrostels.com*

The menu at this main-street restaurant offers a broad selection of seafood, chicken, pasta and specialty prime rib. American menu. Lunch Monday, Wednesday and Friday, dinner. Closed Sunday. Children's menu. Outdoor seating. $$

### ★HOUSE OF HUNAN

*6810 Douglas Ave., Des Moines, 515-276-5556*

Chinese menu. Lunch, dinner. Bar. $

### ★JESSE'S EMBERS

*4810 86th St., Urbandale, 515-251-7175; www.jessesembers.com*

Seafood, steak menu. Lunch, dinner. Closed Sunday. Bar. $$$

### ★THE MACHINE SHED

*11151 Hickman Road, Urbandale, 515-270-6818; www.machineshed.com*

American menu. Breakfast, lunch, dinner. Bar. Children's menu. $$

### ★MAXIE'S

*1311 Grand Ave., West Des Moines, 515-223-1463*

Steak menu. Lunch, dinner. Closed Sunday. Bar. Children's menu. $$

### ★OHANA STEAKHOUSE

*2900 University Ave., West Des Moines, 515-225-3325;*
*www.ohanasteakhouse.com*

Japanese menu. Dinner. Closed Monday; holidays. Bar. Children's menu. $$

### ★SPAGHETTI WORKS

*310 Court Ave., Des Moines, 515-243-2195*

American, Italian menu. Dinner. Bar. Children's menu. Outdoor seating. $$

### ★WATERFRONT SEAFOOD MARKET

*2900 University Ave., West Des Moines, 515-223-5106*

Seafood menu. Lunch, dinner. Closed Sunday. Bar. Children's menu. $$

# DUBUQUE

Facing both Wisconsin and Illinois across the broad Mississippi River, Dubuque became the first known European settlement in Iowa when Julien Dubuque, a French Canadian, came from Quebec in 1788 and leased land from the Native Americans to mine lead. After his death, Native Americans barred settlement until 1833 when the territory was opened under a treaty with Chief Black Hawk. Once a boisterous river and mining town, Dubuque had the first bank and newspaper in what is now Iowa. Its downtown has been extensively rejuvenated in recent years, with a number of restaurants opening in restored buildings.

*Information: Convention and Visitors Bureau, 300 Main St.,*
*563-557-9200, 800-798-8844; www.traveldubuque.com*

## WHAT TO SEE AND DO
### BELLEVUE STATE PARK
*24668 Highway 52, Dubuque, 563-872-4019;*
*www.iowadnr.com/parks*
Approximately 540 acres on a high bluff above the Mississippi. Native American mounds, rugged woodlands, hiking trails, snowmobiling, picnicking, camping, nature center.

### CATHEDRAL SQUARE
*Second and Bluff streets, Dubuque, 563-582-7646*
Surrounding the square are stylized figures of a lead miner, farmer, farmer's wife, priest and river hand. Opposite the square is the architecturally and historically significant St. Raphael's Cathedral.

### CRYSTAL LAKE CAVE
*7699 Crystal Lake Cave Drive, Dubuque, 563-556-6451;*
*www.crystallakecave.com*
A network of passageways carved by underground streams surrounds a lake with glittering stalactites and stalagmites, with water that really is crystal clear. Guided tours. Memorial Day-late October, daily; May, weekends.

### DIAMOND JO CASINO
*Ice Harbor, 400 E. Third St., Dubuque, 563-690-2100, 800-582-5956;*
*www.diamondjo.com*
Casino gambling on the river. 8 a.m.-3 a.m. daily.

### DUBUQUE ARBORETUM AND BOTANICAL GARDENS
*3800 Arboretum Drive, Dubuque, 563-556-2100; www.dubuquearboretum.com*
Features annual and perennial gardens, rose, water, formal gardens; ornamental trees, woodland and prairie wildflower walk. Daily.

### DUBUQUE COUNTY COURTHOUSE
*720 Central Ave., Dubuque, 563-589-4445; www.dubuquecounty.org*
This gold-domed courthouse is on the National Historic Register of Places. Monday-Friday.

★
★
★
★
★

## DUBUQUE MUSEUM OF ART/OLD COUNTY JAIL

*701 Locust St., Dubuque, 563-557-1851*

This museum is housed in a brand-new facility. The gallery is an example of Egyptian Revival architecture. Tuesday-Friday, weekend afternoons.

## EAGLE POINT PARK

*2200 Bunker Hill Road, Dubuque, 563-589-4263; www.dbq.com*

On a high bluff above the Mississippi, this 164-acre park overlooks three states. A Works Progress Administration project, the park's Prairie School pavilions and naturalistic landscaping were designed by Alfred Caldwell, who studied under Frank Lloyd Wright. From the bluff, see a view of barges moving through the lock-and-dam on the river below. Mid-May-mid-October, daily.

## FENELON PLACE ELEVATOR

*512 Fenelon Place, Dubuque, 563-582-6496;*
*www.dbq.com/fenplco*

In operation since 1882, one of the world's shortest, steepest incline railways connects Fenelon Place with Fourth Street, providing a three-state view. Accepts bicycles. April-November, daily 8 a.m.-10 p.m.

## FIELD OF DREAMS MOVIE SITE

*28995 Lansing Road, Dyersville, 563-875-8404; www.fieldofdreamsmoviesite.com*

Background set of the movie *Field of Dreams* including the baseball diamond where visitors can actually play ball. Daily.

## FIVE FLAGS THEATER

*405 Main St., Dubuque, 563-589-4254; www.fiveflagscenter.com*

Designed by Rapp and Rapp, premier theater architects of their day, the Five Flags was modeled after Parisian music halls. Tours by appointment.

## GENERAL ZEBULON PIKE LOCK AND DAM

*3000 Lock and Dam Road, Dubuque, 563-582-1204*

A steady stream of barges and other river traffic moves through lock.

## GRAND OPERA HOUSE

*135 Eighth St., Dubuque, 563-588-1305; www.thegrandoperahouse.com*

This century-old opera house was recently restored and offers a variety of entertainment throughout the year.

## HERITAGE TRAIL

*13606 Swiss Valley Road, Dubuque, 563-556-6745;*
*www.dubuquecounty.com/HeritageTrail.cfm*

This trail provides 26 miles of scenic hiking, biking and cross-country skiing on an old railroad along rugged Little Maquoketa River valley. Level, surfaced trails cross from wooded, hilly, "driftless" areas to rolling prairie near Dyersville. Self-guided tour identifies railroad landmarks, includes water-powered mill sites. Daily.

### JULIEN DUBUQUE MONUMENT

*Grandview Avenue and Julien Dubuque Drive, Dubuque, 563-556-0620*

Tower built in 1897 at the site of Julien Dubuque's mine and the spot where Native Americans buried him in 1810. Provides an excellent view of the Mississippi River.

### MATHIAS HAM HOUSE HISTORIC SITE

*2241 Lincoln Ave., Dubuque, 563-583-2812*

An 1857 Italianate/Victorian mansion with a cupola, this house has spectacular views of the Mississippi River. Built by lead miner Mathias Ham. Also Iowa's oldest log cabin and one-room schoolhouse. June-October, daily; May, weekends only.

### NATIONAL MISSISSIPPI RIVER MUSEUM AND AQUARIUM

*350 E. Third St., Dubuque, 563-557-9545; www.missiissippirivermusem.com*

Complex of six Dubuque County Historical Society museums, all emphasizing the city's river history. Daily.

### SPIRIT OF DUBUQUE

*400 E. Third St., Dubuque, 563-583-8093, 800-747-8093; www.spiritofdubque.com*

Sightseeing and dinner cruises (11/2-hour) on the Mississippi River aboard this paddle wheeler. May-October.

### SUNDOWN MOUNTAIN SKI AREA

*16991 Asbury Road, Dubuque, 563-556-6676, 888-786-3696; www.sundownmtn.com*

Skiing in Iowa? Yep. And at this spot, the lodge is at the top of the run. Five chairlifts, tow rope, patrol, school, rentals, snowmaking. Twenty-one runs; longest run 1/2 mile; vertical drop 475 feet. Late November-mid-March: daily.

### WOODWARD DISCOVERY CENTER

*350 E. Third St., Ice Harbor, Dubuque, 563-557-9545; www.mississippirivermuseum.org*

Dramatizes 300 years of Mississippi River history: Native Americans, explorers, lead miners, boat builders and steamboat captains; lead mines; pilothouse and log raft displays. The aquarium may be the nation's most significant display of river and freshwater creatures, with five huge tanks and live-animal exhibits. This is one of the region's outstanding attractions.

## SPECIAL EVENT

### DUBUQUE COUNTY FAIR

*Dubuque County Fairgrounds, 14569 Olde Highway Road, Dubuque, 563-588-1406*

Recently the fair has had a knack for booking country and contemporary rock acts just as they are hitting it big. Late July.

## HOTELS

### ★★BEST WESTERN MIDWAY HOTEL

*3100 Dodge St., Dubuque, 563-557-8000, 800-336-4392;*
*www.bestwesterniowa.com*

149 rooms. Pets accepted, some restrictions. Complimentary full breakfast. High-speed Internet access. Restaurant, bar. Children's activity center. Fitness room. Indoor pool, whirlpool. Airport transportation available. $

### ★COMFORT INN

*4055 McDonald Drive, Dubuque, 563-556-3006, 800-228-5150;*
*www.choicehotels.com*

52 rooms. Pets accepted, some restrictions; fee. Complimentary continental breakfast. Indoor pool, whirlpool. Airport transportation available. Free High-speed Internet access. $

### ★★DAYS INN

*1111 Dodge St., Dubuque, 563-583-3297, 800-772-3297;*
*www.daysinn.com*

155 rooms. Pets accepted; fee. Complimentary continental breakfast. Restaurant, bar. Fitness room. Outdoor pool. Free High-speed Internet access.

### ★★THE GRAND HARBOR RESORT AND WATERPARK

*350 Bell St., Dubuque, 563-690-4000, 888-690-4006;*
*www.grandharborresort.com*

193 rooms. Restaurant, bar. Children's activity center. Fitness room. Indoor pool, outdoor pool, children's pool, whirlpool. Airport transportation available. $$

### ★HEARTLAND INN DUBUQUE WEST

*4025 McDonald Drive, Dubuque, 563-582-3752, 800-334-3277;*
*www.heartlandinns.com*

85 rooms. Pets not accepted, some restrictions; fee. Complimentary continental breakfast. Indoor pool. Airport transportation available. High-speed Internet access. $

### ★★HOLIDAY INN

*450 Main St., Dubuque, 563-556-2000, 800-465-4329; www.holiday-inn.com*

193 rooms. Pets accepted, some restrictions; fee. Wireless Internet access. Restaurant, bar. Fitness room. Indoor pool, whirlpool. Airport transportation available. Business center. $

### ★★JULIEN INN

*200 Main St., Dubuque, 563-556-4200, 800-798-7098; www.julieninn.com*

137 rooms. Restaurant, bar. Fitness room. Airport transportation available. High-speed Internet access. $

### ★★TIMMERMAN'S HOTEL AND RESORT

*7787 Timmerman Drive, East Dubuque, Illinois, 815-747-3181, 800-336-3181;*
*www.timmermanhotel.com*

74 rooms. Pets accepted, some restrictions; fee. Complimentary continental breakfast. Restaurant, bar. Indoor pool, whirlpool. $

## SPECIALTY LODGINGS
### THE LANDING

*703 S. River Park Drive, Guttenberg, 563-252-1615;*
*www.thelanding615.com*

This limestone structure was erected in the late 1800s and features great views of the Mississippi River. Five rooms. Pets accepted, some restrictions. $$

**THE REDSTONE INN**

*504 Bluff St., Dubuque, 563-582-1894; www.theredstoneinn.com*

This restored 1890s Victorian mansion was built by a prominent Dubuque industrialist as a wedding gift for his daughter. 14 rooms. Pets accepted. Complimentary full breakfast. Wireless Internet access. **$$$**

## RESTAURANTS

### ★★CAFÉ MISSISSIPPI

*431 S. River Park Drive, Guttenberg, 563-252-4405, 866-595-4093;*
*www.cafemississippi.net*

American menu. Lunch, dinner, brunch. Bar. **$$**

### ★★MARIO'S

*13th and Main Street, Dubuque, 563-556-9424; www.mariosdubuque.com*

Italian, American menu. Lunch, dinner. Closed Sunday. Bar. **$$**

### ★YEN CHING

*926 Main St., Dubuque, 563-556-2574*

Chinese menu. Lunch, dinner. Closed Sunday. **$**

# FORT DODGE

Fort Dodge was established to protect settlers. Its commander, Major William Williams, was given a large tract of land as part of his compensation, and here the town was laid out. Fort Dodge was an innocent party to a scientific hoax when a huge slab of gypsum cut here was freighted to Chicago and carved into the celebrated Cardiff Giant, falsely claimed to be a petrified prehistoric man (now at the Farmer's Museum in Cooperstown, New York).

*Information: Chamber of Commerce, 1406 Central Ave.,*
*515-955-5500, 800-765-1438; www.fortdodgechamber.com*

## WHAT TO SEE AND DO

### FORT DODGE HISTORICAL FOUNDATION, FORT MUSEUM AND FRONTIER VILLAGE

*South Kenyon and Museum Road, Fort Dodge, 515-573-4231*

A replica of an 1862 fort, this park houses a museum, trading post, blacksmith shop, general store, log home, drugstore, cabinet shop, newspaper office, church, jail and one-room school. May-October, daily; rest of year, by appointment.

### KALSOW PRAIRIE

*Manson, 15 miles west on Highway 7 to Manson, then 2 miles north on county road*

Approximately 160 acres of preserved, untouched Iowa prairie land.

## HOTEL

### ★★QUALITY INN

*2001 Highway 169 South, Fort Dodge, 515-955-3621; www.qualityinn.com*

102 rooms. Pets accepted. High-speed Internet access. Restaurant, bar. Fitness room. Indoor pool, children's pool. Complimentary breakfast. **$**

# GRINNELL

When Horace Greeley said "Go west, young man, go west and grow up with the country!" he was talking to Josiah Bushnell Grinnell, who took the advice, went west to a bit of prairie between the Iowa and Skunk rivers, and established the town of Grinnell. Today, Grinnell is a thriving college town.

*Information: Chamber of Commerce, 833 Fourth Ave.,*
*641-236-6555; www.grinnellchamber.org*

## WHAT TO SEE AND DO
### GRINNELL COLLEGE

*1121 Park St., Grinnell, 641-269-3400;*
*www.grinnell.edu*

Considered one of the top liberal arts colleges in the United States, this school was founded in 1846 and has fewer than 1,500 students. Tours by appointment.

### GRINNELL HISTORICAL MUSEUM

*1125 Broad St., Grinnell, 641-236-3732;*
*grinnellmuseum.org*

Historical furnishings; relics, documents of J. B. Grinnell and aviator Billy Robinson housed in a late Victorian house. June-August, Tuesday-Sunday afternoons; rest of year, Saturday afternoons or by appointment.

### WELLS FARGO BANK OF IOWA—POWESHIEK COUNTY

*Grinnell, downtown, on corner opposite town square*

The second in the series of "jewel box" banks that architect Louis Henri Sullivan designed late in his career, this building was constructed in 1914. This unique structure, one of the more important designs in the series, has been restored within the confines of a working bank environment. Monday-Friday.

## HOTEL
### ★SUPER 8

*2111 W. St. South, Grinnell, 641-236-7888, 800-800-8000;*
*www.super8.com*

53 rooms. Pets accepted, some restrictions; fee. Complimentary continental breakfast. Pool. High-speed Internet access. $

# HAMPTON

*Information: Chamber of Commerce, 5 First St. S.W.,*
*614-456-5668; www.hamptoniowa.org*

## WHAT TO SEE AND DO
### BEED'S LAKE STATE PARK

*1422 165th St., Hampton, 641-456-2047; www.iowadnr.gov/parks*

Set on 319 acres the park features a dam that creates a 100-acre lake. Swimming, beach, fishing, boating (ramps); hiking, snowmobiling, picnicking, camping (electricity, dump station).

# IOWA CITY

Referred to as "the river city," Iowa City is the home of the University of Iowa and the state's first capital. In its early days, Iowa City boomed as a backwoods metropolis, with the Territorial Legislative Assembly meeting here for the first time in 1841. A Doric stone capitol was erected, but with the shift of population, the legislators moved to Des Moines in 1857. As a conciliatory gesture to Iowa City, they selected it as the site of the new university, the University of Iowa. The city has a small-town feel accented by the kind of cultural amenities and adventurous restaurants that a university presence delivers. In the fall, the town is mesmerized by football when the Hawkeyes are playing at home on Saturdays.

*Information: Iowa City/Coralville Convention and Visitors Bureau, 900 First Ave., Riverview Square, Coralville, 319-337-6592, 800-283-6592; www.iowacitycoralville.org*

## WHAT TO SEE AND DO

### CORALVILLE LAKE

*2850 Prairie du Chien Road, Iowa City, 319-338-3543; www.mvr.usace.army.mil*

This 5,400-acre lake offers swimming, boating and fishing. Flooding that occurred during the summer of 1993 eroded a 15-foot-deep channel exposing the underlying bedrock. Now called Devonian Fossil Gorge, it offers a rare opportunity to view Iowa's geological past. The site is an Army Corps of Engineers project. Daily.

### HERBERT HOOVER NATIONAL HISTORIC SITE

*110 Parkside Drive, West Branch, 319-643-2541; www.nps.gov/heho*

The 187-acre park includes the restored house in which President Hoover was born, the Quaker meeting house where he worshipped as a boy, a school, a blacksmith shop and the graves of President and Lou Henry Hoover. Daily.

### HERBERT HOOVER PRESIDENTIAL LIBRARY-MUSEUM

*210 Parkside Drive, West Branch, 319-643-5301; www.hoover.nara.gov*

Administered by the National Archives and Records Administration. Features a museum with recreated historic settings in China, Belgium, Washington and other places prominent in Hoover's 50 years of public service. Research library by appointment. Daily 9 a.m.-5 p.m.; closed holidays.

### IOWA CHILDREN'S MUSEUM

*1451 Coral Ridge Ave., Coralville, 319-625-5500; www.theicm.org*

Interactive exhibits for kids. Tuesday-Thursday 10 a.m.-6 p.m.; Friday-Saturday 10 a.m.-8 p.m., Sunday 11 a.m.-6 p.m.; closed Monday when area schools are in session.

### KALONA HISTORICAL VILLAGE

*411 Ninth St., Kalona, 319-656-2519; www.kalonaiowa.org*

Amish traditions and lifestyle are preserved in this village containing the Wahl Museum, the Mennonite Museum and Archives, and an implement building; restored 110-year-old depot, log house, one-room school, country store, outdoor bake oven, Victorian house, working windmill, post office and church. Monday-Saturday.

★
★
★
★
★

### PLUM GROVE

*1030 Carroll St., Iowa City, 319-337-6846; www.uiowa.edu*

The 1844 residence of the territory's first governor, Robert Lucas, has been restored and furnished with period furniture. Memorial Day-October, Wednesday-Sunday 1-5 p.m.

### UNIVERSITY OF IOWA

*IMU Madison and Jefferson streets, Iowa City, 319-335-0557,*
*319-335-3500; www.uiowa.edu*

This major state university has more than 28,000 students, 100 major buildings on 1,900 acres, 11 colleges, six schools and 82 departments. Big Ten basketball is played at the Carver-Hawkeye Arena, and Hawkeye football is an annual Iowa City obsession.

### SPECIAL EVENT
#### IOWA ARTS FESTIVAL

*408 S. First Ave., Iowa City, 319-337-7944;*
*www.iowacityjazzfestival.com/artsfest*
Celebration of the arts. Mid-June.

### HOTELS
#### ★★HAMPTON INN

*1200 First Ave., Coralville, 319-351-6600, 800-426-7666;*
*www.hamptoninn.com*

115 rooms. Complimentary continental breakfast. Restaurant. Fitness room. Indoor pool, whirlpool. Airport transportation available. Business center. High-speed Internet access. $

#### ★★HOLIDAY INN

*1220 First Ave., Coralville, 319-351-5049, 800-252-7466;*
*www.holiday-inn.com*

96 rooms. Complimentary continental breakfast. Restaurant. Fitness room. Indoor pool, pets accepted. $

#### ★★★SHERATON IOWA CITY HOTEL

*210 S. Dubuque St., Iowa City, 319-337-4058, 800-848-1335;*
*www.starwoodhotels.com*

Located one block from the University of Iowa, rooms at this hotel have been updated with the chain's signature luxury beds and soaking tubs. 236 rooms. Pets accepted, some restrictions. Restaurant, bar. Fitness room. Indoor pool, whirlpool. Airport transportation available. $$

# MARQUETTE

First known as North McGregor, this town was later renamed for Father Jacques Marquette. He and Louis Jolliet were the first to see Iowa territory from the mouth of the Wisconsin River in 1673. Within a 15-mile radius of the town are hundreds of effigy mounds, fortifications and earthworks.

*Information: McGregor/Marquette Chamber of Commerce,*
*146 Main St., 563-873-2186, 800-895-0910; www.mqtcty.org*

## WHAT TO SEE AND DO
### EFFIGY MOUNDS NATIONAL MONUMENT
*151 Highway 76, Harpers Ferry, 563-873-3491; www.nps.gov*

Preserves traces of indigenous civilization from 2,500 years ago. Mounds built in shapes of animals, birds and other forms. Area divided by Yellow River; Great Bear Mound is the largest known bear effigy in the state, 70 feet across the shoulders, 137 feet long and five feet high. Footpath leads from headquarters to Fire Point Mound Group, to scenic viewpoints overlooking the Mississippi and Yellow rivers. Daily.

### PIKES PEAK STATE PARK
*15316 Great River Road, McGregor, 563-873-2341; www.iowadnr.gov*

Set on 970 acres on bluffs overlooking the Mississippi River. Native American mounds, colored sandstone outcroppings, woods and wildflowers. A trail leads across rugged terrain to Bridal Veil Falls.

### SPOOK CAVE AND CAMPGROUND
*13299 Spook Cave Road, McGregor, 563-873-2144;*
*www.spookcave.com*

Guided 35-minute tour of underground cavern via power boat. Campground has swimming beach, lake fishing, hiking trails and picnic areas. May-October, daily.

## HOTEL
### ★HOLIDAY SHORES
*110 Front St., McGregor, 563-873-3449;*
*www.holidayshoresmotel.com*

33 rooms. Indoor pool, whirlpool. Overlooks the Mississippi River. $

# MARSHALLTOWN

The business center of Marshall County prides itself on its historic courthouse, parks and numerous churches. Perhaps its most famous son is "Cap" Anson, son of the founder, who is celebrated at the Baseball Hall of Fame in Cooperstown, New York.
*Information: Convention & Visitors Bureau, 709 S. Center St.,*
*641-753-6645, 800-697-3155; www.marshalltown.org*

★
★★
★★★
★★
★

## WHAT TO SEE AND DO
### FISHER COMMUNITY CENTER ART GALLERY
*709 S. Center St., Marshalltown, 641-753-9013;*
*www.centraliowaartassociation.com*

Art collection including paintings by Sisley, Utrillo and Cassatt. Daily; closed holidays.

## HOTEL
### ★★BEST WESTERN REGENCY INN
*3303 S. Center St., Marshalltown, 641-752-6321, 800-780-7234;*
*www.bestwestern.com*

105 rooms. Restaurant, bar. Indoor pool, whirlpool, fitness room, High-speed Internet access. Pets accepted. $

# MASON CITY

A Native American uprising slowed growth of the city after the first settlement, but pioneers, many of whom were Masons, gradually returned. The town was first known as Shibboleth, later as Masonic Grove. This is the seat of Cerro Gordo County and was the inspiration for the classic musical *The Music Man*.

*Information: Convention & Visitors Bureau, 15 W. State St.,*
*641-422-1663, 800-423-5724; www.masoncityia.com*

## WHAT TO SEE AND DO
### FRANK LLOYD WRIGHT STOCKMAN HOUSE

*530 First St. N.E., Mason City, 641-421-3666;*
*www.stockmanhouse.org*

The only Prairie School house in Iowa designed by Frank Lloyd Wright, this 1908 structure is one of the few houses built by Wright during this period to address middle-class housing needs. Tours. June-August, Thursday-Sunday; September-October, weekends.

### KINNEY PIONEER MUSEUM

*Highway 18 W., Mason City, 641-423-1258*

Local history, pioneer, military exhibits; antique cars; original log cabin (circa 1854); one-room schoolhouse; old farm machinery, railroad caboose; artifacts, fossils. May-September, Tuesday-Sunday.

### MEREDITH WILLSON BOYHOOD HOME

*314 S. Pennsylvania Ave., Mason City, 641-423-3534*

Birthplace of the author of *The Music Man*. May-October, daily; November-April, weekends.

### MEREDITH WILLSON FOOTBRIDGE

*Second Street S.E., Mason City*

Formerly called the Willow Creek Bridge, the name was inspired by the creator of *The Music Man*.

## HOTEL
### ★COMFORT INN

*410 Fifth St. S.W., Mason City, 641-423-4444, 800-228-5150;*
*www.comfortinn.com*

60 rooms. Complimentary continental breakfast. Indoor pool, whirlpool. Pets not accepted. High-speed Internet access. $

# MUSCATINE

This city produces the famous Muscatine cantaloupes and watermelons. Samuel Clemens, who once lived here, declared Muscatine's summer sunsets unsurpassed.

*Information: Convention and Visitors Bureau, 319 E. Second St.,*
*563-263-8895, 800-257-3275; www.muscatine.com*

## WHAT TO SEE AND DO
### MARK TWAIN OVERLOOK
*Lombard and Second streets, Muscatine*

Three acres with a panoramic view of Mississippi River Valley and downtown Muscatine; picnicking.

### MUSCATINE ART CENTER
*1314 Mulberry Ave., Muscatine, 563-263-8282*

Consists of the Laura Musser Museum and the Stanley Gallery. The museum is housed in an Edwardian mansion; changing art exhibits, special events, Estey player pipe organ with 731 pipes, antiques and historical displays; oriental carpets, furniture, paintings, drawings, prints, sculpture, graphics in permanent collection. Tuesday, Wednesday and Friday10 a.m.-5 p.m.; Thursday until 7 p.m.; Saturday and Sunday 1-5 p.m.; closed Monday and holidays.

## HOTEL
### ★★HOLIDAY INN
*2915 N. Highway 61, Muscatine, 563-264-5550, 800-465-4329;*
*www.holiday-inn.com*

112 rooms. Pets accepted; fee. Restaurant, bar. Fitness room. Indoor pool, children's pool, whirlpool. Business center. Kids eat free. $

# NEWTON

The washing machine industry was born here in 1898, and for years the Maytag Company was the dominant business in the city.

*Information: Convention and Visitors Bureau, 113 First Ave. W.,*
*641-792-0299, 800-798-0299; www.visitnewton.com*

## WHAT TO SEE AND DO
### FRED MAYTAG PARK
*301 S. 11th Ave. West, Newton, 641-792-1470*

Donated by the founder of the Maytag Company. Tennis, picnicking, playground, amphitheater, log cabin. Daily. Pool and water slide (June-August daily).

### JASPER COUNTY HISTORICAL MUSEUM
*I-80 Exit 164, Newton, Iowa, 641-792-9118; www.jaspercountymuseum.net*

Local historical displays include a bas-relief sculpture of the natural history of the county, Victorian home, schoolroom, chapel, tool and farm equipment collections. There's also a Maytag historical display of washing machines. May-September, afternoons.

## HOTELS
### ★★★LA CORSETTE MAISON INN
*629 First Ave. E., Newton, 641-792-6833; www.lacorsette.com*

This historic mission-style mansion from 1909 is decorated with stained glass and oak. Guest suites have French furnishings and wood-burning fireplaces. Five rooms. Complimentary full breakfast. Restaurant. $$

★
★★
★★
★

### ★SUPER 8
*1635 S. 12th Ave. West, Newton, 641-792-8868, 800-800-8000; www.super8.com*
43 rooms. Complimentary continental breakfast. High-speed Internet access. Pets not accepted. **$**

## RESTAURANT
### ★★★LA CORSETTE MAISON INN
*629 First Ave. E., Newton, 641-792-6833; www.lacorsette.com*
Located inside La Corsette Maison Inn, guests are served by tuxedoed waiters and entertained with music from the baby grand piano. Entrées include creations such as roasted pork loin with prune chutney or orange roughy with walnut cream sauce. American menu, French. Lunch, dinner. Reservations recommended. **$$$**

# OKOBOJI
Lake Okoboji and the surrounding area are among the most popular resort areas in Iowa.
*Information: Okoboji Tourism, 243 W. Broadway, 712-332-2209,*
*800-270-2574; www.vacationokoboji.com*

## WHAT TO SEE AND DO
### ARNOLDS PARK AMUSEMENT PARK
*37 Lake St., Arnolds Park, 712-332-2183; www.arnoldspark.com*
Century-old amusement park with classic old rides and newer favorites, plus entertainment and games. Mid-June-mid-August, daily; May-mid-June and late August, weekends; hours vary.

### GULL POINT STATE PARK
*1500 Harpen St., Wahpeton, 712-337-3211; www.iowadnr.gov*
Set on 165 acres on West Okoboji Lake, this park has swimming, fishing, boating, snowmobiling, hiking trails, picnicking and camping.

### OKOBOJI QUEEN II
*37 Lake St., Arnolds Park, 712-332-5159*
Several steamship cruises on West Okoboji Lake are offered in the summer, with a more limited schedule the rest of the year.

## SPECIAL EVENT
### OKOBOJI SUMMER THEATER
*Highway 71, Okoboji, 712-332-7773; www.okoboji.com*
This theater has a new play each week and is operated by Stephens College of Columbia, Missouri. Mid-June-mid-August, Tuesday-Sunday.

## HOTELS
### ★★★ARROWWOOD RESORT AND CONFERENCE CENTER BY CLUBHOUSE
*1405 Highway 71 N., Okoboji, 712-332-2161; www.arrowwood-okoboji.com*
This spacious resort and conference center provides guests with a relaxed environment and a host of activities to choose from, including tennis, swimming or simply taking in the beautiful scenery. 99 rooms. Pets accepted. Restaurant, bar. Fitness room. Two outdoor pools, whirlpool. Golf, 27 holes. Tennis. High-speed Internet access. **$**

### ★★INN AT OKOBOJI

*3301 Lake Shore Drive, Okoboji, 712-332-2113;*
*www.theinnatokoboji.com*

156 rooms. Closed October-April. Restaurant, bar. Children's activity center. Indoor pool, outdoor pool. Golf. Tennis. Business center. $

### OTTUMWA PARK

*105 E. Third St., Ottumwa, 641-682-1307*

This 365-acre recreation area in the center of the city includes camping, fishing, tennis, volleyball, basketball courts, baseball diamond, horseshoes, bocce. April-mid-October, daily.

# SIOUX CITY

At the heart of a tri-state region bordered by the Sioux and Missouri rivers, Sioux City has historically been a hub for shipping, transportation and agriculture. The Lewis and Clark expedition followed the Missouri River; the only fatality of that historic trek is commemorated here with the Sergeant Floyd Monument, the first registered historic landmark in the United States.

Today, the Missouri River is important to the city from a recreational standpoint, with a developed riverfront with parks, a dance pavilion and a riverboat casino. Sioux City also has many theaters, parks, an art center, nature center, historical attractions and festivals and events throughout the year.

*Information: Sioux City Convention Center/Tourism Bureau, 801 Fourth St.,*
*712-279-4800, 800-593-2228; www.siouxcitytourismconvention.com*

## WHAT TO SEE AND DO

### ARGOSY CASINO

*100 Larsen Park Road, Sioux City, 800-424-0080; www.argosy.com/siouxcity*

Tri-level riverboat casino. May-October, daily.

### SERGEANT FLOYD MONUMENT

*Glenn Avenue and Highway 75, Sioux City*

This was the first registered national historic landmark in the United States. The 100-foot obelisk marks the burial place of Sergeant Charles Floyd, the only casualty of the Lewis and Clark expedition.

### SIOUX CITY ART CENTER

*225 Nebraska St., Sioux City, 712-279-6272; www.siouxcityartcenter.org*

Contemporary traveling exhibits and permanent collection. Three-story glass atrium. Special programs. Tuesday, Wednesday, Friday and Saturday 10 a.m.-5 p.m. Thursday 10 a.m.-9 p.m. Sunday 1-5 p.m.; closed Monday.

### SIOUX CITY PUBLIC MUSEUM

*2901 Jackson, Sioux City, 712-279-6174; www.siouxcitymuseum.org*

Exhibits show Sioux City history and life in pioneer days; geological, archaeological and Native American materials. Located in a Romanesque 23-room mansion. Tuesday-Saturday 9 a.m.-5 p.m., Sunday 1-5 p.m.; closed holidays.

### STONE STATE PARK

*500 Talbot Road, Sioux City, 712-255-4698;*
*www.iowadnr.com/parks*

Set on 1,069 acres, the park overlooks the Missouri and Big Sioux River valleys and offers views of three states from Dakota Point Lookout near Big Sioux River. The 10-acre Dorothy Pecant Nature Center is also here. Tuesday-Saturday 9 a.m.-5 p.m., Sunday 1-5 p.m.; closed Monday and holidays.

### WOODBURY COUNTY COURTHOUSE

*620 Douglas St., Sioux City, 712-279-6601*

This courthouse was the largest structure ever completed in the architectural style of Chicago's Prairie School. Designed by Purcell and Elmslie, long-time associates of Louis Sullivan, the city-block-long building was constructed in 1918 of Roman brick and ornamented with massive pieces of terra-cotta, stained glass and relief sculpture by Alfonso Ianelli, who also worked with Frank Lloyd Wright. Both the exterior and highly detailed interior are in near-pristine condition. Courtrooms still contain original architect-designed furniture and lighting fixtures. Monday-Friday.

## HOTELS

### ★★CLARION HOTEL AND CONFERENCE CENTER

*Route 70 and I-295, Cherry Hill, 856-428-2300*

197 rooms. Pets accepted, some restrictions; fee. Restaurant, bar. Fitness room. Indoor pool. Airport transportation available. $

### ★RAMADA CITY CENTRE

*130 Nebraska St., Sioux City, 712-277-1550, 800-272-6232; www.ramada.com*

114 rooms. Free continental breakfast. Free High-speed Internet access. Business center. Fitness center. Pets accepted, some restrictions; fee. Bar. Pool. $

### ★SUPER 8

*4307 Stone Ave., Sioux City, 712-274-1520, 800-800-8000; www.super8.com*

60 rooms. Free continental breakfast. Pets accepted, some restrictions; fee. High-speed Internet access. $

## RESTAURANT

### ★GREEN GABLES

*1800 Pierce St., Sioux City, 712-258-4246*

Steak menu. Lunch, dinner, late-night. Children's menu. $$

# WATERLOO

On both banks of the wide Cedar River, Waterloo has established park and picnic areas, docks and boating facilities along the shoreline. One of the largest tractor production facilities in the world is located here.

*Information: Convention and Visitors Bureau, 215 E. Fourth St.,*
*319-233-8350, 800-728-8431; www.waterloocvb.org*

## WHAT TO SEE AND DO

### GEORGE WYTH MEMORIAL STATE PARK

*3659 Wyth Road, Waterloo, 319-232-5505; www.iowadnr.gov*

The 1,200-acre park includes several lakes. Swimming, fishing, boating, nature, hiking and bicycle trails, snowmobiling, picnicking, camping. Daily 4 a.m.-10.30 p.m.

### GROUT MUSEUM OF HISTORY AND SCIENCE

*503 S. St., Waterloo, 319-234-6357; www.groutmuseumdistrict.org*

Permanent and changing exhibits on regional history and science. Discovery Zone offers many hands-on activities. Pioneer Hall, photo history area, industrial hall; genealogy library. Planetarium shows. Tuesday-Saturday 9 a.m.-5 p.m.

### WATERLOO COMMUNITY PLAYHOUSE

*224 Commercial St., Waterloo, 319-235-0367; www.wcpbhct.org*

Open since 1916, this theater offers seven productions yearly including comedies, dramas, mysteries and classics.

### WATERLOO MUSEUM OF ART

*225 Commercial St., Waterloo, 319-291-4490; www.waterloocenterforthearts.org*

Permanent collections include Haitian, American and regional art plus Grant Wood drawings. Changing exhibits. Gift shop offers works by Midwest artists. Tuesday-Sunday 10 a.m.-4 p.m.

## SPECIAL EVENT

### MY WATERLOO DAYS FESTIVAL

*215 E. Fourth St., Waterloo, 319-233-8431*

Citywide festival features air show, balloon rallies, parade, laser and fireworks show, music, renaissance fair, food. Four days beginning the Thursday after Memorial Day.

## HOTELS

### ★★BEST WESTERN STARLITE VILLAGE

*214 Washington St., Waterloo, 319-235-0321, 800-903-0009;*
*www.bestwestern.com*

219 rooms. Pets accepted; fee. Restaurant, bar. Indoor pool. Airport transportation available. $

### ★HEARTLAND INN WATERLOO CROSSROADS

*1809 LaPorte Road, Waterloo, 319-235-4461, 800-334-3277;*
*www.heartlandinns.com*

112 rooms. Complimentary continental breakfast. High-speed Internet access. Fitness room. Indoor pool. Business center. Pets not accepted. Free local calls. $

### ★HEARTLAND INN WATERLOO GREYHOUND PARK

*3052 Marnie Ave., Waterloo, 319-232-7467, 800-334-3277;*
*www.heartlandinns.com*

54 rooms. Complimentary continental breakfast. High-speed Internet access. Indoor pool, whirlpool. Business center. Pets not accepted. Free local calls. $

# WILLIAMSBURG

This small town, located in the central-eastern half of the state, grew in the 1880s when the railroad passed through town. Today, Interstate 80 (I-80) also runs through the area, drawing visitors to this Welsh, Scottish and German farming community.

*Information: www.williamsburgiowa.org*

## RESTAURANT

### ★★COLONY VILLAGE

*I-80 at Exit 225, Little Amana, 319-668-1223; www.colonyvillage.com*

American, German menu. Breakfast, lunch, dinner. Bar. Children's menu. **$$**

# KANSAS

IN THE MOVIE *THE WIZARD OF OZ*, KANSAS IS A DUSTY, EMPTY LANDSCAPE IN BLACK-AND-white. In real life, no one will deny Kansas has plenty of open space (the state has been using the slogan "As Big As You Think" to promote itself), but the curious visitor will find that Kansas is full of interesting places and natural attractions. And yes, it's in color: the gold and black of sunflowers growing by the thousands in a field, the green of vast swaths of native prairie grass (dappled with splashes of brightly colored wildflowers) and of course, the amber waves of grain—wheat—that is grown on so much of Kansas's ground.

You'll find colors of another kind at the annual Wah-Shun-Gah Days powwow in a Santa Fe Trail town, where tribal dancers in native costumes dip and sway to drums. Or if you like your colors loud and your timing is right, you can catch the spectacle of car racing at the NASCAR track in Kansas City.

Native Americans inhabited Kansas thousands of years before Spanish conquistador Francisco Vasquez de Coronado explored the territory in 1541. Other early explorers of Kansas were Meriwether Lewis and William Clark. Army Captain Zebulon Pike also explored the area, continuing westward to discover what is now Pikes Peak in Colorado.

By the 1840s, traders and immigrants had established the Santa Fe and Chisholm Trails across the region. Kansas's pre-Civil War activities included the exploits of John Brown, who operated part of the Underground Railroad for slaves escaping through Kansas. Many clashes occurred between antislavery and proslavery forces as Kansas was being admitted to the Union. The Abolitionists were determined that Kansas be a "free" state. As railroads expanded westward, the era of cattle drives made such towns as Abilene, Hays, Wichita and Dodge City centers of the legendary Old West, as did such men as Bat Masterson, Wyatt Earp, "Wild Bill" Hickok and the Dalton Gang.

★
★★
★★★
★★
★

Eastern Kansas is green, fertile and hilly, with woods, streams and lakes. Western Kansas is a part of the Great Plains, once the grass-covered haunt of the buffalo. In 1874, Mennonite immigrants from Russia introduced their Turkey Red wheat seed to Kansas soil, helping to establish Kansas as the breadbasket of the nation.

When you want to rub elbows with civilization, Topeka, the state's largest city with a 600,000 metro area population, has galleries and museums. Its historic Delano District, once known for its brothels and saloons, is a place to find martini lounges and jazz. If you're looking for the laid-back vibe of a college town, head to

**FUN FACTS**

The world's largest ball of twine, located in Cawker City, is more than 40 feet in circumference, weighs more than 17,000 pounds and is still growing.

At one time it was against the law to serve ice cream on cherry pie in Kansas.

Lawrence, home of the University of Kansas. While it's now a place of coffeehouses, brewpubs and great ethnic restaurants, Lawrence was where the Abolitionists and pro-slavery forces clashed. More than 150 citizens were killed in the fiery Quantrill's Raiders attack. Finally, at the state's eastern edge, the Kansas City metro area is a bustling cluster of suburbs (including Overland Park, Shawnee, Bonner Springs, Lenexa, Olathe and Leawood) spilling over from the bigger Kansas City on the Missouri side of the border. It's a place full of shopping malls and outlet stores, and restaurants ranging from barbecue to gourmet.

# ABILENE

Once famous as a Kansas "cow town," Abilene in 1867 was the terminal point of the Kansas Pacific (later Union Pacific) Railroad and the nearest railhead for the shipment of cattle brought north over the Chisholm Trail. The number of cattle shipped east from here between 1867 and 1871 has been estimated at more than a million, and often 500 cowboys were paid off at a time. City marshals Tom Smith and "Wild Bill" Hickok brought in law and order in the 1870s. Today, Abilene is a wheat center, perhaps best known as the boyhood home of Dwight D. Eisenhower.

*Information: Convention and Visitors Bureau, 201 N.W. Second St., 785-263-2231, 800-569-5915; www.abileneks.com*

## WHAT TO SEE AND DO

### ABILENE & SMOKY VALLEY RAIL ROAD

*200 S. Fifth St., Abilene, 785-263-1077, 888-426-6687; www.asvrr.org*

This 100-year-old wooden diner coach makes trips through the historic countryside. Memorial Day-Labor Day, Wednesday-Saturday 10 a.m. and 2p.m.; Sunday, 2 p.m.

### DICKINSON COUNTY HISTORICAL MUSEUM

*412 S. Campbell St., Abilene, 785-263-2681; www.heritagecenterdk.com*

Exhibits at this museum depict life in early pioneer days and include antique toys and household items used at the turn of the century. Also onsite is a Heritage Center, carousel and log cabin. Daily.

★
★
★
★
★

### EISENHOWER CENTER

*200 S.E. Fourth St., Abilene, 785-263-4751; www.dwightdeisenhower.com*

President Dwight D. Eisenhower's birthplace is also the location of his presidential library. Visitors can tour the 1887 house where Eisenhower was raised; the interior and most furnishings are original. The museum houses changing exhibits of mementos, souvenirs and gifts received during Eisenhower's career. The library contains presidential papers. President and Mrs. Eisenhower are buried in the Meditation Chapel. Daily.

### LEBOLD MANSION

*106 N. Vine St., Abilene, 785-263-4356; www.abilenekansas.org*

A restored Victorian mansion with period furnishings, this house was built in 1880 by C. H. Lebold. Tours: Tuesday-Sunday 10 a.m.-4 p.m.

## SEELYE MANSION AND MUSEUM

*1105 N. Buckeye Ave., Abilene, 785-263-1084; www.seelyemansion.org*

This 25-room Georgian mansion is listed on the National Register of Historic Places. It was built in 1905 by A. B. Seelye, a patent medicine entrepreneur. The museum depicts a turn-of-the-century medicine business. Daily.

## HOTEL
### ★SUPER 8

*2207 N. Buckeye Ave., Abilene, 785-263-4545, 1-800-800-8000; www.super8.com*

61 rooms. Pets accepted; fee. $

## RESTAURANTS
### ★★BROOKVILLE HOTEL DINING ROOM

*105 E. Lafayette, Abilene, 785-263-2244; www.brookvillehotel.com*

American menu. Dinner. Closed Monday. $$$

### ★★★KIRBY HOUSE

*205 N.E. Third St., Abilene, 1-785-263-7336; www.kirby-house.com*

Built as a home in 1885, this Victorian-style restaurant has a friendly atmosphere popular with large groups and anyone celebrating a special occasion. The menu features American classics like country fried steak. American menu. Lunch, dinner, Sunday brunch. Bar. Children's menu. Closed Sunday. $$

# COLBY

This town is the hub of Northwest Kansas, with cultural, shopping and hospitality facilities. Agribusiness drives the economy.

*Information: Convention and Visitors Bureau, 350 S. Range, 785-460-7643, 800-611-8835; www.colbychamber.com*

## WHAT TO SEE AND DO
### PRAIRIE MUSEUM OF ART & HISTORY

*1905 S. Franklin St., Colby, 785-460-4590; www.prairiemuseum.org*

This museum features rare bisque and china dolls, glass and crystal, Chinese and Japanese artifacts, textiles and furniture. On the museum site are a sod house, restored 1930s farmstead, one-room schoolhouse, a country church and one of the largest barns in Kansas. Daily.

## HOTEL
### ★★QUALITY INN

*1950 S. Range Ave., Colby, 785-462-3933, 800-750-7160; www.qualityinn.com*

117 rooms. Restaurant. Indoor pool. $

★
★★
★★
★

# COUNCIL GROVE

As the last outfitting place on the Santa Fe Trail between the Missouri River and Santa Fe, Council Grove, now a National Historic Landmark, holds historic significance in the development of the West. The town grew up around a Native American campground in a grove of oaks near the Neosho River and has many turn-of-the-century buildings, several parks and two lakes.

*Information: Convention and Visitors Bureau, 207 W. Main St., 800-732-9211; www.councilgrove.com*

## A WALK THROUGH THE OLD WEST

If you're looking for an authentic Old West town, journey to Council Grove, a once busy trading center on the Sante Fe Trail during the 1840s and 1850s. Council Grove contains some of the best-preserved frontier-era architecture in Kansas, and many of the buildings are still used for their original commercial purpose.

Begin your tour at the **Kaw Mission State Historic** Site (*500 N. Mission St.*). Methodist missionaries built this school for native Kaw children in 1851. Today the structure contains a museum dedicated to the Kaw, the Sante Fe Trail and early Council Grove. From here, walk south on Mission Street to Main Street, which follows the route of the Santa Fe Trail through town. **The Cottage House Hotel** (*25 N. Neosho*) is a beautifully maintained Victorian hotel still in operation with wraparound porches and striking Queen Anne turrets and gazebos. Across Main Street, the **Farmers and Drovers Bank** (*201 W. Main St.*) is a handsome landmark of red brick and limestone, with eclectic architectural features including Romanesque arches, stained-glass windows and a Byzantine dome.

One block east on Main Street is another historic structure, which is still in operation. The **Hays House Restaurant** (*112 W. Main St.*) is the oldest continuously operating restaurant west of the Mississippi. Since it was constructed in 1857, the restaurant has served the likes of General George Custer and Jesse James. The ambience is frontier-era, and peach pie is among the favorite offerings. Also on this block of Main Street is the stone **Last Chance Store** (also in operation since 1857) and the **Council Grove National Bank Building.**

Before crossing the Neosho River Bridge, turn south two blocks to the Seth Hays Home. Built in 1867, this home has been preserved and is open to visitors on Sundays and by appointment. Cross the Neosho River on Main Street. In a shelter along the riverbank is the remains of the Council Oak, a once-vast oak tree under which representatives of the United States and the Osage tribe signed a treaty in 1825 that guaranteed settlers safe passage across Indian territory. On the north corner of Main and Union streets is a small park containing the Madonna of the Trail, a statue of a pioneer mother and children erected in 1925 by the Daughters of the American Revolution. Along with a museum of frontier history, the park is home to the Post Office Oak, a 300-year-old burr oak that served as an unofficial post depository for travelers along the Sante Fe Trail. Continue east on Main to Durland Park (at Fifth Street) where Council Grove's first jail, constructed in 1849, still stands. Also in Durland Park are two 19th-century train depots.

## WHAT TO SEE AND DO
### COUNCIL OAK SHRINE
*313 E. Main St., Council Grove*
The treaty of 1825 was signed here between U.S. government commissioners and the Osage.

### CUSTER'S ELM SHRINE
*South Neosho Street, Council Grove*
This elm trunk stands as a shrine to a tree that was 100 feet tall, 16 feet in circumference and reputedly sheltered the camp of General George Custer in 1867 when he was leading an expedition to western Kansas.

### MADONNA OF THE TRAIL MONUMENT
*Corner of Union and Main streets, Council Grove*
One of 12 statues erected in each of the states through which the National Old Trails Roads passed. The Madonna pays tribute to pioneer mothers and commemorates the trails that opened the West.

### POST OFFICE OAK
*East Main Street, Council Grove*
This mammoth oak tree with a cache at its base served as an unofficial post office for pack trains and caravans on the Santa Fe Trail from 1825-1847.

## SPECIAL EVENT
### WAH-SHUN-GAH DAYS
*207 W. Main St., Council Grove, 620-767-5413*
This event is the Kaw Intertribal Powwow and includes a Santa Fe Trail ride and supper, antique tractor pull and street dance. Third weekend in June.

## HISTORIC DODGE CITY
Memorable for buffalo hunts, longhorn cattle and frontier marshals, Dodge City was laid out by construction crews of the Santa Fe Railroad and named for nearby Fort Dodge. Vast herds of buffalo—estimated at 24 million or more—which then covered the surrounding plains, had been hunted here for years. The railroad provided transportation to make the hides commercially profitable. A skilled hunter could earn $100 a day at the industry's height; by 1875 the herds were nearly exterminated. Cattle drives, also stimulated by the railroad, took the buffalo's place in the town's economy. In the 1870s, Dodge City became the cowboy capital of the region. Among its notable peace officers were Bat Masterson and Wyatt Earp. The prevalence of sudden and violent death resulted in the establishment of Boot Hill cemetery. In the mid-1880s the era of the cattle drives ended, and by 1890 much of the grazing land had been plowed for crops. Visitors to Doge City can get a peak into the Wild West's past by exploring the many preserved historic buildings, including those on restored historic Front Street.
Information: Convention & Visitors Bureau, 400 W. Wyatt Earp Blvd., Dodge City; 620-225-8186, 800-653-9378; www.visitdodgecity.org

## RESTAURANT
### ★★HAYS HOUSE HISTORIC RESTAURANT AND TAVERN
*112 W. Main St., Council Grove, 620-767-5911; www.hayshouse.com*
American menu. Breakfast, lunch, dinner, Sunday brunch. Bar. Children's menu.
National Register of Historic Landmarks on Santa Fe Trail. $$

# EL DORADO
El Dorado, the seat of Butler County, is located on the western edge of the Flint Hills.
The city's growth can be attributed to oil—two refineries are located here. Stapleton
No. 1, the area's first gusher, tapped in 1915, is commemorated by a marker at the
northwestern edge of the town.
*Information: Chamber of Commerce, 201 E. Central, El Dorado,*
*316-321-3150; www.eldoradochamber.com*

## WHAT TO SEE AND DO
### EL DORADO STATE PARK
*618 N.E. Bluestem Road, El Dorado, 316-321-7180*
The largest of Kansas's state parks, El Dorado is made up of four areas totaling 4,000
acres. Rolling hills, wooded valleys and open prairie make up the natural environment
of the park. El Dorado Lake is also within the park. Daily.

### KANSAS OIL MUSEUM
*383 E. Central Ave., El Dorado, 316-321-9333; www.kansasoilmuseum.org*
Displays at this museum depict the area's oil, ranching and agricultural history,
including a model rotary drilling rig. Outdoor historic oil field exhibits include a
restored cable-tool drilling rig, shotgun lease house and antique engines. Monday-
Saturday 9 a.m.-5 p.m.

## HOTEL
### ★★BEST WESTERN RED COACH INN
*2525 W. Central St., El Dorado, 316-321-6900, 800-362-2034; www.bestwestern.com*
73 rooms. Pets accepted, some restrictions; fee. Restaurant. Fitness room. Indoor
pool, whirlpool. $

# EMPORIA
This was the home of one of America's most famous newspaper editors, William
Allen White. His *Emporia Gazette* editorials, written from the 1890s to the 1940s,
attracted nationwide attention and earned White a Pulitzer Prize. Emporia is the seat
of Lyon County and on the edge of the Flint Hills area.
*Information: Convention & Visitors Bureau, 719 Commercial St., Emporia,*
*620-342-1600, 800-279-3730; www.emporiakschamber.org*

## WHAT TO SEE AND DO
### DAVID TRAYLOR ZOO OF EMPORIA
*75 Soden Road, Emporia, 620-341-4365; www.emporiazoo.org*
This zoo has nearly 400 specimens of birds, mammals and reptiles representing more
than 80 species housed in natural habitats. Drive or walk-through. Daily.

### EMPORIA GAZETTE BUILDING

*517 Merchant St., Emporia, 620-342-4800*

This building houses William Allen White's widely-quoted newspaper. Located here is a small one-room museum that displays newspaper machinery used in White's time. Call for hours.

### FLINT HILLS NATIONAL WILDLIFE REFUGE

*530 W. Maple Ave., Hartford, 620-392-5553; www.fws.gov/flinthills*

Consisting of 18,500 acres located on the upstream portion of John Redmond River, this park offers hiking and camping. Wild food gathering is permitted. Bald eagles can be spotted in fall and winter. Fishing and hunting in legal seasons. Monday-Friday 8 a.m.-4:30 p.m. Some portions closed during fall migration of waterfowl.

### NATIONAL TEACHERS HALL OF FAME

*1200 Commercial, Emporia, 620-341-5660; www.nthf.org*

This organization is committed to drawing the public's attention to exceptional teachers through a museum, teacher's resource center and an induction ceremony that recognizes five of the nation's most outstanding Pre-Kindergarten through Grade 12 educators each year. Monday-Saturday.

## HOTEL

### ★★BEST WESTERN HOSPITALITY HOUSE

*3021 W. Highway 50, Emporia, 620-342-7587, 800-362-2036; www.bestwestern.com*

143 rooms. Pets accepted, some restrictions. Complimentary continental breakfast. Restaurant. Bar. Fitness room. Indoor pool, whirlpool. Business center. $

# HAYS

Fort Hays, a former military post on the old frontier, gave this railroad town its name. Oil, grain, cattle, educational and medical facilities, and tourism are important to the area.

*Information: Convention and Visitors Bureau, 2700 Pine St., Hays, 785-628-8202, 800-569-4505; www.haysusa.com*

## WHAT TO SEE AND DO

### ELLIS COUNTY HISTORICAL SOCIETY MUSEUM

*100 W. Seventh St., Hays, 785-628-2624; www.elliscountyhistoricalmuseum.org*

More than 26,000 items are on display in this museum including antique toys and games, musical instruments and rotating exhibits including quilts from the 1800s to present. Also here are a one-room schoolhouse and the oldest stone church in Ellis County. June-August, Tuesday-Friday, also Saturday afternoons; rest of year, Tuesday-Friday.

### HISTORIC FORT HAYS

*1472 Highway 183 Alternate, Hays, 785-625-6812; www.kshs.org/places/forthays*

This former U.S. Army post was in use from 1865-1889 as a base for defending the railroad that ran through the area. Wild West legends Wild Bill Hickok and Buffalo Bill Cody are just some of the figures who passed through the fort. March-November, Tuesday-Saturday 9 a.m.-5 p.m., Sunday 1-5 p.m., December-February, Wednesday-Saturday 10 a.m.-5 p.m. Group tours by appointment.

**STERNBERG MUSEUM OF NATURAL HISTORY**

*3000 Sternberg Drive, Hays, 785-628-4286; www.fshu.edu/sternberg*

This museum features natural history, paleontological and geological collections. Tuesday-Sunday; closed Monday.

## SPECIAL EVENTS
### PIONEER DAYS AT HISTORIC FORT HAYS

*1472 Highway 183 Alternate, Hays, 785-625-6812*

Two full days are filled with demonstrations of butter churning, tatting, rope making, rug weaving, whittling and stone post cutting at this annual event. Third week in September.

### WILD WEST FESTIVAL

*Frontier Park, 2700 Vine St., Hays, 785-628-8202; www.wildwestfestival.com*

This annual event features family-oriented activities, concerts, food booths and a fireworks display. Early July.

## HOTELS
### ★HAMPTON INN

*4002 General Hays Road, Hays, 785-621-4444, 800-426-7866; www.hamptoninn.com*

80 rooms. Complimentary continental breakfast. $

### ★★HOLIDAY INN

*3603 Vine St., Hays, 785-625-7371; www.holiday-inn.com*

191 rooms. Restaurant. Bar. Fitness room. Indoor pool, whirlpool. Airport transportation available. $

## RESTAURANT
### ★GUTIERREZ

*1106 E. 27 St., Hays, 785-625-4402; www.thelocalsfavorite.com*

Mexican, American menu. Lunch, dinner. Bar. Children's menu. Daily. $$

# HUTCHINSON

In 1887, drillers for natural gas discovered some of the world's richest rock salt deposits under the town of Hutchinson. Today, the town is a major salt-producing center.

*Information: Greater Hutchinson Convention and Visitors Bureau, 117 N. Walnut, Hutchinson, 620-662-3391, 800-691-4262; www.hutchchamber.com*

## WHAT TO SEE AND DO
### HISTORIC FOX THEATRE

*18 E. First Ave., Hutchinson, 620-663-5861; www.hutchinsonfox.com*

This theater exemplifies Art Deco architecture and is on the National Register of Historic Places. Professional entertainment, classic and independent film and arts education programs are offered.

## HOTELS

### ★★GRAND PRAIRIE HOTEL AND CONVENTION CENTER

*1400 N. Lorraine St., Hutchinson, 620-669-9311, 800-362-5018;*
*www.grandprairiehotel.com*

218 rooms. Pets accepted; fee. Kids play station; convention center; Restaurant. Indoor pool. **$**

### ★SUN DOME

*11 Des Moines Ave., South Hutchinson, 620-663-4444;*

96 rooms. Pets accepted, some restrictions. Complimentary breakfast. Restaurant. Business center. High-speed Internet access. **$**

# IOLA

Most of the expansion of this small eastern Kansas town happened after natural gas was discovered in the area in the 1900s. The town retains its historic feel with a preserved downtown with Victorian buildings.
*Information: Chamber of Commerce, 208 W. Madison, 620-365-5252;*
*www.iola.com/guide.html*

## WHAT TO SEE AND DO

### OLD JAIL MUSEUM

*203 N. Jefferson Ave., Iola, 620-365-3051;*
*www.kansastravel.org*

A historic building, this jail has been restored and is now open for tours. May-September, Tuesday-Saturday.

### BOYHOOD HOME OF MAJOR GENERAL FREDERICK FUNSTON

*207 N. Jefferson, Iola, 620-365-3051; www.skyways.lib.ks.us*

This house, built in 1860, was the home of Fred Funston, a decorated soldier noted for directing the recovery efforts following the San Francisco earthquake of 1906. Originally located on a homestead about five miles north of Iola, the house has been restored according to the Victorian décor of the 1880s and 1890s. Many original family items are on display. May-October; Wednesday-Saturday 12:30-4:30 p.m. November-April; Tuesday-Saturday 2-4 p.m.

## HOTEL

### ★★BEST WESTERN INN

*1315 N. State St., Iola, 620-365-5161, 800-769-0007; www.bestwestern.com*
58 rooms. Pets accepted, some restrictions; fee. Restaurant. Outdoor pool. **$**

# LAWRENCE

Lawrence had a stormy history in the territorial years. It was founded by the New England Emigrant Aid Company, which aimed to populate the area with antislavery proponents transplanted from New England and other "free states" as a means of warding off slavery. The center of Free State activities, the town was close to a state of war from 1855 until the Free Staters triumphed in 1859. The Confederate guerrilla leader, William Quantrill, made one of his most spectacular raids on Lawrence in 1863, burning the town and killing 150 citizens. After the Civil War,

**KANSAS**

★
★
★
★

the town experienced a gradual and peaceful growth. It is the site of the University of Kansas.

*Information: Convention and Visitors Bureau, 402 N. Second St., Lawrence, 785-865-4499; www.visitlawrence.com*

## WHAT TO SEE AND DO
### HASKELL INDIAN NATIONS UNIVERSITY
*155 Indian Ave., Lawrence, 785-749-8404; www.haskell.edu*
This school was founded in 1884 to provide education for Native Americans. More than 120 tribes are represented among the students. The campus is a registered historic landmark. The American Indian Athletic Hall of Fame is located here.

### LAWRENCE ARTS CENTER
*940 New Hampshire St., Lawrence, 785-843-2787; www.lawrenceartscenter.com*
Galleries featuring the work of local artists and craftspeople; performance hall for theater, dance, and music; art classes and workshops for all ages. Monday-Saturday 9 a.m.-5 p.m.

### OLD WEST LAWRENCE HISTORIC DISTRICT
*402 N. Second St., Lawrence, 785-865-4499*
Take a self-guided tour through this area of notable 19th-century homes.

### UNIVERSITY OF KANSAS
*Corner of 15th and Iowa streets, Lawrence, 785-864-2700; www.ku.edu*
With 26,000 students, this university stretches over a 1,000-acre campus. Kansas Jayhawks athletics (especially basketball) are a prime attraction in Lawrence. Some campus attractions include the Campanile Bell Tower, Museum of Natural History, Museum of Anthropology and Spencer Museum of Art. All buildings are closed on holidays.

## HOTELS
### ★BEST WESTERN LAWRENCE
*2309 Iowa St., Lawrence, 785-843-9100; www.bestwestern.com*
100 rooms. Pets accepted; fee. Complimentary continental breakfast. High-speed Internet access. Fitness room. Indoor pool, whirlpool. Business center. **$**

### ★★★ELDRIDGE HOTEL
*701 Massachusetts St., Lawrence, 785-749-5011, 800-527-0909; www.eldridgehotel.com*
This hotel, with a history dating to the Civil War, is located in the heart of quaint downtown Lawrence, near the University of Kansas. The setting is charming, but the décor is crisp and contemporary. The original ceilings and woodwork have been nicely maintained. 48 rooms, all suites. Wireless Internet access. Restaurant. Bar. **$$**

### ★★HOLIDAY INN LAWRENCE
*200 McDonald Drive, Lawrence, 785-841-7077; www.holiday-inn.com/lawrenceks*
192 rooms. Pets accepted; fee. Wireless Internet access. Restaurant. Bar. Indoor pool, whirlpool. Airport transportation available. Business center. **$**

## SPECIALTY LODGING
### HALCYON HOUSE BED AND BREAKFAST
*1000 Ohio St., Lawrence, 785-841-0314, 888-441-0314;*
*www.thehalcyonhouse.com*
This Victorian inn was built in 1885 but has been updated with modern touches like high-speed Internet access. 9 rooms. Children over 12 years only. Complimentary full breakfast. High-speed Internet access. Victorian inn built in 1885. **$**

# LEAVENWORTH
Leavenworth was the first incorporated town in Kansas Territory. At first strongly pro-slavery, Leavenworth had many border conflicts, but during the Civil War it was loyal to the Union. In the years just before the war, the town was the headquarters for a huge overland transportation and supply operation sending wagons and stagecoaches northwest on the Oregon Trail and southwest on the Santa Fe Trail. Fort Leavenworth, adjoining the city, is the oldest military post west of the Mississippi River that has been in continuous operation (since 1827). A federal penitentiary is on the grounds adjacent to the fort.
*Information: Leavenworth Convention and Visitors Bureau, 518 Shawnee St.,*
*Leavenworth, 913-682-4113, 800-844-4114; www.lvarea.com*

## WHAT TO SEE AND DO
### FORT LEAVENWORTH
*600 Thomas Ave., Fort Leavenworth, 913-684-5604*
Features of interest at this base are the U.S. Army Command and General Staff College, U.S. Disciplinary Barracks, National Cemetery, Buffalo Soldier Monument and branches of the Oregon and Santa Fe trails. The Frontier Army Museum features artifacts of pioneer history and the Army of the West. Daily.

### FRONTIER ARMY MUSEUM
*Fort Leavenworth, Reynolds Avenue, Leavenworth, 913-684-3767*
Discover the history of Fort Leavenworth and the United States Regular Army on the Frontier. See historic army uniforms, weapons and equipment, including a 1917 JN4D Jenny biplane and the carriage that Abraham Lincoln traveled in when he visited in 1859. Monday-Friday 9 a.m.-4 p.m., Saturday 10 a.m.-4 p.m.

### PARKER CAROUSEL
*320 S. Esplanade, Leavenworth, 913-682-1331; www.firstcitymuseums.org*
This restored 1913 carousel features hand-carved, one-of-a-kind horses. Thursday-Saturday, 11 a.m.-5 p.m., Sunday 1-5 p.m.

## HOTEL
### ★DAYS INN
*3211 S. Fourth St., Highway 7/73, south of Leavenworth, 913-651-6000;*
*www.daysinn.com*
52 rooms. Pets allowed. Complimentary continental breakfast. Outdoor pool. High-speed Internet access. **$**

63

**KANSAS**

★
★
★
★
★

# LEAWOOD

A Kansas City suburb was established after World War II and grew after the building of several housing developments. It's now one of the fastest growing cities in Kansas.

*Information: City of Leawood; 4800 Town Center Drive, Leawood,*
*913-339-6700; www.leawood.org*

## RESTAURANTS

### ★GATES BAR-B-Q

*103 Road, Leawood, 913-383-1752; www.gatesbbq.com*
American menu. Lunch, dinner, late-night. Closed holidays. **$$**

### ★★★HEREFORD HOUSE

*5001 Town Center Drive, Leawood, 913-327-0800; www.herefordhouse.com*
Jack Webb founded the original branch of this steakhouse in Kansas City in 1957. Now, this Town Center Plaza location is one of three, with charcoal-grilled steaks and friendly, no-hassle service. Steak menu. Lunch, dinner. Bar. Children's menu. Outdoor seating. **$$$**

### ★★YAHOOZ

*4701 Town Center Drive, Leawood, 913-451-8888; www.eatpbj.com*
American, steak menu. Lunch, dinner, Sunday brunch. Bar. Children's menu. Reservations recommended. Outdoor seating. Daily. **$$$**

# LIBERAL

Liberal's name comes from the generosity of one of its first settlers, S.S. Rogers. Although water was scarce in southwestern Kansas, Rogers never charged parched and weary travelers for the use of his well—a "liberal" fee.

*Information: Tourist Information Center, 1 Yellow Brick Road, 620-626-0170;*
*www.liberal.net*

## WHAT TO SEE AND DO

### CORONADO MUSEUM

*567 E. Cedar St., Liberal, 620-624-7624;*
*www.sewardcountymuseum.com*
Displays at this museum depict early life of in Liberal. Some exhibits trace Francisco Coronado's route through Kansas. Also included are Dorothy's House from *The Wizard of Oz* and an animated display of the story. Memorial Day-Labor Day, Monday-Saturday 9 a.m.-6 p.m., Sunday, 1-6 p.m. Labor Day-Memorial Day, Tuesday-Saturday 9 a.m.-5 p.m., Sunday 1-5 p.m.

### MID-AMERICA AIR MUSEUM

*2000 W. Second St., Liberal, 620-624-5263;*
*www.kansastravel.org/airmuseum.htm*
See an aviation collection of 100 aircraft including civilian aircraft, military aircraft from World War II and planes of the Korean and Vietnam era. Also here is the Liberal Army Airfield exhibit. Daily; closed holidays.

# MANHATTAN

Manhattan is a thriving center for trade, education, government, health care and entertainment. Several early settlements were combined to form Manhattan. Lying in a limestone bowl-shaped depression resulting from glacial action, the town developed as a trading center for farm products. Kansas State University is located in Manhattan.

*Information: Convention and Visitors Bureau, 501 Poyntz Ave., Manhattan,*
*785-776-8829; www.manhattan.org*

## WHAT TO SEE AND DO
### KANSAS STATE UNIVERSITY

*119 Anderson hall, Manhattan, 785-532-6250, 800-432-8270; www.ksu.edu*
With more than 20,000 students, this campus, established around 1863, has buildings constructed of native limestone.

### SUNSET ZOO

*2333 Oak St., Manhattan, 785-587-2737; www.ci.manhattan.ks.us/sunsetzoo*
A zoo with more than 300 animals, residents here include Brownie, thought to be the oldest living grizzly bear in the world. He's kept company by snow leopards, cheetahs, red pandas, bobcats, reptiles, birds and more. Daily.

### TUTTLE CREEK STATE PARK

*5800 A River Pond Road, Manhattan, 785-539-7941;*
*www.stateparks.com/tuttle_creek.html*
This 1,200-acre park is located on a 13,350-acre lake. There is a special observation area with distant views of the Blue River Valley and Randolph Bridge, the largest in Kansas. Beach, bathhouse, fishing, boating, camping.

## HOTELS
### ★★CLARION HOTEL

*530 Richards Drive, Manhattan, 785-539-5311; www.choicehotels.com*
196 rooms. Pets accepted, some restrictions; fee. Wireless Internet access. Two restaurants, bar. Fitness room. Indoor pool, children's pool, whirlpool. Business center. $

### ★★HOLIDAY INN MANHATTAN AT THE CAMPUS

*1641 Anderson Ave., Manhattan, 785-539-7531, 800-111-000; www.holiday-inn.com*
113 rooms. Pets accepted. Restaurant. Bar. Wireless Internet access. Fitness room. Outdoor pool. Business center. $

## RESTAURANT
### ★★★HARRY'S

*418 Poyntz Ave., Manhattan, 785-537-1300; www.harrysmanhattan.com*
The historic Wareham hotel is the setting for this restaurant, named in honor of the hotel's first owner, Harry Wareham. Though the restaurant has been restored to look much as it did when it first opened in the 1920s, the menu is decidedly up-to-date, with dishes such as risotto and fried smoked portobellos, or grilled lobster salad with spicy roma tomato chutney. American menu. Lunch, dinner. Closed Sunday. Bar. Children's menu. Business casual attire. Reservations recommended. $$$

65

**KANSAS**

★
★
★
★
★

# MCPHERSON

Both the city and the county bear the name of Civil War hero General James Birdseye McPherson, who was killed in the Battle of Atlanta in 1864. This small town of 14,000 residents has a historic downtown and a restored opera house dating to the 1880s.
*Information: Convention and Visitors Bureau, 306 N. Main St., 620-241-3340,*
*800-324-8022; www.mcphersonks.org*

## WHAT TO SEE AND DO
### MAXWELL WILDLIFE REFUGE
*101 N. Main St., Canton, 620-628-4455, 800-324-8022;*
*www.mcphersonks.org/community/parks.php*
This 2,800-acre prairie provides a natural environment for elk, deer and buffalo. The refuge has an observation tower, a 46-acre fishing lake, boat ramp and nature trail. Daily.

## HOTEL
### ★★BEST WESTERN HOLIDAY MANOR
*2211 E. Kansas Ave., McPherson, 620-241-5343, 888-841-0038;*
*www.bestwestern.com*
109 rooms. Pets accepted, some restrictions; fee. Restaurant. Indoor pool, outdoor pool, whirlpool. $

# OVERLAND PARK

The suburb Overland Park, which wasn't incorporated until 1960, is located directly south of Kansas City and has a historic downtown.
*Information: Convention and Visitors Bureau, 9001 W. 110th St.,*
*Overland Park, 913-491-0123, 800-262-7275; www.opcvb.org*

## WHAT TO SEE AND DO
### DEANNA ROSE CHILDREN'S FARMSTEAD
*138th Street and Switzer Road, Overland Park, 913-897-2360; www.opkansas.org*
Feed and pet farm animals, hop on a horse-drawn wagon or walk through a replica of an early 1900s Kansas farmhouse at this farmstead. April-October, daily. Closed. November-March.

### OVERLAND PARK ARBORETUM AND BOTANICAL GARDENS
*8909 W. 179th St., Overland Park, 913-685-3604; www.opkansas.org*
This park features 300 acres of land, including three miles of hiking trails (some wheelchair accessible) through gardens. Naturalized areas feature a Meadow Garden, Butterfly Garden and Woodland Garden. Guided tours by appointment. Daily, weather permitting.

## HOTELS
### ★★COURTYARD KANSAS CITY OVERLAND PARK/CONVENTION CENTER
*11001 Woodson Ave., Overland Park, 913-317-8500, 800-321-2211;*
*www.courtyard.com*
168 rooms. High-speed Internet access. Restaurant. Fitness room. Indoor pool, whirlpool. Business center. $

### ★★DOUBLETREE HOTEL OVERLAND PARK-CORPORATE WOODS

*10100 College Blvd., Overland Park, 913-451-6100, 800-222-8733;*
*www.doubletree.com*

356 rooms. Restaurant. Bar. High-speed Internet access. Fitness room. Indoor pool, whirlpool. Airport transportation available.

### ★★EMBASSY SUITES HOTEL KANSAS CITY-OVERLAND PARK

*10601 Metcalf Ave., Overland Park, 913-649-7060, 800-362-2779;*
*www.embassysuites.com*

200 rooms, all suites. Complimentary full breakfast. Wireless Internet access. Restaurant. Bar. Fitness room. Indoor pool, whirlpool. Business center. $

### ★★HAMPTON INN KANSAS CITY/OVERLAND PARK

*10591 Metcalf Frontage Road, Overland Park, 913-341-1551, 800-426-7866;*
*www.hamptoninn.com*

134 rooms. Complimentary continental breakfast. Wireless Internet access. Restaurant. Bar. Outdoor pool, whirlpool. Business center. $

### ★★HOLIDAY INN OVERLAND PARK-WEST

*8787 Reeder Road, Overland Park, 913-888-8440, 888-825-7538;*
*www.holiday-inn.com*

191 rooms. High-speed Internet access. Restaurant. Bar. Fitness room. Indoor pool, outdoor pool, whirlpool. Business center. $

### ★LA QUINTA INN & SUITES OVERLAND PARK

*10610 Marty St., Overland Park, 913-648-5555; www.lq.com*

143 rooms. Complimentary breakfast. Pets accepted. Outdoor pool. High-speed Internet access. $

### ★★★OVERLAND PARK MARRIOTT

*10800 Metcalf Ave., Overland Park, 913-451-8000, 800-228-9290;*
*www.overlandparkmarriott.com*

Located in an industrial area of Overland Park, this well-landscaped suburban hotel can be easily seen from the Interstate (I-435). The Metcalf South Mall is approximately one mile away, and the convention center is within two miles of the hotel. 391 rooms. High-speed Internet access. Three restaurants, bar. Fitness room. Indoor pool, outdoor pool, whirlpool. Airport transportation available. Business center. $$

## RESTAURANTS

### ★★FIORELLA'S JACK STACK BARBECUE

*9520 Metcalf Ave., Overland Park, 913-385-7427; www.jackstackbbq.com*

American, barbecue menu. Lunch, dinner. Daily. Closed holidays. Bar. Children's menu. Casual attire. $$

### ★★IL TRULLO

*9056 Metcalf Ave., Overland Park, 913-341-3773; www.iltrullo-kc.com*

Italian menu. Lunch, dinner. Closed Sunday-Monday. Bar. Children's menu. Casual attire. Reservations recommended. $$

**KANSAS**

★
★
★
★
★

### ★★INDIA PALACE
*9914 W. 87th St., Overland Park, 913-381-1680*
Indian menu. Lunch, dinner. $$

### ★★★J. GILBERT'S WOOD FIRED STEAKS AND SEAFOOD
*8901 Metcalf Ave., Overland Park, 913-642-8070; www.jgilberts.com*
The restaurants in this minichain (there are locations in Ohio, Virginia and Connecticut) all have a fireplace as their focal point, a visual reminder of this eatery's dedication to preparing simply delicious wood-fired steaks. The prime Kansas City strip is a favorite, while dishes like pan-seared halibut satisfy those who are less carnivorous. Steak menu. Dinner. Daily. Closed holidays. Bar. Children's menu. Casual attire. Reservations recommended. Outdoor seating. $$$

### ★★JOHNNY CASCONE'S
*6863 W. 91st St., Overland Park, 913-381-6837; www.cascones.com*
Italian menu. Lunch, dinner. Bar. Children's menu. Casual attire. Reservations recommended. $$

### ★★K. C. MASTERPIECE BARBECUE & GRILL
*10985 Metcalf Ave., Overland Park, 913-345-2255; www.masterpiecebbq.com*
American, barbecue menu. Lunch, dinner. Bar. Restaurant, Children's menu. Casual attire. $$

### ★★★NIKKO JAPANESE STEAKHOUSE
*10800 Metcalf Road, Overland Park, 913-451-8000; www.marriott.com*
A Japanese steakhouse complete with tableside teppanyaki chefs, this restaurant is located inside the Marriott hotel. Entrées, from steak to seafood and more, come with soup, salad, shrimp, steamed rice and vegetables. Japanese menu. Dinner. Children's menu. Valet parking. $$

### ★★RAOUL'S VELVET ROOM
*7222 W. 119th St., Overland Park, 913-469-0466; www.raoulsvelvetroom.com*
American menu. Dinner, late-night. Bar. Casual attire. Reservations recommended. Outdoor seating. $$

### ★SUSHI GIN
*9559 Nall Ave., Overland Park, 913-649-8488; www.sushigin.com*
Japanese menu. Lunch, dinner. Bar. Children's menu. $$

### ★★YIA YIA'S EUROBISTRO
*4701 W. 119th St., Overland Park, 913-345-1111; www.kansascitymenus.com/yiayias*
Continental, seafood menu. Lunch, dinner, Sunday brunch. Bar. Children's menu. Casual attire. Reservations recommended. Outdoor seating. $$

# PRAIRIE VILLAGE

This Kansas City suburb began in the 1940s as a planned community designed by J.C. Nichols, who also created nearby Country Club Plaza, the nation's first suburban shopping center.

www.pvkansas.com

## RESTAURANT

### ★★★TATSU'S

*4603 W. 90th St., Prairie Village, 913-383-9801; www.tatsus.com*

This quiet French restaurant grew from a small pastry and lunch shop opened by chef/owner Tatsu Arai in 1980. Since then, it has become a top Kansas City dining destination. The classic French cuisine includes dishes such as beef bourguignon, poached salmon with champagne sauce or lemon butter sauce and roasted boneless duck breast with peppercorn cream sauce. French menu. Lunch, dinner. Bar. **$$**

# SALINA

Salina got its start as a trading post for gold hunters stopping through on their way to Pikes Peak. The arrival of the Union Pacific Railroad in 1867 brought new growth, and the wheat crops in the 1870s established a permanent economy. Alfalfa, now one of the state's major crops, was first introduced in Kansas by a Salina resident in 1874. The city was rebuilt in 1903 after the Smoky Hill flood destroyed most of the community. Aviator Steve Fossett made history in 2005 when he launched the first solo, nonstop, round-the-world, nonrefueled flight in the Virgin Atlantic GlobalFlyer from the Salina airport.

*Information: Chamber of Commerce, 120 W. Ash, Salina, 785-827-9301; www.salinakansas.org*

## WHAT TO SEE AND DO

### SALINA ART CENTER

*242 S. Santa Fe, Salina, 785-827-1431; www.salinaartcenter.org*

This center features art exhibits as well as a hands-on art laboratory for children. The cinema shows current art house releases. Wednesday-Saturday 12-5 p.m., Sunday 1-5 p.m.

### SMOKY HILL MUSEUM

*211 W. Iron Ave., Salina, 785-309-5776; www.smokyhillmuseum.org*

Area history is told through photos and artifacts at this museum. Changing exhibits are featured, as is a general store period room. Tuesday-Friday 12-5 p.m., Saturday 10 a.m.-5 p.m., Sunday 1-5 p.m.

## HOTEL

### ★★HOLIDAY INN SALINA

*1616 W. Crawford St., Salina, 785-823-1739, 888-465-4329; www.holiday-inn.com/salinaks*

192 rooms. Pets accepted; fee. Wireless Internet access. Two restaurants, bar. Fitness room. Indoor pool, whirlpool. Airport transportation available. **$**

**KANSAS**

★
★
★
★
★

## RESTAURANT

### ★GUTIERREZ

*640 Westport Blvd., Salina, 785-825-1649; www.gutzsalina.com*

Mexican menu. Lunch, dinner. Bar. Children's menu. Casual attire. **$$**

# SHAWNEE

This Kansas City suburb was founded in the 1850s and features many parks, an outdoor pioneer museum and a historic downtown.

*Information: Shawnee Convention Visitor's Bureau, 15100 W. 67th St.,*

*913-631-6545, 888-550-7282; www.shawneekscvb.com*

## RESTAURANTS

### ★★LEONA YARBROUGH'S

*10310 Shawnee Mission Parkway, Shawnee, 913-248-0500;*

*www.yarbroughrestaurant.com*

American menu. Restaurant, Lunch, dinner. Children's menu. **$$**

### ★★PAULO & BILL

*16501 Midland Drive, Shawnee, 913-962-9900; www.pauloandbill.com*

Italian, American menu. Lunch, dinner. Closed holidays. Bar. Children's menu. Outdoor seating. **$$**

# TOPEKA

The capital city of Kansas is located on the Kansas River (locally called the Kaw). World-famous psychiatric clinic and research center, the Menninger Foundation, is located here, and Herbert Hoover's vice president, Charles Curtis, who was part Kaw and a descendant of one of Topeka's earliest settlers, was born here.

*Information: Convention and Visitors Bureau, 1275 S.W. Topeka Blvd.,*

*785-234-1030, 800-235-1030; www.topeka.org*

## WHAT TO SEE AND DO

### BROWN V. BOARD OF EDUCATION NATIONAL HISTORIC SITE

*1515 S.E. Monroe St., Topeka, 785-354-4273; www.nps.gov/brvb*

This site commemorates the U.S. Supreme Court's groundbreaking 1954 decision declaring segregation in public schools unconstitutional. Here you'll find Monroe Elementary School, one of Topeka's four formerly segregated elementary schools for African-American children, along with interpretive exhibits and educational programs. Monday-Friday 8 a.m.-4 p.m.; closed federal holidays.

### CEDAR CREST GOVERNOR'S MANSION

*1 S.W. Cedar Crest Road, Topeka, 785-296-3636;*

*www.governor.ks.gov/cedarcrest/index.html*

This massive house features period architecture with Loire Valley overtones spread out on 244 acres. Built in 1928 and bequeathed to the state in 1955, it became the governor's residence in 1962. Guided tours, Monday afternoons.

## WILDLIFE ON THE PRAIRIE

East central Kansas boasts beautiful tallgrass prairies, some of the few remaining in the United States. Take this drive in early spring, when the old grass is burned to make way for spring growth, or in early summer, when wildflowers are abundant. Head west from Topeka on I-70 to Manhattan. Nearby, the Konza Prairie is a major site for prairie research, with hiking and wildlife-watching. Continue south on Highway 177 to the Tallgrass Prairie National Preserve near Strong Falls. Covered-wagon train trips are offered at El Dorado, northeast of Wichita on Highway 177. From Wichita, take I-135 north to McPherson and visit the McPherson-Maxwell Game Preserve, with one of the states' largest bison herds, as well as elk, deer and buffalo. Return to I-70 at Salina, then head back east to your starting point.

### COMBAT AIR MUSEUM

*Forbes Field, Hangars 602 and 604, J St., Topeka, 785-862-3303;*
*www.combatairmuseum.org*

Jets, cargo transports, fighters and trainers from 1917-1980 are displayed here, as well as military artifacts. Guided tours, by appointment. Summer, Monday-Saturday 9 a.m.-4:30 p.m.; winter, 12-4:30 p.m. Closed holidays.

### GAGE PARK

*9635 S.W. Gage Blvd., Topeka, 785-368-9180; www.topeka.org*

Tennis, swimming, softball and volleyball facilities are available here, along with playground equipment for different ages and abilities. The newly restored carousel was built in 1908 and operates from 10 a.m.-8 p.m. during the summer and on weekends only in September and October. This park is also home to the Topeka Zoo.

### KANSAS STATE HISTORICAL SOCIETY

*6425 S.W. Sixth Ave., Topeka, 785-272-8681; www.kshs.org*

The Kansas Museum of History includes the Library of Kansas and information on Native American and Western history and genealogy. Tuesday-Saturday.

### STATE CAPITOL

*300 W. 10th St., Topeka, 785-296-3966; www.governor.ks.gov*

The design of this building was based on the U.S. Capitol. On the grounds are statues of Lincoln and Pioneer Woman, both by Topeka-born sculptor Merrell Gage. Murals on the second floor are by John Steuart Curry; those on the first floor are by David H. Overmyer. Monday-Friday.

### TOPEKA ZOO

*635 S.W. Gage Blvd., Topeka, 785-368-9180; www.topeka.org/zoo*

An orangutan and gorilla exhibit, black bear exhibit, lion display, tropical rain forest and more are featured at this museum. Daily 10 a.m.-5 p.m.

71

KANSAS

★
★
★
★
★

## ACROSS THE PRAIRIE LANDSCAPE

This loop trail passes through prairie landscapes and across the Kansas of past, present and future. Begin in Wichita, the state's largest city. The city's historic role as a cow capital along the Chisholm Trail is preserved at the Old Cowtown Museum, a historic village with 40 buildings from the city's early boom years in the 1870s. Nearby is the Wichita Art Museum, with a fine collection of American Impressionists and a grand outdoor sculpture garden. Gardeners will enjoy Botanica, The Wichita Garden, which has a number of theme gardens.

Drive northeast on I-35 to Cassoday, home to several good antique stores, and join Highway 177 northbound. Known as the Flint Hills Scenic Byway, this route passes through a rugged landscape of rolling hills, mesas and virgin prairie. Stop in Cottonwood Falls to visit the Chase County Courthouse, which is the oldest in Kansas. The building was constructed from local limestone in a striking French Renaissance style.

Just north is the Tallgrass Prairie National Preserve, which protects 11,000 acres of native prairie grassland that is home to 40 species of grasses, 200 species of birds, 30 species of mammals and up to 10-million insects per acre. A number of trails lead across the plains, which in spring are carpeted with wildflowers. The preserves headquarters are located at the Z Bar Ranch, an imposing stone ranch house cum mansion from the 1880s.

Council Grove is one of Kansas's most historic towns. In fact, the entire settlement has been designated a National Historic Landmark. Council Grove was the last provisioning stop on the old Sante Fe Trail between the Missouri River and Sante Fe, and the town is filled with landmarks of the frontier West.

Continue north on Highway 57 to Junction City, located at the confluence of the Republican and Smoky Hill rivers. The town owes its existence to Fort Riley, founded in 1853 to protect pioneers traveling along the Sante Fe and Oregon trails. The fort, just north of town along Highway 57, contains a number of historic sites, including the state's first territorial capital, an early home of General George Custer and the U.S. Cavalry Museum, which chronicles the history of the mounted horse soldier from the Revolutionary War to 1950.

Continue east on I-70 to Abilene, famous as an Old West cow town and as the boyhood home of President Dwight D. Eisenhower. In addition to the frontier and presidential museums you would expect, Abilene offers a couple of unusual attractions, including dinner excursions on an antique train and the American Indian Art Center, which represents 90 artists from 30 Native American nations.

## SPECIAL EVENTS
### HUFF 'N PUFF HOT AIR BALLOON RALLY
*Lake Shawnee, Topeka, 785-554-2003; www.huff-n-puff.org*
Dozens of hot air balloons take to the skies in this annual event. September.

### WASHBURN SUNFLOWER MUSIC FESTIVAL

*1700 S.W. College Ave., Topeka, 785-670-1511; www.sunflowermusicfestival.org*

This annual festival features international symphonic musicians performing nightly. First two weeks in June.

## HOTELS
### ★★CLUBHOUSE INN & SUITES TOPEKA

*924 S.W. Henderson Road, Topeka, 785-273-8888, 800-258-2466; www.clubhouseinn.com*

121 rooms. Wireless Internet access. Pets accepted, some restrictions; fee. Complimentary full breakfast. Restaurant, bar. Outdoor pool, whirlpool. Business center. $

### ★★DAYS INN TOPEKA

*1510 S.W. Wanamaker Road, Topeka, 785-272-8538, 800-329-7466; www.daysinn.com*

62 rooms. Pets accepted; fee. Complimentary continental breakfast. Restaurant. Bar. High-speed Internet access. Indoor pool, whirlpool. Business center. $

### ★★RAMADA DOWNTOWN TOPEKA

*420 S.E. Sixth Ave., Topeka, 785-234-5400, 800-272-6232; www.ramada.com*

214 rooms. Pets accepted, some restrictions; fee. Complimentary full breakfast. High-speed Internet access. Restaurant, bar. Fitness room. Indoor pool, outdoor pool, whirlpool. Business center. $

## RESTAURANTS
### ★CARLOS O'KELLY'S

*3425 S. Kansas Ave., Topeka, 785-266-3457; www.carlosokellys.com*

Mexican menu. Lunch, dinner. Bar. Children's menu. Casual attire. $$

### ★★MCFARLAND'S

*4133 S.W. Gage Center Drive, Topeka, 785-272-6909*

American menu. Lunch, dinner. Closed Monday. Bar. Children's menu. $$

# WICHITA

The largest city in Kansas has a metropolitan flavor, with its tall buildings and wide streets. Still a major marketing point for agricultural products, the city is now best known as an aircraft production center. McConnell Air Force Base is here.

The town's first settlers were the Wichita, who built a village of grass lodges on the site. The following year James R. Mead set up a trading post and in 1865 sent his assistant, Jesse Chisholm, on a trading expedition to the Southwest. His route became famous as the Chisholm Trail, over which longhorn cattle were driven through Wichita to the Union Pacific at Abilene. As the railroad advanced to the southwest, Wichita had its turn as a "cow capital" in the early 1870s. By 1880, farmers drawn by the land boom had run fences across the trail and the cattle drives were shifted west to Dodge City. Wheat production and the discovery of oil after World War I revived the city.

*Information: Convention and Visitors Bureau, 100 S. Main, 316-265-2800, 800-288-9424; www.visitwichita.com*

## WHAT TO SEE AND DO
### ALLEN-LAMBE HOUSE MUSEUM AND STUDY CENTER
*255 N. Roosevelt St., Wichita, 316-687-1027; www.allenlambe.org*
Designed in 1915 by Frank Lloyd Wright as a private residence, this structure is considered the last of Wright's prairie houses. The house features furniture designed by Wright in collaboration with interior designer George M. Niedecken. Guided tours by appointment only, minimum of five people.

### BOTANICA, THE WICHITA GARDENS
*701 Amidon, Wichita, 316-264-0448; www.botanica.org*
Displays of exotic flowers and plants native to Kansas fill this botanical garden. April-December, daily; rest of year, Monday-Friday.

### CHENEY STATE PARK
*16000 N.E. 50 St., Cheney, 316-542-3664*
A 1,913-acre park on a 9,537-acre lake, this area is popular with sailboat and windsurfing enthusiasts. Large-scale regattas are a featured part of the many lake activities. Beach, bathhouse, fishing, boating, picnicking, concessions, camping.

### CORBIN EDUCATION CENTER
*1845 Fairmount, Wichita*
This Prairie-style structure, located on the campus of Wichita State University, was designed by Frank Lloyd Wright.

### LAKE AFTON PUBLIC OBSERVATORY
*25000 W. 39th St. South, Wichita, 316-978-7827; www.webs.wichita.edu/lapo*
Public programs offer the opportunity to view a variety of celestial objects through a 16-inch reflecting telescope. Programs begin 30 minutes after sunset. September-May, Friday-Saturday; June-August, Friday-Sunday; closed December 23-January 1.

### MID-AMERICA ALL-INDIAN CENTER MUSEUM
*650 N. Seneca, Wichita, 316-262-5221; www.theindiancenter.org*
This museum features changing exhibits of past and present Native American art. Tuesday-Saturday 10 a.m.-4 p.m.

### OLD COWTOWN MUSEUM
*1865 Museum Blvd., Wichita, 316-660-1871; www.oldcowtown.org*
This 40-building historic village museum depicts Wichita life in the 1870s. The Diamond W Chuckwagon Supper features all-you-can-eat barbecue and a performance by the Prairie Wranglers, a country-western band. October, Thursday-Monday 10 a.m.-4 p.m., Sunday, 11 a.m.-4 p.m.; November-April, Tuesday-Saturday 10 a.m.-4 p.m.; closed Sunday-Monday.

### SEDGWICK COUNTY ZOO
*5555 Zoo Blvd., Wichita, 316-660-9453; www.scz.org*
See animals in their natural habitats at this Wichita zoo. A new Asian tiger exhibit is being constructed and is expected to open in 2009. Daily.

### WICHITA ART MUSEUM

*1400 W. Museum Blvd., Wichita, 316-268-4921; www.wichitaartmuseum.org*

This museum features traveling exhibits, a collection of American art, paintings and sculpture by Charles M. Russell, pre-Columbian art and works by contemporary and historic Kansas artists. Tuesday-Sunday; closed holidays.

### WICHITA CENTER FOR THE ARTS

*9112 E. Central Ave., Wichita, 316-634-2787; www.wcfta.com*

With changing and permanent exhibits, this center features a gallery, theater and art school. Tuesday-Sunday.

### WICHITA-SEDGWICK COUNTY HISTORICAL MUSEUM

*204 S. Main St., Wichita, 316-265-9314; www.wichitahistory.org*

Local history, Native American artifacts, period rooms, a costume collection and more on are display at this museum. Tuesday-Friday 11 a.m.-4 p.m., Saturday-Sunday 1-5 p.m.

## SPECIAL EVENT
### WICHITA RIVER FESTIVAL

*1820 E. Douglas Ave., Wichita, 316-267-2817; www.wichitariverfestival.com*

This annual festival includes a twilight pop concert and fireworks, antique bathtub races, a hot air balloon launch, athletic events and entertainment. Mid-May.

## HOTELS
### ★DAYS INN WICHITA WEST

*550 S. Florence St., Wichita, 316-942-1717, 800-329-7466; www.daysinn.com*

42 rooms. Complimentary continental breakfast. High-speed Internet access. **$**

### ★★HOLIDAY INN WICHITA

*549 S. Rock Road, Wichita, 316-686-7131, 888-465-4329; www.holiday-inn.com*

250 rooms. Pets accepted, some restrictions; fee. Wireless Internet access. Restaurant. Bar. Fitness room. Indoor pool, outdoor pool, whirlpool. Airport transportation available. Business center. **$**

### ★★★HYATT REGENCY WICHITA

*400 W. Waterman, Wichita, 316-293-1234, 800-633-7313; www.ichita.hyatt.com*

Perched on the Arkansas River, this contemporary hotel has updated rooms with duvet-topped beds. The Southwinds Bar and Grill serves red meat of every kind (the grilled spicy cowboy ribeye steak is a standout) in an upscale setting. 303 rooms. Restaurant. Bar. Fitness room. Indoor pool. Business center. **$**

### ★INN & SUITES WICHITA

*515 S. Webb Road, Wichita, 316-684-1111, 800-258-2466; www.clubhouseinn.com*

119 rooms. Pets accepted; fee. Complimentary full breakfast. Wireless Internet access. Outdoor pool, whirlpool. **$**

**KANSAS**

★
★
★
★
☆

### ★★★MARRIOTT WICHITA

*9100 E. Corporate Hills Drive, Wichita, 316-651-0333, 800-610-0673;*
*www.marriott.com*

After a complete renovation in 2007, this hotel is now a smoke-free environment with updated guest rooms that feature luxury beds, flatscreen TVs and wireless Internet access. The Black Angus Grille serves steakhouse classics, while Corrigan's Sports Bar is a prime place for catching up on the latest scores and noshing on pub fare. 294 rooms. Restaurant. Bar. Fitness room. Indoor pool, outdoor pool, whirlpool. Airport transportation available. Business center. **$$**

### ★QUALITY SUITES AIRPORT

*658 Westdale Drive, Wichita, 316-945-2600, 800-318-2607; www.qualityinn.com*

50 rooms, all suites. Pets accepted, some restrictions; fee. Complimentary full breakfast. Wireless Internet access. Fitness room. Outdoor pool. Airport transportation available. **$**

## RESTAURANT
### ★★★OLIVE TREE

*2949 N. Rock Road, Wichita, 316-636-1100; www.olivetree-bistro.com*

This family-owned, European-style bistro has an extensive wine list and a menu with both small and large plates of Mediterranean-inspired dishes. Entrées are eclectic and include everything from Thai green curry made with eggplant to fennel pollen roasted chicken. American menu. Dinner, late-night, Sunday brunch. **$$**

**KANSAS**

★
★★
★★
★

# MISSOURI

WHEN THE UNITED STATES PURCHASED ALL OF THE VAST FRENCH TERRITORY OF LOUISIANA in 1803, Missouri, with its strategic waterways and the already-thriving town of St. Louis, became a gateway to the West and remained one throughout the entire westward expansion. Its two largest cities, St. Louis and Kansas City, sit on its eastern and western edges like bookends. St. Louis was the Midwest's first great city, the center of commerce and transportation thanks to its location on two major rivers. Kansas City was once the quintessential cow town and, the Gateway Arch notwithstanding, was the true way station to the West—to cattle trails and to the frontier.

Today, Missouri offers a diverse array of sights. St. Louis and Kansas City have fine dining (and great barbecue), nightlife and music (especially blues and jazz). St. Louis has a world famous zoo and one of the largest city parks in the nation. It has a significant art museum as well as the International Bowling Hall of Fame. St. Louis, home to the Cardinals and a legion of knowledgeable fans, is often hailed as the nation's best baseball town. Kansas City has the world's first planned shopping center (Country Club Plaza), a 60-acre water park, and did we mention barbecue?

For outdoor recreation, Missouri could vie for the title of Land of Awesome Lakes. Its largest one, Lake of the Ozarks, is 92 miles end to end and has 1,150 miles of shoreline. There's also the 55,000-acre Truman Lake, part of the Harry S. Truman State Park, southeast of Kansas City, and Pomme de Terre Lake, 78 acres of water near Springfield.

Then there are the rivers, and we don't just mean the Mississippi and Missouri. Four state parks dot the Meramec River, which runs for nearly 100 miles. Nearly 90 percent of the river is shallow, which makes it a perfect waterway for float trips. Another of Missouri's river gems is the Black, running through Poplar Bluff and north into the Arcadia Valley. It, too, promises great floating.

Wherever you are in the state, there's something to explore. Around Hannibal by the Mississippi, you can recapture Mark Twain's riverboat days. Along the Missouri River in St. Joseph, the flavor is more Lewis and Clark and pioneers. Southwest is Springfield, a gateway to both the Ozarks and to Branson, that one-of-a-kind capital of cornpone, country and crooning. In the middle is Jefferson City, a prototypical sleepy capital town with a beautiful capitol standing astride the Missouri River.

*www.mo.gov/*

**★ FUN FACTS**

Famous Missourians include Mark Twain, Walter Cronkite and Harry S. Truman.

No one is sure how the state's nickname, "The Show Me State" originated. Most think it has something to do with Missourians' stubborn need for proof.

The state takes its name for a branch of the Sioux tribe who lived in the area.

The rivalry between the University of Missouri and the University of Kansas is the second oldest in the nation.

**MISSOURI**

★
★
★
★
★

## MISSOURI'S EL CAMINO REAL

Originally an Indian trail, this route became the El Camino Real, laid out during the late 18th-century when Spain ruled the North American territory west of the Mississippi. Leave St. Louis on Interstate 55 (I-55) south to exit 186, then drive east to Highway 61. Head south on Highway 61 to Kimmswick, a little town on the Mississippi that thrived from the 1860s to the end of the 19th century, when it was a busy center for riverboat traffic.

Lucianna Gladney Ross, daughter of the founder of the 7Up softdrink company, discovered the handsome but dilapidated town and spearheaded a movement to restore it to its original condition. Today, Kimmswick is part open air museum, part shopping boutique. Many of the older buildings contain restaurants, antique stores and other specialty retail shops. The Old House Restaurant (Second and Elm streets) was once a stagecoach stop and tavern frequented by Ulysses S. Grant. It features old-fashioned home-cooked meals and desserts.

Just west of Kimmswick, the 425-acre Mastodon Historic Site preserves an important archaeological area that contains the bones of American mastodons. The fossil remains of these and other now extinct animals were first found in the early 1800s in what is now called the Kimmswick Bone Bed. The area became known as one of the most extensive Pleistocene bone beds in the country, attracting archaeological and paleontological interest from around the world. A museum tells the natural and cultural story of the area.

Follow Highway 61 south along the Mississippi to Ste. Genevieve, founded in the 1750s as a French village. Ste. Genevieve is one of the oldest European settlements west of the Mississippi and contains an important collection of French Colonial architecture. Now a National Historic District, the entire town gives testament to the lasting quality of French craftsmanship.

South of Perryville to the east of Highway 66 is a cluster of villages settled by Germans: Altenburg, Frohna and Wittenberg. Altenburg has a collection of original structures from the 1830s and a museum that commemorates the early Lutheran farming history of the area. Continue south on Highway 66, and follow Highway 177 east to Trail of Tears State Park. This 3,415-acre park is a memorial to the Cherokee Indians who died during a forced relocation to Oklahoma. The park's many trails are good for hiking, and the bluffs and cliffs along the river are roosting sites for bald eagles.

Follow Highway 177 to Cape Girardeau, which began as a furtrading fort. The town sweeps up from the Mississippi to a high promontory, with a number of 19th century buildings along the waterfront, and has the distinction of being the hometown of Rush Limbaugh.

From Cape Girardeau, follow Highway 61 south to New Madrid. In 1789, this site was selected to be the capital of the colony that Spain hoped to establish in the Louisiana Territory. Not much became of Spain's plans for this colony, and now New Madrid is most famous for the devastating 1811 earthquake that centered on the New Madrid Fault. With an estimated magnitude reaching more than eight on the Richter scale, this earthquake was one of the largest in recent geologic history. *Approximately 190 miles.*

MISSOURI

★
★ ★
★ ★ ★
★ ★
★

# BONNE TERRE

French settlers named this town Bonne Terre, meaning "good earth," when they discovered the abundance of lead ore in the area.

*Information: Chamber of Commerce, 11 S.W. Main St., 573-358-4000;*
*www.bonneterrechamber.com*

## WHAT TO SEE AND DO
### BONNE TERRE MINE TOURS
*39 N. Allen St., Bonne Terre, 573-358-2148; www.2dive.com*
A one-hour walking tour takes visitors through lead and silver mines that operated from 1864-1962. See historic mining tools, ore cars, ore samples, an underground lake, flower garden and museum exhibits. May-September, daily; rest of year, Friday-Monday.

### MARK TWAIN NATIONAL FOREST
*Highway 8, Bonne Terre, 573-438-5427; www.fs.fed.us*
This park has a swimming beach, boat launch, nature trails and camping. Daily.

### WASHINGTON STATE PARK
*Highway 21, DeSoto, 636-586-2995; www.parks.wa.gov*
A more than 1,400-acre park containing petroglyphs (interpretations available). Swimming pool, fishing, canoeing on Big River; hiking trails, playground, cabins, camping. Daily.

# BRANSON

The resort town of Branson has become a mecca for fans of country music and old-fashioned acts. Variety shows, comedy acts and performers of all ages hit the stages of the many theaters in town nightly.

*Information: Branson/Lakes Area Chamber of Commerce, 269 Highway 248,*
*417-334-4084, 800-214-3661; www.branson.com*

## WHAT TO SEE AND DO
### ANDY WILLIAMS MOON RIVER THEATER
*2500 W. Highway 76, Branson, 417-334-4500; www.andywilliams.com*
This theater is the domain of 1960s singer Andy Williams, who is sometimes joined on stage by guest performers, which in the past have included Charo and Glen Campbell. April-December.

### BALDKNOBBERS JAMBOREE
*2835 W. 76 Country Blvd., Branson, 417-334-4528,*
*800-998-8908; www.baldknobbers.com*
This country music variety show features comedy, music and skits. March-mid-April, Friday-Saturday; mid-April-mid-December, Monday-Saturday.

### BRANSON SCENIC RAILWAY
*206 E. Main St., Branson, 417-334-6110, 800-287-2462; www.bransontrain.com*
Forty-mile roundtrip through Ozark Foothills. Mid-March-mid-December, schedule varies; closed holidays.

MISSOURI

★
★
★
★
★

### COLLEGE OF THE OZARKS

*100 Opportunity Ave., Point Lookout, 417-334-6411, 800-222-0525; www.cofo.edu*

Established in 1906, this is a small liberal arts college of 1,500 where students work, rather than pay, for their education.

### DUTTON FAMILY THEATER

*3454 W. Highway 76, Branson, 417-332-2772; www.theduttons.com*

A musical variety show featuring all seven members of the Dutton family and their spouses playing a variety of instruments. April-December.

### ELVIS AND THE SUPERSTARS SHOW

*205 S. Commercial, Branson, 417-336-2112, 800-358-4795; www.elvisinbranson.com*

A musical tribute to Elvis Presley, this show features an impersonator belting out tunes by the King from his early days to Vegas years. Year-round.

### GRAND COUNTRY MUSIC HALL

*1945 W. Highway 76, Branson, 417-335-2484, 1-888-514-1088; www.grandcountry.com*

Shows at this performance space include everything from *Amazing Pets* to the *Ozarks Mountain Jamboree.*

### HUGHES BROTHERS CELEBRITY THEATRE

*3425 W. Highway 76, Branson, 417-334-0076; www.hughes-brothers.com*

The five Utah-born Hughes brothers, along with their wives and children, entertain six days a week in this musical variety show.

### JIMMY OSMOND'S AMERICAN JUKEBOX SHOW

*3600 W. Highway 76, Branson, 417-336-6100; www.osmondfamilytheater.com*

The youngest Osmond performs hit songs from the '40s to the present. April-December.

### JIM STAFFORD THEATRE

*3440 W. Highway 76, Branson, 417-335-8080; www.jimstafford.com*

Novelty singer Jim Stafford, who had several hits in the '70s, performs at this theater.

### PRESLEY'S COUNTRY JUBILEE

*2920 W. Highway 76, Branson, 417-334-4874, 800-335-4847; www.presleys.com*

Four generations of a family perform country music and more. March-mid-December.

### RIPLEY'S BELIEVE IT OR NOT! MUSEUM

*3326 W. Highway 76, Branson, 417-337-5300; www.ripleys.com*

This outpost of the curiosities museum has hundreds of exhibits in eight galleries. Daily, 9:30 a.m.-11 p.m.

### SHEPHERD OF THE HILLS

*5586 W. Highway 76, Branson, 417-334-4191; www.oldmatt.com*

Jeep-drawn conveyance tours include authentically furnished Old Matt's Cabin, home of the prominent characters in Harold Bell Wright's Ozark novel *The Shepherd of the Hills.* Late April-late October, daily.

MISSOURI

★
★ ★
★ ★
★ ★
★

## WIDE OPEN COUNTRY

The beautiful Ozark hills drew people to southwest Missouri long before Branson became famous for its country music theaters. From Springfield, drive 41 miles south on Highway 65 to Branson. Touring options here include a railroad that travels through the Ozarks to Arkansas, and the Ducks, amphibious vehicles that roll around town and onto Table Rock Lake. Other area attractions beyond the music theaters packing Highway 76 (Country Boulevard) include the Shepherd of the Hills homestead and outdoor theater and Silver Dollar City theme park. Once you've had your fill of Branson, head east out of town on Highway 76, a scenic stretch through part of the Mark Twain National Forest, then take Highway 5 north. Stop at Mansfield to see the Laura Ingalls Wilder farm, where the author wrote the Little House books. Return to Springfield via Highway 60 west. *Approximately 150 miles.*

### SHOWBOAT BRANSON BELLE

*4800 State Highway 165, Branson, 417-336-7171, 800-475-9370; www.showboatbransonbelle.com*
Lunch and dinner cruises depart from Highway 165 near Table Rock Dam. April-December, daily.

### STONE HILL WINERY

*601 Highway 165, Branson, 417-334-1897; www.stonehillwinery.com*
Guided tours and bottling demonstrations. Daily; closed holidays.

### TABLE ROCK DAM AND LAKE

*4600 Highway 165, Branson, 417-334-4101; www.swl.usace.army.mil/parks/tablerock*
This 43,100-acre reservoir, formed by impounding waters of White River, offers swimming, waterskiing, scuba diving; fishing for bass, crappie, and walleye; boating; hunting for deer, turkey, rabbit and waterfowl; picnicking; playgrounds and camping. Daily.

## SPECIAL EVENT
### FESTIVAL OF AMERICAN MUSIC AND CRAFTSMANSHIP

*399 Indian Point Road, Branson, 800-475-9370; www.silverdollarcity.com*
Celebrating arts, crafts and cooking from across America, with demonstrations, exhibits and entertainment. Early September-late October.

## HOTELS
### ★★BEST WESTERN MOUNTAIN OAK LODGE

*8514 Highway 76, Branson, 417-338-2141, 800-868-6625; www.bestwestern.com*
145 rooms. Complimentary continental breakfast. Restaurant, bar. Indoor pool. $

### ★★★BIG CEDAR LODGE

*612 Devils Pool Road, Ridgedale, 417-335-2777; www.bigcedarlodge.com*
Guests can stay in one of three lodges, a cabin or a cottage. The resort offers boating and swimming on the lake, tennis, golf, horseback riding, a 10,000-acre nature park

with hiking trails and more. 224 rooms. Restaurant, bar. Children's activity center. Fitness room. Two outdoor pools. Tennis. $

### ★★★CHATEAU ON THE LAKE

*415 N. Highway 265, Branson, 417-334-1161, 888-333-5253;*
*www.chateauonthelake.com*

Chateau on the Lake has a mountaintop location overlooking Table Rock Lake. The resort is located close to town, and features a spa and salon, as well as an old-fashioned soda fountain. 300 rooms. Pets accepted, some restrictions; fee. Restaurant, bar. Fitness room. Indoor pool, outdoor pool, whirlpool. Spa. Tennis. Business center. $$

### ★★CLARION HOTEL AT THE PALACE

*2820 W. Highway 76, Branson, 417-334-7666, 800-725-2236;*
*www.choicehotels.com*

166 rooms. Complimentary continental breakfast. Restaurant, bar. Indoor pool, whirlpool. Fitness center. $

### ★★DAYS INN

*3524 Keeter St., Branson, 417-334-5544, 800-329-7466; www.daysinnbranson.com*

424 rooms. Pets accepted; fee. Complimentary continental breakfast. Restaurant. Outdoor pool, children's pool, whirlpool. $

### ★HAMPTON INN

*3695 W. Highway 76, Branson, 417-337-5762, 800-426-7866;*
*www.hamptoninn.com*

110 rooms. Complimentary continental breakfast. High speed Internet access. Indoor pool, whirlpool. Fitness center. $

### ★★★LODGE OF THE OZARKS ENTERTAINMENT COMPLEX

*3431 W. Highway 76, Branson, 417-334-7535, 877-866-2219;*
*www.lodgeoftheozarks.com*

This hotel offers large rooms and is walking distance from theaters, shopping and other attractions. 190 rooms. Complimentary continental breakfast. Wireless Internet access. Restaurant, bar. Indoor pool, whirlpool. $

### ★★RADISSON HOTEL BRANSON

*120 S. Wildwood Drive, Branson, 417-335-5767, 800-333-3333;*
*www.radisson.com/bransonmo*

472 rooms. Restaurant, bar. High-speed Internet access. Fitness room. Indoor pool, outdoor pool, whirlpool. $

### ★RAMADA INN

*1700 W. Highway 76, Branson, 417-334-1000, 800-641-4106;*
*www.ramadabranson.com*

296 rooms. Pets accepted; fee. Outdoor pool. $

### ★★★THOUSAND HILLS GOLF AND CONFERENCE RESORT

*245 S. Wildwood Drive, Branson, 417-336-5873, 877-262-0430;*
*www.thousandhills.com*

This sprawling resort has both cabins and condominiums available for rent alongside the Thousand Hills Golf Course. Most have jacuzzi tubs, fireplaces and fully stocked kitchens. The resort also has a fitness center, indoor and outdoor pools and tennis courts. Pets not accepted. Golf. Fitness center. **$$$**

## RESTAURANTS

### ★★CANDLESTICK INN

*127 Taney St., Branson, 417-334-3633; www.candlestickinn.com*
Seafood, steak menu. Lunch, dinner. Bar. Children's menu. **$$$**

### ★MR G'S CHICAGO-STYLE PIZZA

*201 N. Commercial, Marvel Cave Park, 417-335-8156*
Italian menu. Lunch, dinner. Bar. **$**

### PANCHOVILLA

*2819 Highway 76 W. Branson, 417-334-4548*
American menu. Lunch, dinner. Closed December-January. Children's menu. **$$**

# CAPE GIRARDEAU

On early maps, a rocky promontory on the Mississippi River, 125 miles below St. Louis, was labeled Cape Girardot (or Girardeau), named for a French ensign believed to have settled there about 1720. In 1792, an agent for the Spanish government, Louis Lorimier, set up a trading post at the site of the present city and encouraged settlement.

Cape Girardeau's location assured flourishing river traffic before the Civil War. The war, however, ended river trade and the earliest railroads bypassed the town, triggering further decline. In the late 1880s, the arrival of new railroads and the 1928 completion of a bridge across the Mississippi contributed to industrial growth and the widening of Cape Girardeau's economic base. Southeast Missouri State University, which has a mural in its library depicting the history of the area, is located in the town.

*Information: Convention and Visitors Bureau, 400 Broadway,*
*573-335-1631, 800-777-0068; www.capegirardeaucvb.org*

## WHAT TO SEE AND DO

### BOLLINGER MILL STATE HISTORIC SITE

*113 Bollinger Mill Road, Cape Girardeau, 573-243-4591; www.mostateparks.com*
This day-use park features a historic 19th-century gristmill and the oldest covered bridge in the state. Guided tours are available. Daily.

### CAPE RIVER HERITAGE MUSEUM

*538 Independence, Cape Girardeau, 573-334-0405*
Exhibits on Cape Girardeau's early heritage, 19th-century industry, education and culture. March-December, Friday-Saturday; also by appointment.

### COURT OF COMMON PLEAS BUILDING

*Spanish and Themis streets, Cape Girardeau*

Central portion built around 1854 to replace previous log structure. During the Civil War, cells in the basement housed prisoners. Outstanding view of the Mississippi River from the park.

### GLENN HOUSE

*325 S. Spanish St., Cape Girardeau, 573-334-1177; www.glennhouse.org*

A Victorian house with period furnishings, memorabilia of the Mississippi River and the steamboat era is displayed here. April-December, Friday-Sunday.

### OLD ST. VINCENT'S CHURCH

*131 S. Main St., Cape Girardeau, 573-335-1631; www.oldstvincents.com*

English Gothic Revival church showing Roman influences. More than 100 medieval-design plaster masks. Hand-carved doors. Tours by appointment.

### ST. LOUIS IRON MOUNTAIN AND SOUTHERN RAILWAY

*Intersection of Highways 61 and 25, Jackson, 573-243-1688,*
*800-455-7245; www.slimrr.com*

A 1946 steam locomotive pulls vintage 1920s cars through scenic woodlands. Trips range from 80 minutes to five hours. April-October, Saturday-Sunday.

### TRAIL OF TEARS STATE PARK

*429 Moccasin Spring, Cape Girardeau, 573-334-1711;*
*www.mostateparks.com/trailoftears.htm*

A more than 3,000-acre park on limestone bluffs overlooking the Mississippi River, this park commemorates the forced migration of the Cherokee Nation over the Trail of Tears to Oklahoma. Daily.

## HOTELS

### ★★DRURY INN

*104 S. Vantage Drive, Cape Girardeau, 573-334-7151, 800-378-7946;*
*www.druryhotels.com*

139 rooms. Pets accepted, some restrictions. Complimentary full breakfast. Wireless Internet access. Restaurant, bar. Fitness room. Outdoor pool, children's pool. $

### ★★HOLIDAY INN

*3253 William St., Cape Girardeau, 573-334-4491, 888-465-4329; www.holidayinn.com*

102 rooms. Restaurant, bar. High-speed Internet access. Fitness room. Indoor pool, outdoor pool, children's pool. $

### ★PEAR TREE INN

*3248 William St., Cape Girardeau, 573-334-3000, 800-378-7946;*
*www.druryhotels.com*

78 rooms. Pets accepted, some restrictions. Complimentary continental breakfast. Wireless Internet access. Outdoor pool, children's pool. $

## RESTAURANTS
### ★BG'S OLDE TYME DELI & SALOON
*205 S. Plaza Way, Cape Girardeau, 573-335-8860*
American menu. Lunch, dinner. Bar. Children's menu. $

### ★BROUSSARD'S CAJUN CUISINE
*120 N. Main St., Cape Girardeau, 573-334-7235; www.broussardscajuncuisine.com*
Cajun/Creole menu. Lunch, dinner. Bar. $$

# CARTHAGE
Carthage was founded as the seat of Jasper County in 1842. The first major Civil War battle west of the Mississippi River was fought here July 5, 1861. Belle Starr, a Confederate spy and outlaw, lived here as a girl. Annie Baxter, the first woman in the United States to hold elective office, was elected County Clerk in Carthage in 1890, and James Scott, a ragtime musician and composer, began his career here in 1906. Many interesting Victorian houses can still be found in Carthage.
*Information: Chamber of Commerce, 107 E. Third St.,*
*417-358-2373; www.carthagenow.com*

## WHAT TO SEE AND DO
### BATTLE OF CARTHAGE CIVIL WAR MUSEUM
*205 E. Grant, Carthage; www.carthage-mo.gov*
Features artifacts, a wall-sized mural and a diorama depicting the progress of the battle. Daily.

### JASPER COUNTY COURTHOUSE
*302 S. Main, Carthage, 417-358-0441*
Built in 1894 of Carthage marble, the Courthouse features a mural by Lowell Davis depicting local history. Monday-Friday.

## HOTEL
### ★CARTHAGE INN
*2244 Grand Ave., Carthage, 417-358-2499, 888-454-2499; www.carthageinn.com*
40 rooms. Pets accepted, some restrictions; fee. Complimentary continental breakfast. Wireless Internet access. $

## SPECIALTY LODGING
### GRAND AVENUE BED AND BREAKFAST
*1615 Grand Ave., Carthage, 417-358-7265, 888-380-6786; www.grand-avenue.com*
This bed and breakfast is housed in a Queen Anne-style house built in 1890. Four rooms. Complimentary full breakfast. High-speed Internet access. Outdoor pool. $

## RESTAURANT
### ★★BAMBOO GARDEN
*102 N. Garrison Ave., Carthage, 417-358-1611*
Chinese menu. Lunch, dinner. $

MISSOURI

★
★
★
★
★

# CHESTERFIELD

This is suburb was under water during the Great Flood of 1993 due to parts being located in the Chesterfield Valley. It is the largest city west of St. Louis.
www.chesterfieldmochamber.com

## RESTAURANTS

### ★★ANNIE GUNN'S

*16806 Chesterfield Airport Road, Chesterfield, 636-532-7684;*
*www.smokehousemarket.com*
American menu. Lunch, dinner, late-night. Bar. Outdoor seating. **$$$**

### ★★PAUL MANNO'S

*75 Forum Center, Chesterfield, 314-878-1274*
Italian menu. Dinner. Closed Sunday; also late June-early July. Bar. Business casual attire. Reservations recommended. **$$**

# CHILLICOTHE

Chillicothe, seat of Livingston County, is a Shawnee word meaning "our big town." It was named for Chillicothe, Ohio. Sloan's Liniment was developed here about 1870 by Earl Sloan. An Amish community located approximately 25 miles northwest of town, near Jamesport, has many interesting shops.
*Information: Chamber of Commerce, 715 Washington St.,*
*660-646-4050, 877-224-4554; www.chillicothemo.com*

★
★
★
★
★

## WHAT TO SEE AND DO

### GENERAL JOHN J. PERSHING BOYHOOD HOME STATE HISTORIC SITE

*1000 Pershing Drive, Laclede, 660-963-2525; www.mostateparks.com/pershingsite.htm*
This 11-room house, built in 1858, was the childhood home of the World War I hero. Also here is a statue of "Black Jack" Pershing, a Wall of Honor and the relocated Prairie Mound School, the one-room schoolhouse where Pershing taught before entering West Point. Daily.

### PERSHING STATE PARK

*29277 Highway 130, Chillicothe, 660-963-2299; www.stateparks.com*
This 3,527-acre memorial to General John J. Pershing offers fishing, canoeing, hiking trails, picnicking, camping. North of the park is the Locust Creek covered bridge, the longest of four remaining covered bridges in the state. Daily.

## HOTELS

### ★BEST WESTERN CHILLICOTHE INN & SUITES

*1020 S. Washington St., Chillicothe, 660-646-0572, 800-990-9150;*
*www.bestwestern.com*
58 rooms. Pets accepted; fee. Complimentary continental breakfast. High-speed Internet access. Outdoor pool. **$**

### ★★GRAND RIVER INN

*606 W. Business 36, Chillicothe, 660-646-6590, 888-317-8290;*
*www.grandriverinn.com*
60 rooms. Pets accepted; fee. Complimentary continental breakfast. Restaurant, bar. Outdoor pool, whirlpool, fitness center. $

# COLUMBIA

An educational center from its earliest years, Columbia is the home of Columbia College, Stephens College and the University of Missouri, the oldest state university west of the Mississippi. Established as Smithton, the town was moved a short distance to ensure a better water supply and renamed Columbia. In 1822, the Boone's Lick Trail was rerouted to pass through the town. Classes began at the University of Missouri in 1841, and the town has revolved around the institution ever since. The School of Journalism, founded in 1908, was the first degree-granting journalism school in the world.

*Information: Convention and Visitors Bureau, 300 S. Providence Road,*
*573-875-1231, 800-652-0987; www.visitcolumbiamo.com*

## WHAT TO SEE AND DO
### EDISON ELECTRIC DYNAMO
*Lobby of University of Missouri Engineering Building,*
*E. Sixth Street and Stewart Road, Columbia*
The recently restored dynamo, given to the university in 1882 by its inventor, Thomas Alva Edison, was used on campus in 1883 for the first demonstration of incandescent lighting west of the Mississippi. Monday-Friday.

### ELLIS LIBRARY
*Lowry Mall between Memorial Union and Jesse Hall, Ninth Street and Conley Avenue,*
*Columbia, 573-882-4391; www.mulibraries.missouri.edu/containing*
One of the largest libraries in the Midwest, it features a rare-book room containing a page from a Gutenberg Bible. The State Historical Society of Missouri, located on the east ground wing, has early newspapers and works by Missouri artists.

### MUSEUM OF ANTHROPOLOGY
*100 Swallow Hall, Columbia, 573-882-3764; www.anthromuseum.missouri.edu*
Artifacts from 9000 B.C. to the present. Monday-Friday.

### MUSEUM OF ART AND ARCHAEOLOGY
*1 Pickard Hall, Columbia, 573-882-3591*
Comprehensive collection including more than 13,000 objects from around the world; from the Paleolithic period to the present. Cast gallery has items made from original Greek and Roman sculptures. Tuesday-Sunday.

### NIFONG PARK
*3700 Ponderosa St., Columbia, 573-443-8936; www.gocolumbiamo.com*
The park includes a visitor center, restored 1877 Maplewood house (April-October, Sunday, limited hours), Maplewood Barn Theater (summer), Boone County Historical Society Museum, petting zoo, lake and picnicking. Park, daily.

**MISSOURI**

### SHELTER GARDENS

*1817 W. Broadway, Columbia, 573-445-8441*

Miniature mid-American environment with a pool and stream, domestic and wild flowers, more than 300 varieties of trees and shrubs, rose garden. Concerts in summer. Daily, weather permitting.

### STEPHENS COLLEGE

*1200 E. Broadway, Columbia, 573-442-2211; www.stephens.edu/*

On this 240-acre campus is the Firestone Baars Chapel on Walnut Street, designed in 1956 by Eero Saarinen. Monday-Friday.

### UNIVERSITY OF MISSOURI-COLUMBIA

*311 Jesse Hall, Columbia, 573-882-6333; www.missouri.edu*

This 1,334-acre campus with more than 22,000 students contains numerous collections, exhibits, galleries and attractions.

## HOTELS
### ★★HOLIDAY INN

*2200 I-70 Drive S.E., Columbia, 573-445-8531, 800-465-4329;*
*www.holiday-inn.com*

311 rooms. Pets accepted. Restaurant, bar. Fitness room. Indoor pool, outdoor pool, whirlpool. Adjacent to Exposition Center. $

### ★★QUALITY INN

*1612 N. Providence Road, Columbia, 573-449-2491,*
*800-228-5751; www.qualityinn.com*

142 rooms. Pets accepted, some restrictions; fee. Restaurant, bar. Fitness room. Indoor pool, whirlpool. $

## RESTAURANTS
### ★★BOONE TAVERN

*811 E. Walnut St., Columbia, 573-442-5123; www.boonetavern.com*

American menu. Lunch, dinner. Closed holidays. Bar. Children's menu. Outdoor seating. $$

### ★FLAT BRANCH PUB & BREWING

*115 S. Fifth St., Columbia, 573-499-0400; www.flatbranch.com*

American menu. Lunch, dinner. Bar. Children's menu. Outdoor seating. $$

# ELLISVILLE

This town is located 13 miles west of St. Louis. Though it was settled in the 1830s, it was not incorporated until 1932.

*www.ellisville.mo.us*

## RESTAURANT
### ★★★AGOSTINOS
*280 Long Road, Chesterfield, 636-391-5480; www.agostinoscatering.com*

The owners, Agostino and Rosa, were born and raised in Palermo, Sicily, and their upbringings are reflected in the cuisine and service of this fine Italian restaurant. Italian menu. Lunch, dinner, late-night. Bar. Jacket required (dinner). **$$**

# EXCELSIOR SPRINGS

Excelsior Springs was established in 1880 when two settlers, Anthony W. Wyman and J. V. D. Flack, discovered various natural springs on Wyman's property. Today the city is a health resort offering visitors bottled water from the springs and medicinal baths in the city-operated bathhouse.

*Information: Chamber of Commerce, 101 E. Broadway, 816-630-6161;*
*www.exsmo.com*

## WHAT TO SEE AND DO
### EXCELSIOR SPRINGS HISTORICAL MUSEUM
*101 E. Broadway, Excelsior Springs, 816-630-0101*

Includes murals, a bank, antiques, antique bedroom, doctor's office, dental equipment. Tuesday-Saturday.

### JESSE JAMES'S FARM
*Jesse James Farm Road, Excelsior Springs, 816-736-8500*

This house is where outlaw James was born and raised with his brother Frank. Daily.

### WATKINS WOOLEN MILL STATE PARK AND STATE HISTORIC SITE
*26600 Park Road N. Lawson, 816-580-3387;*
*www.mostateparks.com*

Woolen factory and gristmill built and equipped in 1860 and still contains original machinery. Original owner's house, summer kitchen, ice house, smokehouse and school. Guided tours daily.

## HOTEL
### ★★★THE INN ON CRESCENT LAKE
*1261 St. Louis Ave., Excelsior Springs, 816-630-6745, 866-630-5253;*
*www.crescentinn.com*

This inn was built in 1915 on 22 acres of landscaped yard, surrounded by two cresent-shaped ponds. The rooms are individually decorated and have private baths. 10 rooms. Children over 12 years only. Complimentary full breakfast. Restaurant. Fitness room. Outdoor pool. **$**

# FULTON

Named in honor of Robert Fulton, inventor of the steamboat, this town was home to both architect General M. F. Bell, who designed many of Fulton's historic buildings, and Henry Bellaman, author of the best-selling novel *King's Row,* which

★
★
★
★
★

## GEORGE WASHINGTON CARVER NATIONAL MONUMENT

Born a slave on the farm of Moses Carver, George Washington Carver (1864-1943) rose to become an eminent teacher, humanitarian, botanist, agronomist and pioneer conservationist. Carver was the first African American to graduate from Iowa State University. He received both a bachelor's and a master's degree in science. He then headed the Department of Agriculture at Booker T. Washington's Tuskegee Institute in Alabama.

Authorized as a national monument in 1943, this memorial to Carver honors a vital part of the American historical heritage. The visitor center contains a museum and audioviasual presentation depicting Carver's life and work. A self-guided trail passes the birthplace site, the statue of Carver by Robert Amendola, the restored 1881 Moses Carver house, the family cemetery and the woods and streams where Carver spent his boyhood. Daily.

Information: 5646 Carver Road, Diamond, 417-325-4151; www.nps.gov/gwca

depicted life in Fulton at the turn of the century. The town is home to Westminster College, William Woods University and the Missouri School for the Deaf.

*Information: Kingdom of Callaway Chamber of Commerce, 409 Court St.,*
*573-642-3055, 800-257-3554; www.keystofulton.com*

### WHAT TO SEE AND DO
#### WESTMINSTER COLLEGE
*501 Westminster Ave., Fulton, 573-642-3361*
Winston Churchill delivered his "Iron Curtain" address here on March 5, 1946.

#### WINSTON CHURCHILL MEMORIAL AND LIBRARY
*Seventh Street and Westminster Avenue, Fulton, 573-592-5369;*
*www.churchillmemorial.org*
To memorialize Churchill's "Iron Curtain" speech, the bombed ruins of Sir Christopher Wren's 17th-century Church of St. Mary, Aldermanbury, were dismantled, shipped from London to Westminster College, reassembled and finally restored. The church was rehallowed in 1969 with Lord Mountbatten of Burma and Churchill's daughter, Lady Mary Soames, in attendance. The undercroft of the church houses a museum, gallery and research library with letters, manuscripts, published works, photos, memorabilia. Daily.

## HANNIBAL

Hannibal is world-famous as the hometown of the great novelist Samuel Clemens (Mark Twain) as well as the setting of *The Adventures of Tom Sawyer,* which records many actual events of Clemens' boyhood. He served his printer's apprenticeship here and gained a fascination with steamboats in the days when the river was the source of the town's prosperity.

*Information: Visitors and Convention Bureau, 505 N. Third St.,*
*573-221-2477; www.visithannibal.com*

## WHAT TO SEE AND DO
### BECKY THATCHER HOUSE
*209-211 Hill St., Hannibal*
House where Laura Hawkins (Becky Thatcher) lived during Samuel Clemens' boyhood; upstairs rooms have authentic furnishings. Daily.

### JOHN M. CLEMENS JUSTICE OF THE PEACE OFFICE
*205 Hill St., Hannibal*
Restored courtroom where Twain's father presided as justice of the peace.

### MARK TWAIN CAVE
*7097 Country Road 453, Hannibal, 573-221-1656*
This is the cave in *The Adventures of Tom Sawyer* in which Tom and Becky Thatcher were lost and where Injun Joe died. Tours daily; closed holidays.

### MARK TWAIN MUSEUM AND BOYHOOD HOME
*208 Hill St., Hannibal, 573-221-9010*
Museum houses Mark Twain memorabilia, including books, letters, photographs and family items. Daily.

### MARK TWAIN RIVERBOAT EXCURSIONS
*Center St., Hannibal, 573-221-3222, 800-621-2322*
One-hour cruises on the Mississippi River; also two-hour dinner cruises. Early May-October, daily.

### MOLLY BROWN BIRTHPLACE AND MUSEUM
*600 Butler St., Hannibal, 573-221-2100*
Antique-filled home has memorabilia of the "unsinkable" Molly Brown, who survived the *Titanic* disaster. April-May, September-October, weekends; June-August, daily.

**MISSOURI**

### PILASTER HOUSE AND GRANT'S DRUGSTORE
*Hill and Main streets, Hannibal*
The Clemens family lived in this Greek Revival house, which contains a restored old-time drugstore, pioneer kitchen, doctor's office and quarters where John Clemens, Twain's father, died.

★
★
★
★
★

### ROCKCLIFFE MANSION
*Hill Street, Hannibal, 573-221-4140*
Restored Beaux Arts mansion overlooking the river; 30 rooms, many original furnishings. Samuel Clemens addressed a gathering here in 1902. Guided tours. Daily.

## SPECIAL EVENT
### TOM SAWYER DAYS
*505 N. Third St., Hannibal, 573-221-2477; www.hannibaljaycees.org/tomsawyer.hrm*
National fence painting contest; frog jumping; entertainment. Four days early in July.

# MARK TWAIN'S HANNIBAL

Start a tour of Hannibal, an old Mississippi riverboat town and hometown to Samuel Longhorn Clemens—better known as Mark Twain—at the **Hannibal Convention and Visitors Bureau** (*505 N. Third St.*). Towering above the visitor center is the Mark Twain Lighthouse, located at the crest of Cardiff Hill. This is the largest inland lighthouse in the United States, offering great views of Hannibal and the Mississippi from the top.

A block south of the Visitors Bureau is the **Mark Twain Boyhood Home and Museum** (*208 Hill St.*), which features the original 1843 Clemens home, restored to look as it did when Twain lived here in the 1840s. Next door (*211 Hill St.*) is the **period home of Laura Hawkins,** Mark Twain's childhood sweetheart and the inspiration for the character Becky Thatcher in Twain's novels. On the corner of Hill and Main streets is the Clemens Law office, where Twain's father, J. M. Clemens, presided as Hannibal's justice of the peace. Attached to the building is a historic courtroom, which served as the model for scenes from *The Adventures of Tom Sawyer.* At the base of Cardiff Hill at Main Street is the Tom and Huck Statue, which commemorates Twains most famous characters, Huck Finn and Tom Sawyer. Frederick Hibbard sculpted this bronze statue in 1926.

Stretching along Main Street are a number of historic buildings and shops. Follow Main Street south, passing boutiques in historic storefronts. A worthy stop is **Mrs. Clemens' Antique Mall** (*305 N. Main*), which features two floors of antiques and an icecream parlor. At Bird and Main streets stands the handsome Pilaster House/Grant's Drug Store, dating from the 1830s. The Clemens family lived here briefly in the 1940s, and Judge Clemens died here in 1847. Today, the building is preserved as an 1890s apothecary.

At Main and Center streets is the Mark Twain Museum, a restored structure that contains a collection of original Norman Rockwell paintings used for illustrated editions of *Adventures of Huckleberry Finn*. The museum also serves as a memento of Hannibal's riverboat past.

★
★★
★★
★

## HOTELS

### ★★★GARTH WOODSIDE MANSION BED AND BREAKFAST

*11069 New London Road, Hannibal, 573-221-2789, 888-427-8409;*
*www.hannibal-missouri.com*

With eight guest rooms, each with its own private bath, this Second Empire/Victorian mansion where Mark Twain was often a guest is located on 33 acres of grass, woodland, gardens and ponds. Eight rooms. Complimentary full breakfast. High-speed Internet access. $

### ★HOTEL CLEMENS

*401 N. Third St., Hannibal, 573-248-1150; www.hotelclemens.us*
78 rooms. Complimentary continental breakfast. Indoor pool, whirlpool. Airport transportation available. $

### ★SUPER 8
*120 Huckleberry Heights Drive, Hannibal, 573-221-5863,*
*800-800-8000; www.super8.com*
59 rooms. Pets accepted, some restrictions; fee. Complimentary continental breakfast.
Outdoor pool. **$**

## RESTAURANT
### ★LOGUE'S
*121 Huckleberry Heights Drive, Hannibal, 573-248-1854*
American menu. Breakfast, lunch, dinner. Children's menu. **$**

# HERMANN

German immigrants, unhappy with the English atmosphere of Philadelphia, bought
this land and founded the town with the purpose of maintaining their German culture.
Grape cultivation and winemaking started early and thrived until Prohibition. Today
the town has several working wineries and plenty of German-influenced buildings,
restaurants and shops.
*Information: 573-486-2744, 800-932-8687; www.hermannmo.com*

## WHAT TO SEE AND DO
### DEUTSCHHEIM STATE HISTORIC SITE
*109 W. Second St., Hermann, 573-486-2200;*
*www.mostateparks.com*
This site includes the authentically furnished Pommer-Gentner House on Market
Street and Strehly House and Winery (circa 1840-1867) on West Second Street.
Kitchen, herb and flower gardens; special events. Tours. Daily.

### GRAHAM CAVE STATE PARK
*217 Highway TT, Montgomery, 573-564-3476;*
*www.mostateparks.com*
Native Americans occupied this cave approximately 10,000 years ago. About 350
acres with fishing, nature trails, playground, camping. Daily.

### HERMANNHOF WINERY
*330 E. First St., Hermann, 573-486-5959*
This 150-year-old winery includes 10 wine cellars. Sausage making; cheeses. Sampling. Daily.

### HISTORIC HERMANN MUSEUM
*312 Schiller St., Hermann, 573-486-2017*
Heritage Museum in 1871 building, with artifacts of early settlers; River Room
depicts the history of early river men; children's museum has toys, furniture of 1890s;
handmade German bedroom set; 1886 pump organ. Mechanism of town clock may be
seen. April-October, Tuesday-Sunday.

**MISSOURI**

## SPECIAL EVENT
### GREAT STONE HILL GRAPE STOMP
*Stone Hill Winery and Restaurant, 1110 Stone Hill Highway, Hermann,*
*800-909-9463; www.stonehillwinery.com*
Jump into in a barrel full of juicy grapes to celebrate the beginning of grape harvest.
Second Saturday in August.

## HOTEL
### ★HERMANN MOTEL
*112 E. 10th St., Hermann, 573-486-3131; www.hermannmotel.com*
24 rooms. $

## RESTAURANT
### ★★VINTAGE
*1110 Stone Hill Highway, Hermann, 573-486-3479, 800-909-9463;*
*www.stonehillwinery.com*
American, German menu. Lunch, dinner. Closed mid-December-mid-February. Chil-
dren's menu. Reservations recommended. $$

# INDEPENDENCE
Independence was an outfitting point for westbound wagon trains from 1830-1850.
The scene of much of the Mormon Wars in the early 1830s, it was ravaged by raiders
and occupied by Union and Confederate troops during the Civil War. Today it's best
known as the hometown of President Harry S. Truman.
*Information: Tourism Division, 111 E. Maple, 816-325-7111, 800-748-7323*

★
★
★
★
★

## WHAT TO SEE AND DO
### 1859 MARSHAL'S HOME AND JAIL MUSEUM
*217 N. Main St., Independence, 816-252-1892; www.jchs.org*
Restored building contains dungeon-like cells, marshal's living quarters, regional his-
tory museum. One-room schoolhouse. April-October, daily; November-December
and March, Tuesday-Sunday.

### BINGHAM-WAGGONER ESTATE
*313 W. Pacific, Independence, 816-461-3491; www.planetware.com*
Famous Missouri artist George Caleb Bingham lived here from 1864-1870; also the
homestead of the Waggoner family, millers of "Queen of the Pantry" flour. April-
October, daily.

### FORT OSAGE
*105 Osage, Sibley, 816-795-8200*
Restoration of one of the first U.S. outposts in the Louisiana Territory following the
purchase from France. Built in 1808 by William Clark of the Lewis and Clark expe-
dition, the fort includes officers' quarters, soldiers' barracks, trading post, factor's
house, museum; costumed guides. Mid-April-mid-November, Wednesday-Sunday;
rest of year, Saturday-Sunday.

### HARRY S. TRUMAN COURTROOM AND OFFICE MUSEUM

*Jackson County Courthouse, 112 W. Lexington, Independence, 816-795-8200*

Restored office and courtroom where Truman began his political career as presiding county judge. Tours. Sunday-Thursday, by appointment.

### HARRY S. TRUMAN NATIONAL HISTORIC SITE (TRUMAN HOUSE)

*Main and Truman streets, Independence, 816-254-9929; www.nps.gov/hstr*

This was Truman's residence from the time of his marriage to Bess Wallace in 1919 until his death in 1972. An excellent example of late 19th-century Victorian architecture. The house, built by Bess Truman's grandfather, was the birthplace of Margaret Truman and served as the summer White House from 1945-1953. Memorial Day-Labor Day, daily; rest of year, Tuesday-Sunday.

### NATIONAL FRONTIER TRAILS CENTER

*318 W. Pacific, Independence, 816-325-7575; www.ci.independence.mo.us*

Partially restored flour mill at the site of the Santa Fe, California and Oregon trails serves as a museum, interpretive center, library and archive of westward pioneer expansion. Daily.

### TRUMAN FARM HOME

*12301 Blue Ridge Blvd., Grandview, 816-254-2720; www.planetware.com*

Harry Truman lived in this two-story, white frame house in the decade preceding World War I. During these years—"the best years," according to Truman—he farmed the surrounding 600 acres, worked as a mason and postmaster, served as a soldier and courted Bess Wallace. Interior features period furnishings, including original family pieces. Mid-May-late August, Friday-Sunday.

### TRUMAN PRESIDENTIAL MUSEUM AND LIBRARY

*500 W. Highway 24, Independence, 816-268-8200; www.trumanlibrary.org*

Includes presidential papers, mementos of public life and a reproduction of President Truman's White House office. Graves of President and Mrs. Truman in courtyard. Museum, daily; closed holidays. Library, Monday-Friday.

## SPECIAL EVENT

### SANTA-CALI-GON

*210 W. Truman Road, Independence, 816-252-4745*

Celebration commemorating the Santa Fe, California and Oregon trails. Contests, arts and crafts, square dancing. Labor Day weekend.

## HOTEL

### ★COMFORT INN EAST

*4200 S. Noland Road, Independence, 816-373-8856; www.choicehotels.com*

170 rooms. Pets accepted; fee. Complimentary continental breakfast. Indoor pool, outdoor pool, whirlpool. **$**

**95**

**MISSOURI**

★
★
★
★
★

## SPECIALTY LODGING
### WOODSTOCK INN BED AND BREAKFAST
*1212 W. Lexington Ave., Independence, 816-833-2233, 800-276-5202;*
*www.independence-missouri.com*
11 rooms. Complimentary full breakfast. High-speed Internet access. In a historic area of town near the Truman house and library. **$**

## RESTAURANTS
### ★★RHEINLAND
*208 N. Main St., Independence, 816-461-5383*
German menu. Breakfast, lunch, dinner, brunch. Children's menu. **$$**

### ★★SALVATORE'S
*12801 Highway 40 E. Independence, 816-737-2400; www.salvatores.us*
Italian menu. Lunch, dinner. Bar. Children's menu. Outdoor seating. **$$**

### ★★★V'S ITALIANO
*10819 Highway 40 E., Independence, 816-353-1241; www.vsrestaurant.com*
This family-style Italian restaurant serves up heaping portions of classic dishes like veal parmigiana and osso bucco. Entrées come with fresh slices of Italian rum cake. American, Italian menu. Lunch, dinner, Sunday brunch. Bar. Children's menu. Casual attire. **$$**

# JEFFERSON CITY
Jefferson City was chosen for the state capital in 1826. Near a river landing, it consisted of a foundry, a shop and a mission. Government business drives this small historic town. Named for Thomas Jefferson, it is known locally as "Jeff City."
*Information: Jefferson City Convention and Visitors Bureau, 213 Adams St.,*
*573-634-3616, 800-769-4183; www.jeffcitymo.org*

## WHAT TO SEE AND DO
### COLE COUNTY HISTORICAL SOCIETY MUSEUM
*109 Madison St., Jefferson City, 573-635-1850; www.colecohistsoc.org*
One of three four-story row houses built in the Federal style, this museum features Victorian furnishings and household items, plus inaugural gowns from Missouri's first ladies dating from 1877. Tuesday-Saturday.

### GOVERNOR'S MANSION
*100 Madison St., Jefferson City, 573-751-7929; www.missourimansion.org*
This Renaissance Revival house was designed by George Ingham Barnett and features period furnishings, stenciled ceilings, period wall coverings and late 19th-century chandeliers. Tours Tuesday and Thursday; closed August and December.

### JEFFERSON LANDING STATE HISTORIC SITE
*Jefferson and Water streets, Jefferson City, 573-751-3475*
Restored mid-1800s riverboat landing. Lohman Building features exhibits and audio-visual presentation on the history of Jefferson City and the Missouri Capitol. Union Hotel contains a gallery of exhibits by local artisans. Tuesday-Saturday.

## STATE CAPITOL

*High Street and Broadway, Jefferson City, 573-751-4127*

On a bluff overlooking the Missouri River, this building of Carthage stone is the third state capitol in Jefferson City; both predecessors burned. A Thomas Hart Benton mural is in the House Lounge, on the third floor west wing. Also here are paintings by N. C. Wyeth and Frank Brangwyn. Daily.

## HOTELS

### ★★BEST WESTERN CAPITAL INN

*1937 Christy Drive, Jefferson City, 573-635-4175, 800-780-7234;*
*www.bestwestern.com*

79 rooms. Pets accepted, some restrictions. Complimentary continental breakfast. Restaurant, bar. Indoor pool. $

### ★★★CAPITOL PLAZA HOTEL

*451 W. McCarty St., Jefferson City, 573-635-1234,*
*800-338-8088; www.jqhhotels.com*

This full-service hotel offers renovated guest rooms, a pool, whirlpool and cascading waterfall in the atrium, a restaurant, café and lounge and more. It is located across from the Truman building and near attractions. 200 rooms. Pets accepted, some restrictions; fee. Restaurant, bar. Fitness room. Indoor pool. $

### ★★HOTEL DEVILLE

*319 W. Miller St., Jefferson City, 573-636-5231, 800-392-3366;*
*www.devillehotel.com*

97 rooms. Restaurant, bar. Outdoor pool. $

## RESTAURANT

### ★★MADISON'S CAFÉ

*216 Madison St., Jefferson City, 573-634-2988; www.madisonscafe.com*

Italian menu. Lunch, dinner. Children's menu. Casual attire. $$

# JOPLIN

The discovery of lead here convinced an early settler to establish a town. As the mining boom continued, another community, Murphysburg, grew up on the west side of Joplin Creek. The two towns were rivals until 1873 when both agreed to merge. Today Joplin, one of Missouri's larger cities, is home to many manufacturing industries.

*Information: Convention and Visitors Bureau, 602 S. Main St.,*
*417-625-4789, 800-657-2534; www.joplincvb.com*

## WHAT TO SEE AND DO

### DOROTHEA B. HOOVER HISTORICAL MUSEUM

*W. Seventh Street and Schifferdecker Avenue, Joplin, 417-623-1180;*
*www.joplinmuseum.org*

Period rooms with late 19th-century furnishing; miniatures, including a circus, photographs, musical instruments, Victorian doll house and playhouse; antique toys; dolls; Native American artifacts; cut glass.

### THOMAS HART BENTON EXHIBIT

*303 E. Third St., Joplin*

Includes the mural, *Joplin at the Turn of the Century, 1896-1906,* as well as photographs, clay models, personal letters and other paintings by Benton. Monday-Friday.

## HOTELS

### ★DRURY INN

*3601 S. Range Line Road, Joplin, 417-781-8000, 800-378-7946;*
*www.druryhotels.com*

109 rooms. Pets accepted. Complimentary continental breakfast. Fitness room. Indoor pool, whirlpool. $

### ★★HOLIDAY INN

*3615 Range Line Road, Joplin, 417-782-1000, 800-465-4329;*
*www.holiday-inn.com*

262 rooms. Pets accepted, some restrictions. Restaurant, bar. Fitness room. Indoor pool, outdoor pool, whirlpool. $

## RESTAURANTS

### ★KITCHEN PASS

*1212 S. Main St., Joplin, 417-624-9095; www.kitchenpass.net*

Seafood, steak menu. Lunch, dinner. Closed Sunday; holidays. Bar. Children's menu. $$

### ★WILDER'S

*1216 Main St., Joplin, 417-623-7230*

Seafood, steak menu. Dinner. Bar. Sunday closed. $$$

# KANSAS CITY

Kansas City was developed as a steamboat landing for the town of Westport, four miles south on the Santa Fe Trail, and a competitor with Independence as the trail's eastern terminus and outfitting point. The buildings that sprang up along this landing eclipsed Westport, which was eventually incorporated into the new city. Kansas City's roaring overland trade was disturbed by the border warfare of the 1850s and the Civil War, but peace and the railroads brought new prosperity. A network of railway lines following the natural water-level routes that converge at the mouth of the Kansas River made Kansas City a great terminus.

Famous for their "booster" spirit, its citizens were aroused to the need for civic improvement in the 1890s by the crusade of William Rockhill Nelson, the *Kansas City Star* publisher. As a result, today's Kansas City boasts 52 boulevards totaling 155 miles and more fountains than any city except Rome. It's also known around the world for its superb barbecue and its rhythm and blues scene.

*Information: Kansas City Convention & Visitors Bureau, 1100 Main St.,*
*816-221-5242, 800-767-7700; www.visitkc.com*

# WHAT TO SEE AND DO

## ARABIA STEAMBOAT MUSEUM

*400 Grand Blvd., Kansas City, 816-471-4030; www.1856.com*

Excavated pioneer artifacts from the steamboat *Arabia,* which went down in 1856. The boat, discovered in 1988, carried 200 tons of cargo. Replica of main deck; hands-on displays. Daily.

## ART AND DESIGN CENTER

*4510 State Line Road, Kansas City*

More than 20 shops and galleries located in an historic area.

## CITY MARKET

*Main to Grand streets, Third-Fifth streets, Kansas City*

Outdoor farmers market since early 1800s. April-September, daily. Indoor farmers market, year-round, daily.

## COUNTRY CLUB PLAZA

*4745 Central St., Kansas City, 816-753-0100*

The nation's first planned shopping center (built in 1922) consists of 55 acres encompassing more than 180 shops and 25 restaurants in and around Spanish/Moorish-style arcaded buildings. The plaza features tree-lined walks, statues, fountains and murals; recreations of Spain's Seville light and Giralda tower; horse-drawn carriage rides; free entertainment. Daily.

## CROWN CENTER

*2450 Grand, Kansas City, 816-274-8444; www.crowncenter.com*

This entertainment complex offers shopping, theaters, restaurants and hotels around a landscaped central square; exhibits and ice skating (mid-November-March). Shops daily.

## JESSE JAMES BANK MUSEUM

*103 N. Water St., Liberty, 816-781-4458*

Restored site of the first daylight bank robbery by the James gang in 1866. Jesse James memorabilia; hand-scribed bank ledger books and other relics of early banking. Monday-Saturday.

## JOHN WORNALL HOUSE MUSEUM

*6115 Wornall Road, Kansas City, 816-444-1858; www.wornallhouse.org*

Restored farmhouse interprets the lives of prosperous Missouri farm families from 1830-1865; herb garden. Tuesday-Sunday; closed January.

## KALEIDOSCOPE

*2450 Grand Blvd., Kansas City, 816-274-8300; www.hallmarkkaleidoscope.com*

Participatory creative art exhibit for children ages 5-12. Discovery Room features hands-on creative area. Mid-June-August, Monday-Saturday; rest of year, Saturday or by appointment. Adults may view activity through one-way mirrors. Three 90-minute sessions per day; tickets available half-hour before each session.

**MISSOURI**

★
★
★
★
★

### KANSAS CITY CHIEFS (NFL)

*Arrowhead Stadium, 1 Arrowhead Drive, Kansas City, 816-920-9300,*
*800-676-5488; www.kcchiefs.com*
Professional football team.

### KANSAS CITY MUSEUM

*Union Station, 3218 Gladstone Blvd., Kansas City, 816-483-8300;*
*www.kcmuseum.com*
Science, history and technology exhibits housed in former estate of lumber million-
aire Robert A. Long; re-creation of 1821 trading post, 1860 storefront and functioning
1910 drugstore; planetarium; gift shop. Tuesday-Sunday.

### KANSAS CITY ROYALS (MLB)

*Kauffman Stadium, 1 Royal Way, Kansas City, 816-921-8000; www.kcroyals.com*
Professional baseball team.

### KANSAS CITY WIZARDS (MLS)

*Arrowhead Stadium, 1 Arrowhead Drive, Kansas City, 816-920-9300;*
*www.kcwizards.com*
Professional soccer team.

### KANSAS CITY ZOO

*Swope Park, 6800 Zoo Drive, Kansas City, 816-513-5700; www.kansascityzoo.org*
Explore 200 acres landscaped to resemble natural animal habitats. Sea lion and wild
bird shows; IMAX theater; miniature train, pony and camel rides. Daily.

### NELSON-ATKINS MUSEUM OF ART

*4525 Oak St., Kansas City, 816-751-1278; www.nelson-atkins.org*
Collections range from Sumerian art of 3000 BC to contemporary paintings and
sculpture; period rooms; decorative arts; Kansas City Sculpture Park featuring Henry
Moore sculpture garden. Tuesday-Sunday.

### UNION CEMETERY

*227 E. 28th St., Kansas City*
Some notables buried here include artist George Caleb Bingham and Alexander
Majors, founder of the Pony Express; graves of more than 1,000 Civil War soldiers.

### WESTPORT

*Broadway and Westport Road, Kansas City*
Renovated 1830s historic district includes specialty shops, galleries and restaurants;
Pioneer Park traces Westport's role in the founding of Kansas City. Daily.

### WORLDS OF FUN

*4545 N.E. Worlds of Fun Ave., Kansas City, 816-454-4545; www.worldsoffun.com*
A 170-acre entertainment complex with amusement rides, live entertainment, children's area, special events, restaurants; includes looping steel and wooden roller
coasters. Late May-August, daily; April and September-October, weekends.

**100**

**MISSOURI**

★
★
★
★

## SPECIAL EVENTS
### KANSAS CITY PRO RODEO
*Benjamin Ranch, 6401 E. 87th St., Kansas City, 816-761-1234*
Saddle bronco riding, steer wrestling, bareback riding, barrel racing, calf roping and bull riding are some of the events held at the Benjamin Ranch. Fourth of July week.

### KANSAS CITY SYMPHONY
*1020 Central St., Kansas City, 816-471-0400; www.kcsymphony.org*
Concert series of symphonic and pop music. Friday-Sunday, some Wednesdays.

### LYRIC OPERA
*1029 Central St., Kansas City, 816-471-4933*
Opera productions in English. Performances on Monday, Wednesday, Friday-Saturday, April-May and mid-September-mid-October; holiday production in December.

### MISSOURI REPERTORY THEATRE
*Center for the Performing Arts, 4949 Cherry St., Kansas City,*
*816-235-2700; www.kcrep.org*
Professional equity theater company; classic and contemporary productions. Annual performance of *A Christmas Carol.* September-May, Tuesday-Sunday.

### STARLIGHT THEATER
*Swope Park, 4600 Starlight Road, Kansas City, 816-363-7827*
Outdoor amphitheater featuring Broadway musicals and contemporary concerts. Performances nightly. Early June-August.

### ST. PATRICK'S DAY PARADE
*Pershing and Grand streets, Kansas City, 816-931-7373, 816-373-5405;*
*www.kcirishparade.com*
One of the nation's largest, this St. Patrick's Day parade is approximately one mile long and features a variety of themed floats, bands and performers. March.

## HOTELS
### ★BAYMONT INN
*2214 Taney St., North Kansas City, 816-221-1200, 800-301-0200;*
*www.baymontinn.com*
93 rooms. Complimentary continental breakfast. $

### ★★DOUBLETREE HOTEL
*1301 Wyandotte St., Kansas City, 816-474-6664, 800-222-8733; www.doubletree.com*
388 rooms. Pets accepted, some restrictions; fee. Restaurant, bar. Fitness room. Outdoor pool. Business center. $$

### ★★★HOTEL PHILLIPS
*106 W. 12th St., Kansas City, 816-221-7000, 800-433-1426; www.hotelphillips.com*
Located downtown, this boutique hotel is a convenient base. While the historic Art Deco integrity of this 1931 landmark has been preserved, modern amenities have been added to the rooms and suites. Phillips Chophouse has a 1930s feel. Live music

★
★
★
★
☆

can be heard at 12 Baltimore Café and Bar. 217 rooms. Two restaurants, two bars. High-speed Internet access. Fitness room. Airport transportation available. Business center. $$

### ★★★HOTEL SAVOY
*219 W. Ninth St., Kansas City, 816-842-3575, 800-728-6922; www.bandbonline.com*
This restored 1888 landmark building features original architectural details such as stained and leaded glass, tile floors and tin ceilings. The Savoy Grille is located on the property, and many attractions are nearby. 22 rooms. Complimentary full breakfast. Restaurant, bar. $

### ★★★HYATT REGENCY CROWN CENTER
*2345 McGee St., Kansas City, 816-421-1234, 888-591-1234; www.hyatt.com*
Connected to the Crown Center by an elevated walkway and located near the Truman Sports Complex, an amusement park and the international airport, this hotel is convenient and comfortable. 733 rooms. Five restaurants, bars. Wireless Internet access. Fitness room. Outdoor pool, whirlpool. Tennis. Business center. Airport transportation available. $$

### ★★★★INTERCONTINENTAL KANSAS CITY AT THE PLAZA
*401 Ward Parkway, Kansas City, 816-756-1500, 888-424-6835;*
*www.ichotelsgroup.com*
This elegant and contemporary hotel is located within the Plaza shopping and dining area. It has a 24-hour business center and a fitness center with outdoor pool and spa treatments. The Oak Room restaurant serves steaks and chops. 366 rooms. Pets accepted; fee. High-speed Internet access. Restaurant, bar. Fitness room. Outdoor pool, children's pool. Airport transportation available. Business center. $$

### ★★★MARRIOTT KANSAS CITY AIRPORT
*775 Brasilia Ave., Kansas City, 816-464-2200, 1-800-810-2771; www.marriott.com*
Located on the Kansas City International Airport's grounds, this hotel has been updated with luxury bedding and High-speed Internet access. 378 rooms. Restaurant, bar. Fitness room. Indoor pool, whirlpool. Business center. Airport transportation available. $$

### ★★★MARRIOTT KANSAS CITY COUNTRY CLUB PLAZA
*4445 Main St., Kansas City, 816-531-3000, 800-228-9290; www.marriott.com/mcipl*
Situated 10 minutes from downtown, this hotel is within walking distance of the city's top shopping and restaurants. A non-smoking hotel, this location has updated rooms with luxury bedding. 295 rooms. Wireless Internet access. Restaurant, bar. Fitness room. Indoor pool, whirlpool. Airport transportation available. Business center. $

### ★★★MARRIOTT KANSAS CITY DOWNTOWN
*200 W. 12th St., Kansas City, 816-421-6800, 800-228-9290; www.marriott.com*
This large hotel is located downtown near the city market, casinos and family attractions. 983 rooms. Pets accepted; fee. Wireless Internet access. Two restaurants, two bars. Fitness room (fee). Indoor pool. Business center. Airport transportation available. $$

### ★★QUARTERAGE HOTEL

*560 Westport Road, Kansas City, 816-931-0001, 800-942-4233;*
*www.quarteragehotel.com*

123 rooms. Complimentary full breakfast. High-speed Internet access. Fitness center. Spa. Business center. Airport transportation available. **$**

### ★★★THE RAPHAEL HOTEL

*325 Ward Parkway, Kansas City, 816-756-3800, 800-821-5343; www.raphaelkc.com*

This hotel is located in the midtown area near shops, restaurants and other attractions. 123 rooms. High-speed Internet access. Restaurant, bar. Airport transportation available. Business center. **$$**

### ★★★SHERATON SUITES COUNTRY CLUB PLAZA

*770 W. 47th St., Kansas City, 816-931-4400, 800-325-3535; www.sheraton.com*

This is an all-suite hotel offering many facilities, including a restaurant, lounge, indoor and outdoor heated pools, whirlpool and weight room. The hotel is located near sports, cultural and family attractions. 257 rooms, all suites. Pets accepted. High-speed Internet access. Restaurant, bar. Fitness room. Indoor pool, outdoor pool, whirlpool. Business center. Airport transportation available. **$**

### ★★★THE WESTIN CROWN CENTER

*1 Pershing Road, Kansas City, 816-474-4400, 800-228-3000;*
*www.westin.com/crowncenter*

Located in the downtown area within Hallmark's Crown Center, where visitors will find shops, restaurants and theaters, this hotel is also near the Liberty Memorial and the Bartle Convention Center. 729 rooms. Pets accepted, some restrictions. High-speed Internet access. Two restaurants, two bars. Children's activity center. Fitness room (fee). Outdoor pool, whirlpool. Tennis. Business center. Airport transportation available. **$$**

## SPECIALTY LODGING

### SOUTHMORELAND ON THE PLAZA

*116 E. 46th St., Kansas City, 816-531-7979; www.southmoreland.com*

Each room in this quiet bed and breakfast is uniquely furnished and decorated. Rooms feature either a fireplace, Jacuzzi tub or a private deck. The property is located near the Country Club Plaza shopping district and other attractions. 13 rooms. Children over 13 years only. Complimentary full breakfast. Wireless Internet access. **$**

## RESTAURANTS

### ★★★★THE AMERICAN RESTAURANT

*200 E. 25th St., Kansas City, 816-545-8001; www.theamericankc.com*

The flagship restaurant of the Crown Center, the American has attracted Kansas City diners for 40 years. With a concept designed by the legendary James Beard, the father of American cooking, and Joe Baum, the restaurateur of the former Windows on the World in New York City, the restaurant is as elegant as ever, with downtown views, polished service, and one of the city's best wine lists. The kitchen staff, led by executive chef Celina Tio, prepares American fare using local seasonal produce. American menu. Lunch, dinner. Closed Sunday. Bar. Children's menu. Business casual attire. Reservations recommended. Valet parking. **$$$**

**MISSOURI**

★
★
★
★
★

### ★★★ANDRE'S TEAROOM

*5018 Main St., Kansas City, 816-561-6484, 800-892-1234;*
*www.andreschocolates.com*

An offshoot of legendary Swiss chocolate maker Andres Bollier's candy shop, this tearoom serves continental favorites such as leek and gruyere pie or vol au vent in a quaint setting. After lunch, stock up on truffles or a linzer torte to take home. Continental menu. Lunch. Closed Sunday-Monday. Business casual attire. $

### ★ARTHUR BRYANT'S BARBEQUE

*1727 Brooklyn Ave., Kansas City, 816-231-1123; www.arthurbryantsbbq.com*
American menu. Lunch, dinner. Closed holidays. Casual attire. $

### ★★★BLUESTEM

*900 Westport Road, Kansas City, 816-561-1101; www.bluestemkc.com*

Bluestem is the product of two acclaimed chefs, Colby and Megan Garrelts, who worked at such restaurants as Aureole in Las Vegas and Tru in Chicago. The space is divided into a 40-seat restaurant, clad in cobalt blue walls and warm candlelight, and an adjacent wine bar that offers more casual fare. A three-, five- or seven-course prix menu is available, as well as a twelve-course tasting menu. Entrées might include a torchon of foie gras, wild Tasmanian salmon with oxtail or LaBelle duck with sweet potato gnocchi and apple emulsion. Desserts are outstanding, simplistic in their approach but full of intense flavors. American menu. Dinner, brunch. Bar. Business casual attire. Reservations recommended. $$$

★
★
★
★
★

### ★★BUGATTI'S LITTLE ITALY

*3200 N. Ameristar Drive, Kansas City, 816-414-7000; www.ameristarcasinos.com*
Italian menu. Breakfast, lunch, dinner, brunch. Bar. $$

### ★★CALIFORNOS

*4124 Pennsylvania, Kansas City, 816-531-1097; www.californos.com*
American menu. Lunch, dinner. Closed Sunday; holidays. Bar. Casual attire. Reservations recommended. Valet parking. Outdoor seating. $$

### ★★CASCONE'S ITALIAN RESTAURANT

*3733 N. Oak, Kansas City, 816-454-7977; www.cascones.com*
Italian menu. Lunch, dinner. Bar. Children's menu. Casual attire. Reservations recommended. Outdoor seating. $$

### ★★CHAPPELL'S

*323 Armour Road, North Kansas City, 816-421-0002; www.chappellsrestaurant.com*
Steak menu. Lunch, dinner. Closed Sunday. Bar. Children's menu. Casual attire.

### ★★CLASSIC CUP CAFÉ

*301 W. 47th St., Kansas City, 816-753-1840; www.classiccup.com*
American menu. Breakfast, lunch, dinner, Sunday brunch. Bar. Casual attire. Outdoor seating. $$

### ★★★EBT

*1310 Carondelet Drive, Kansas City, 816-942-8870; www.ebtrestaurant.com*

Mid-1900s sandstone columns and two ornate brass elevators provide the setting for this restaurant, with dishes such as pistachio-encrusted salmon and pepper steak. Tableside presentations are offered, and there is an extensive wine list. American menu. Lunch, dinner. Closed Sunday and Monday. Bar. Children's menu. Business casual attire. Reservations recommended. $$$

### ★★FIGLIO

*209 W. 46th Terrace, Kansas City, 816-561-0505; www.dineoutinkc.com*

Italian menu. Lunch, dinner, brunch. Bar. Children's menu. Casual attire. Reservations recommended. Valet parking. Outdoor seating. $$

### ★★FIORELLA'S JACK STACK BARBECUE

*13441 Holmes St., Kansas City, 816-942-9141, 877-419-7427;*
*www.jackstackbbq.com*

American menu. Lunch, dinner. Bar. Children's menu. Casual attire. Reservations recommended. Outdoor seating. $$

### ★★GAROZZO'S RISTORANTE

*526 Harrison, Kansas City, 816-221-2455; www.garozzos.com*

Italian menu. Lunch, dinner. Bar. Children's menu. Casual attire. Reservations recommended. $$

### ★★GOLDEN OX

*1600 Genessee St., Kansas City, 816-842-2866; www.goldenox.com*

Steak menu. Lunch, dinner. Bar. Children's menu. Casual attire. $$$

### ★★★GRAND STREET CAFÉ

*4740 Grand St., Kansas City, 816-561-8000; www.eatpbj.com*

A stylish and modern botanical theme is found throughout this dining room. Double cut pork chops with cinnamon apples and brown sugar jus, caramelized sea scallops with Maine lobster butter and a crispy potato pancake, and grilled filet mignon with a veal demi-cabernet sauce and French green beans are among the menu items. Brunch is popular. A small, cozy patio with eight tables offers al fresco dining. American menu. Lunch, dinner, Sunday brunch. Bar. Children's menu. Business casual attire. Reservations recommended. Outdoor seating. $$$

### ★★HARDWARE CAFÉ

*5 E. Kansas Ave., Liberty, 816-792-3500*

American menu. Breakfast, lunch, dinner. Closed Sunday. Children's menu. Old-fashioned soda fountain, historical building. No credit cards accepted. $$

### ★★JESS & JIM'S STEAK HOUSE

*517 E. 135th St., Kansas City, 816-941-9499, 816-942-2959;*
*www.jessandjims.com*

Steak menu. Lunch, dinner. Bar. Children's menu. Casual attire. $$$

**MISSOURI**

### ★★★JJ'S
*910 W. 48th St., Kansas City, 816-561-7136; www.jjs-restaurant.com*
Upscale European fare is served at this friendly bistro. Entrées spotlight fresh, local
ingredients and might include Kansas City strip steak with smoked gouda mashed
potatoes. American menu. Lunch, dinner. Bar. Business casual attire. Reservations
recommended. Valet parking. $$$

### ★L.C.'S BAR-B-Q
*5800 Blue Parkway, Kansas City, 816-923-4484*
American menu. Lunch, dinner. Closed Sunday. $$

### ★★★LE FOU FROG
*400 E. Fifth St., Kansas City, 816-474-6060; www.lefoufrog.com*
This French bistro is a good place to dine when seeing a show at the convention center. Sauces are light and presentation is excellent. Portions are big, from the escargot
to the steak au poivre. French menu. Lunch, dinner. Closed Monday. Bar. Casual
attire. Reservations recommended. Valet parking. Outdoor seating. $$$

### ★★★LIDIA'S KANSAS CITY
*101 W. 22nd St., Kansas City, 816-221-3722; www.lidiasitaly.com*
Created by the acclaimed New York restaurateur Lidia Bastianich, this trendy restau-
rant offers a rustic atmosphere, with rough brick walls and exposed wooden beams.
The menu is classic, with dishes such as salmon alla griglia. Italian menu. Lunch,
dinner. Bar. Children's menu. Business casual attire. Reservations recommended.
Outdoor seating. $$

### ★★MACALUSO'S ON 39TH
*1403 W. 39th St., Kansas City, 816-561-0100; www.macalusoson39th.com*
Italian menu. Dinner. Closed Sunday. Bar. Casual attire. Reservations recom-
mended. $$$

### ★★★THE MAJESTIC STEAKHOUSE
*931 Broadway, Kansas City, 816-471-8484; www.majesticsteakhouse.com*
The historic Fitzpatrick Saloon building in downtown Kansas City is home to one
of the best, most entertaining steakhouses in town. It's also a great place to indulge
in a cigar. The restaurant features turn-of-the-century décor with stained-glass win-
dows, ceiling fans and an ornate tin ceiling. Steak menu. Lunch, dinner. Bar. Business
casual attire. Reservations recommended. $$$

### ★★★MARINA GROG & GALLEY
*22 A St., Lees Summit, 816-578-5511; www.marinagrogandgalley.com*
Take in beautiful lake views from the elegant dining room. Seafood menu. Dinner.
Bar. Children's menu. Outdoor seating. $$$

### ★★★O'DOWD'S LITTLE DUBLIN
*4742 Pennsylvania Ave., Kansas City, 816-561-2700; www.odowdslittledublin.com*
This authentic Irish pub, with much of its interior built in Ireland then shipped here,
serves the best fish and chips in town. Irish menu. Lunch, dinner, late-night. Closed

Memorial Day. Bar. Children's menu. Casual attire. Reservations recommended. Outdoor seating. Wireless Internet access. $

### ★PHOENIX PIANO BAR & GRILL
*302 W. Eighth St., Kansas City, 816-472-0001; www.phoenixjazz.net*
American menu. Lunch, dinner, late-night. Closed Sunday. Piano bar; pictures of famous jazz musicians. Casual attire. Outdoor seating. $$

### ★★★PLAZA III STEAKHOUSE
*4749 Pennsylvania Ave., Kansas City, 816-753-0000; www.plazaiiisteakhouse.com*
The epitome of the Kansas City steakhouse, this restaurant serves USDA prime aged cuts of Midwestern beef, chops, fresh fish and lobster. Lunch includes the famous steak soup. Steak menu. Lunch, dinner. Bar. Children's menu. Business casual attire. Reservations recommended. Valet parking. $$$

### ★★★RAPHAEL DINING ROOM
*325 Ward Parkway, Kansas City, 816-756-3800, 800-821-5343; www.raphaelkc.com*
Housed in the Raphael Hotel, this restaurant has an elegant dining room and refined service. The Kansas City strip steak with port wine sauce and melted gorgonzola is a menu standout. International menu. Breakfast, lunch, dinner. Bar. Business casual attire. Reservations recommended. Valet parking. $$$

### ★SMUGGLER'S INN
*1650 Universal Plaza Drive, Kansas City, 816-483-0400*
American menu. Lunch, dinner. Bar. $$

# LAKE OZARK
This resort community rests on the huge, man-made reservoir Lake of the Ozarks. In summer the area is packed with tourists who come to boat and float on the lake or stay in its many resorts.
*www.funlake.comi*

## WHAT TO SEE AND DO
### JACOB'S CAVE
*23114 Highway TT, Versailles, 573-378-4374; www.jacobscave.com*
Famous for its depth illusion, reflective pools, prehistoric bones and the world's largest geode. Daily 9 a.m.-5 p.m.; closed holidays.

### LAKE OF THE OZARKS
*Highway 54, Lake Ozark; www.funlake.com*
Completed in 1931, the 2,543-foot-long Bagnell Dam impounds the Osage River to form this 54,000-acre recreational lake, which has an irregular 1,150-mile shoreline. Fishing, boating and swimming are excellent here.

### LAKE OF THE OZARKS STATE PARK
*403 Highway 134, Kaiser, 573-348-2694*
This more than 17,000-acre park, the largest in the state, has 89 miles of shoreline with two public swimming and boat launching areas. On the grounds is a large cave with streams of water that continuously pour from stalactites.

## HOTEL
### ★★★THE LODGE OF FOUR SEASONS
*Horseshoe Bend Parkway, Lake Ozark, 573-365-3000, 800-843-5253,*
*888-265-5500; www.4seasonsresort.com*
Located in the Ozark Hills, the property overlooks the winding shoreline. Many of the rooms and two- and three-bedroom condominiums have views of the lake or Japanese garden and pool. A golf course and health spa are on the premises. 350 rooms. Restaurant, bar. High-speed Internet access. Children's activity center. Fitness room, spa. Outdoor pool, children's pool, whirlpool. Golf. Airport transportation available. **$$**

## RESTAURANTS
### ★★BENTLEY'S
*Highway 54 Business, Lake Ozark, 573-365-5301;*
*www.bentleysrestaurantmo.com*
Seafood, steak menu. Dinner. Closed Sunday; holidays. Bar. Children's menu. Casual attire. **$$**

### ★★J.B. HOOK'S GREAT OCEAN FISH & STEAKS
*2260 Bagnell Dam Blvd., Lake Ozark, 573-365-3255; www.jbhooks.com*
Seafood, steak menu. Lunch, dinner. Bar. Outdoor seating (lunch only). **$$**

# LEBANON
Lebanon was founded in the mid-1800s beside an Indian trail that today is Interstate 44 (I-44). As the seat of the newly-created Laclede County, the town was originally called Wyota. The name was changed when a respected minister asked that it be renamed after his hometown of Lebanon, Tennessee.
*Information: Lebanon Area Chamber of Commerce, 500 E. Elm St.,*
*417-588-3256; www.lebanonmissouri.com*

## WHAT TO SEE AND DO
### BENNETT SPRING STATE PARK
*26248 Highway 64A, Lebanon, 417-532-4307, 1-800-334-6946;*
*www.bennettspringstatepark.com*
Nearly 3,100 acres. Swimming pool, trout fishing (March-October); picnicking, store, dining lodge, camping, cabins. Restaurant. Nature center. Daily.

## SPECIAL EVENT
### HILLBILLY DAYS
*Bennett Springs State Park, Lebanon, 417-588-3256*
Arts and crafts, contests, country music, antique cars. Father's Day weekend.

## HOTEL
### ★★BEST WESTERN WYOTA INN
*1225 Millcreek Road, Lebanon, 417-532-6171, 800-780-7234, 1-866-996-8246;*
*www.bestwestern.com*
52 rooms. Pets accepted, some restrictions; fee. Complimentary continental breakfast. High-speed Internet access. Restaurant. Outdoor pool. **$**

# LEXINGTON

This historic city with more than 110 antebellum houses was founded by settlers from Lexington, Kentucky, and was the site of a three-day battle during the Civil War. Many of the Union Army's entrenchments are still visible today. Situated on bluffs overlooking the Missouri River, Lexington was an important river port during the 19th-century. Today the area is one of the state's largest producers of apples.

*Information: Tourism Bureau, 817 Main St., 660-259-4711; www.historiclexington.com*

## WHAT TO SEE AND DO
### BATTLE OF LEXINGTON STATE HISTORIC SITE
*Extension Highway N. Lexington, 660-259-4654; www.mostateparks.com*
The site of one of the Civil War's largest western campaign battles (September 18-20, 1861). Anderson House, which stood in the center of the battle and changed hands from north to south three times, has been restored. Daily.

### LAFAYETTE COUNTY COURTHOUSE
*1001 Main St., Lexington, 660-259-4315; www.lafayettecountymo.com*
Built in 1847, this is the oldest courthouse in constant use west of the Mississippi. It has a Civil War cannonball embedded in the east column. Monday-Friday.

### LEXINGTON HISTORICAL MUSEUM
*215 W. Main St., Lexington, 859-254-0530; www.lexingtonhistorymuseum.org*
Built as a Presbyterian church in 1846, this structure contains Pony Express and Battle of Lexington relics, photographs and other historical Lexington items. Mid-April-mid-October, daily.

## RESTAURANT
### ★LONG BRANCH
*28855 Sunset Drive, Macon, 660-385-4600*
Lunch, dinner. Bar. Children's menu. $$

# NEVADA

Settled by families from Kentucky and Tennessee, Nevada became known as the "bushwhackers capital" due to the Confederate guerrillas headquartered here during the Civil War. The town was burned to the ground in 1863 by Union troops and was not rebuilt until after the war. Today Nevada is a shopping and trading center for the surrounding area.

*Information: Nevada-Vernon Chamber of Commerce, 201 E. Cherry, 417-667-5300, 800-910-4276; www.nevada-mo.com*

## WHAT TO SEE AND DO
### BUSHWHACKER MUSEUM
*212 W. Walnut 417-667-9602;*
*www.bushwhacker.org*
The museum, operated by the Vernon County Historical Society, includes a restored 19th-century jail as well as Civil War relics, period clothing and tools. May-September, daily 10 a.m.-4 p.m.; October, weekends.

## MISSOUREE OR MISSOURAH?

As in many states, you might need to check with a local to learn how to pronounce the name of the town in which you're standing. New Madrid is "New MAD-drid," Versailles is "Ver-SAILS." But while town names usually have an undisputed, if vexing (Iowa's Des Moines is "duh-MOYN") right way to say them, it won't do you much good to ask someone how to say "Missouri." On TV, East Coast anchormen and pundits seem to grapple with a foreign language as they strain to utter the state's name in the "authentic" way: "Miz-zur-uh" (as opposed to Miz-zur-ee). But is it? Even though in any Missouri political race, there are always candidates who try to establish their native's credentials and just-folks image with the "-uh" ending, if you ask someone who lives in the state the right way to say it, the answer is far from clear. Some say the "-uh" locution reigns in the south of the state, but you will find plenty of natives there who go with "-ee." Others say it's a western thing, but there are lots of self-declared "Missouree" natives in Kansas City. The consensus seems to be, especially around St. Louis, that while the "-uh" has a lot of adherents among older generations in rural areas, you won't stand out like a lost tourist if you go with "Missouree," the most common pronunciation. Just don't push it by saying, "Show me."

### SPECIAL EVENT
**BUSHWHACKER DAYS**

*225 W. Austin., Nevada, 417-667-5300; www.bwdays.com*

Parade; arts and crafts, antique machine and car shows; street square dance, midway. Mid-June.

### HOTELS
**★DAYS INN**

*2345 E. Marvel Road, Nevada, 417-667-6777, 800-329-7466; www.daysinn.com*

46 rooms. Pets accepted; fee. Complimentary continental breakfast. High-speed Internet access. Restaurant. Outdoor pool, whirlpool. Spa. Fitness center. **$**

**★SUPER 8**

*2301 E. Austin St., Nevada, 417-667-8888, 1-800-800-8000; www.super8.com*

59 rooms. Pets accepted, some restrictions; fee. Complimentary continental breakfast. High-speed Internet access. Indoor pool, whirlpool. **$**

# OSAGE BEACH

A major resort community on the Lake of the Ozarks, the town came into existence with the 1931 completion of the lake.

*Information: Lake Area Chamber of Commerce, 1 Willmore Lane, Lake Ozark, 573-964-1008, 800-451-4117; www.lakeareachamber.com*

# HOTELS
### ★★DOGWOOD HILLS RESORT INN
*1252 Highway KK, Osage Beach, 573-348-1735, 800-220-6571;*
*www.dogwoodhillsresort.com*
47 rooms. Pets accepted; fee. High-speed Internet access. Restaurant (March-October), bar. Outdoor pool, whirlpool. Golf. **$**

### ★★INN AT GRAND GLAIZE
*5142 Highway 54, Osage Beach, 573-348-4731, 800-348-4731;*
*www.innatgrandglaize.com*
1,591 rooms. Restaurant, bar. Wireless Internet access. Fitness room. Outdoor pool, children's pool, whirlpool. **$**

### ★★★TAN-TAR-A RESORT
*Highway KK, Osage Beach, 573-348-3131, 1-800-826-8272; www.tan-tar-a.com*
This property is on the scenic Lake of the Ozarks and offers more than 30 recreational activities, including indoor and outdoor pools, waterskiing, a full spa, jogging, golf and more. The hotel is near many area restaurants and attractions. 365 rooms. Restaurant, bar. Children's activity center. Fitness room. One indoor pool, four outdoor pools, two children's pools, whirlpool. Golf. Tennis. **$**

# RESTAURANTS
### ★★THE BRASS DOOR
*5167 Highway 54, Osage Beach, 573-348-9229; www.the-brass-door.com*
Steak, seafood. menu. Dinner. Children's menu. **$$$**

### ★★DOMENICO'S CARRY-OUT PIZZA
*4737 Highway 54, Osage Beach, 573-348-2844*
Italian, American menu. Dinner. Closed holidays. Bar. Children's menu. **$$**

### ★★HAPPY FISHERMAN
*4676 Highway 54, Osage Beach, 573-348-3311*
American menu. Dinner. Closed mid-December-January. Bar. Children's menu. **$$**

### ★★POTTED STEER
*5085 Highway 54, Osage Beach, 573-348-5053, 573-365-5743;*
*www.blueheronpottedsteer.com*
Dinner. Closed Sunday-Monday. Bar. **$$**

### ★★VISTA GRANDE
*4579 Highway 54, Osage Beach, 573-348-1231;*
*www.vistagrandemexicanrestaurant.com*
American, Mexican menu. Lunch, dinner. Bar. Children's menu. **$$**

# PILOT KNOB
This village of less than 700 people was the site of the Civil War Battle of Pilot Knob. Union and Confederate forces clashed over control of nearby Fort Davidson in 1864.

MISSOURI

★
★
★
★
★

## WHAT TO SEE AND DO
### JOHNSON'S SHUT-INS STATE PARK
*Highway North, Middle Brook, 573-546-2450; www.mostateparks.com*
This nearly 8,500-acre area, left in its wilderness state, has a spectacular canyon-like defile along the river. The park is at the southern end of the 20-mile-long Ozark backpacking trail, which traverses Missouri's highest mountain, Taum Sauk. Swimming, fishing, hiking, picnicking, playground, improved camping. Daily.

## HOTEL
### ★★WILDERNESS LODGE
*Peola Road, Lesterville, 573-637-2295, 888-969-9129;*
*www.wildernesslodgeresort.com*
27 rooms. Restaurant (public by reservation), bar. Internet access. Outdoor pool. Business center. $

# ROLLA
According to legend, this town was named by a homesick settler from Raleigh, North Carolina, who spelled the name as he pronounced it. Called "the child of the railroad" because it began with the building of the St. Louis-San Francisco Railroad, the town is located in a scenic area with several streams nearby. Mark Twain National Forest maintains its headquarters in Rolla.
*Information: Rolla Area Chamber of Commerce, 1301 Kings Highway, 573-364-3577,*
*888-809-3817; www.rollachamber.org*

★
★★
★★★
★☆

## WHAT TO SEE AND DO
### MARAMEC SPRING PARK AND REMAINS OF OLD IRONWORKS
*21880 Maramec Spring Drive, Rolla, 573-265-7387*
The spring discharges an average of 96-million gallons per day. The ironworks was first established in 1826; the present furnace was built in 1857. Nature center; observation tower; two museums. Daily.

### MARK TWAIN NATIONAL FORESTS
*401 Fairgrounds Road, Rolla, 573-364-4621; www.fs.fed.us*
More than 192,000 acres; cradles the headwaters of the Gasconade, Little Piney and Big Piney rivers. Paddy Creek Wilderness Area covers about 6,800 acres with 30 miles of hiking and riding trails.

### ST. JAMES WINERY
*540 Sidney St., 573-265-7912, 800-280-9463; www.stjameswinery.com*
Dry and semidry wines, sparkling wines, concord, catawba and berry wines are all produced here. Daily 8 a.m.-10 p.m.

## HOTELS
### ★BEST WESTERN COACHLIGHT
*1403 Martin Springs Road, Rolla, 573-341-2511, 800-780-7234; www.bestwestern.com*
88 rooms. Pets accepted, some restrictions. Complimentary continental breakfast. High-speed Internet access.

### ★DRURY INN

*2006 N. Bishop Ave., Rolla, 573-364-4000, 800-378-7946; www.druryhotels.com*
86 rooms. Pets accepted, some restrictions. Complimentary continental breakfast. High-speed Internet access. Outdoor pool. **$**

### ★★ZENO'S MOTEL AND STEAK HOUSE

*1621 Martin Springs Drive, Rolla, 573-364-1301; www.zenos.biz.*
51 rooms. Restaurant, bar. Indoor pool, outdoor pool, whirlpool. Fitness center. **$**

## RESTAURANT
### ★JOHNNY'S SMOKE STAK

*201 Highway 72, Rolla, 573-364-4838*
American menu. Lunch, dinner. Children's menu. **$**

# SEDALIA

Known as the "queen city of the prairies," Sedalia was a prosperous railhead town in the 1800s with great cattle herds arriving for shipment to eastern markets. During the Civil War, the settlement functioned as a military post. A monument at Lamine and Main Streets marks the site of the Maple Leaf Club, one of the city's many saloons that catered to railroad men. The monument is dedicated to Scott Joplin, who composed and performed the "Maple Leaf Rag" here, triggering the ragtime craze at the turn of the 20th century. Whiteman Air Force Base is 21 miles west of Sedalia.
*Information: Chamber of Commerce, 600 E. Third St.,*
*660-826-2222, 800-827-5295; www.sedaliachamber.com*

## WHAT TO SEE AND DO
### BOTHWELL LODGE STATE HISTORIC SITE

*19349 Bothwell State Park, Sedalia, 660-827-0510; www.mostateparks.com*
An Arts and Crafts house built between 1897 and 1928 for a local businessman, the lodge is open for tours. The park includes approximately 180 acres, with hiking trails and picnic areas. Daily.

### PETTIS COUNTY COURTHOUSE

*415 S. Ohio, Sedalia, 660-826-4892; www.pettiscomo.com*
Historic courthouse contains local artifacts and exhibits. Monday-Friday.

### SEDALIA RAGTIME ARCHIVES

*State Fair Community College Library, Maple Leaf Room,*
*3201 W. 16th St., Sedalia, 660-530-5800*
Includes original sheet music, piano rolls, tapes of interviews with Eubie Blake. Monday-Friday; closed school holidays.

## SPECIAL EVENTS
### MISSOURI STATE FAIR

*2503 W. 16th St., Sedalia, 660-530-5600, 660-827-8150; www.mostatefair.com*
One of the country's leading state fairs, this event has been held here since 1901. Stage shows, rodeo, competitive exhibits, livestock, auto races. August.

**MISSOURI**

★
★
★
★
★

**SCOTT JOPLIN RAGTIME FESTIVAL**

*321 S. Ohio, Sedalia, 660-826-2271, 866-218-6258; www.scottjoplin.org*
Entertainment by ragtime greats. Early June.

## HOTEL
### ★★BEST WESTERN STATE FAIR MOTOR INN
*3120 S. Limit Ave., Sedalia, 660-826-6100, 1-800-780-7234; www.bestwestern.com*
117 rooms. Pets accepted, some restrictions. Complimentary breakfast. High-speed
Internet access. Restaurant, bar. Fitness room. Indoor pool, children's pool, whirlpool.
Airport transportation available. $

# SIKESTON

Although settlers were in this region before the Louisiana Purchase, John Sikes estab-
lished the town of Sikeston in 1860 on El Camino Real, the overland route from St.
Louis to New Orleans, at the terminus of the Cairo and Fulton Railway (now the
Union Pacific).

*Information: Sikeston-Miner Convention and Visitors Bureau,*
*1 Industrial Drive, 888-309-6591; www.sikeston.net*

## SPECIAL EVENTS
### BOOTHEEL RODEO
*1220 N. Ingram Road, Sikeston, 573-471-7196, 800-455-2855; www.sikestonrodeo.com*
Country music and rodeo events; parade. First full week in August.

## HOTELS
### ★★BEST WESTERN COACH HOUSE INN
*220 S. Interstate Drive, Sikeston, 573-471-9700, 877-471-9700; www.bestwestern.com*
61 rooms. Pets accepted, some restrictions; fee. Complimentary breakfast. High-speed
Internet access. Restaurant, bar. Outdoor pool. $

### ★DRURY INN
*2602 E. Malone Ave., Sikeston, 573-471-4100, 800-378-7946; www.druryhotels.com*
80 rooms. Pets accepted, some restrictions. Complimentary continental breakfast.
Wireless Internet access. Indoor pool, outdoor pool, whirlpool. Business center. $

## RESTAURANTS
### ★FISHERMAN'S NET
*915 S. Kings Highway, Sikeston, 573-471-8102; www.fishermansnet.net*
Seafood menu. Lunch, dinner. Closed Sunday-Monday. Children's menu. Wireless
Internet access. $

### ★LAMBERT'S
*2305 E. Malone Ave., Sikeston, 573-471-4261; www.throwedrolls.com*
American menu. Lunch, dinner. Children's menu. No credit cards accepted. $$

# SPRINGFIELD

In the southwest corner of the state and at the northern edge of the Ozark highlands,
Springfield, known as Ozark Mountain Country's Big City, is near some of Missouri's

most picturesque areas. A few settlers came here as early as 1821, but settlement was temporarily discouraged when the government made Southwestern Missouri a reservation. Later, the tribes were moved west and the town developed. Its strategic location made it a military objective in the Civil War. Confederates took the town in the Battle of Wilson's Creek, August 10, 1861; Union forces recaptured it in 1862. "Wild Bill" Hickok, later one of the famous frontier marshals, was a scout and spy for Union forces headquartered in Springfield. Perhaps the city's most famous native son is actor Brad Pitt, who grew up here and later attended the University of Missouri in Columbia.

*Information: Convention and Visitors Bureau, 3315 E. Battlefield Road, 417-881-5300, 800-678-8767; www.springfieldmo.org*

## WHAT TO SEE AND DO
### BASS PRO SHOPS OUTDOOR WORLD SHOWROOM AND FISH AND WILDLIFE MUSEUM
*1935 S. Campbell Ave., Springfield, 417-887-7334; www.outdoor-world.com*
This 300,000-square-foot sporting goods store features a four-story waterfall, indoor boat and RV showroom, art gallery and indoor firing range. The restaurant has a 30,000-gallon saltwater aquarium. Daily. Monday-Saturday 7 a.m.-10 p.m., Sunday 9 a.m.-7 p.m.

### DICKERSON PARK ZOO
*3043 N. Fort, Springfield, 417-864-1800, 417-833-1570; www.dickersonparkzoo.org*
Animals are housed at this zoo in naturalistic settings. Features an elephant herd; train rides. Daily. April-September, 9 a.m.-5 p.m.; October-March, 10 a.m.-4 p.m.

### DISCOVERY CENTER
*438 St. Louis St., Springfield, 417-862-9910; www.discoverycenter.org*
This interactive hands-on museum includes its "Discovery Town Theatre" where kids can be a star on stage, create a newspaper, run a make-believe TV station or dig for dinosaur bones. Tuesday-Sunday.

### LAURA INGALLS WILDER-ROSE WILDER LANE MUSEUM AND HOME
*3068 Highway A, Mansfield, 417-924-3626, 877-924-7126; www.lauraingallswilderhome.com*
The house where Laura Ingalls Wilder wrote the Little House books houses artifacts and memorabilia of the author, her husband Almanzo and daughter Rose Wilder Lane. Included are four handwritten manuscripts and many items mentioned in Wilder's books, including Pa's fiddle. Daily. March-mid-November, 9 a.m.-5 p.m.; June-August, until 5.30 p.m.

## HOTELS
### ★BEST WESTERN DEERFIELD INN
*3343 E. Battlefield St., Springfield, 417-887-2323, 877-822-6560; www.bestwestern.com*
103 rooms. Complimentary continental breakfast. High-speed Internet access. Fitness center. Business services. Indoor pool. $

★
★
★
★
★

### ★BEST WESTERN ROUTE 66 RAIL HAVEN

*203 S. Glenstone Ave., Springfield, 417-866-1963, 800-780-7234, 800-304-0021;*
*www.bestwestern.com*

93 rooms. Complimentary continental breakfast. High-speed Internet access. Outdoor pool, whirlpool. $

### ★★CLARION HOTEL

*3333 S. Glenstone Ave., Springfield, 417-883-6550, 800-756-7318;*
*www.clarionhotel.com*

192 rooms. Pets accepted; fee. High-speed Internet access. Restaurant, bar. Outdoor pool. Fitness center. $

### ★HAMPTON INN

*222 N. Ingram Mill Road, Springfield, 417-863-1440, 800-426-7866;*
*www.hamptoninn.com*

99 rooms. Complimentary continental breakfast. High-speed Internet access. Restaurant. Fitness room. Outdoor pool, whirlpool. $

### ★★★SHERATON HAWTHORN PARK HOTEL

*2431 N. Glenstone Ave., Springfield, 417-831-3131, 800-223-0092; www.sheraton.com*
201 rooms. Restaurant, bar. Internet access. Fitness room. Indoor pool, outdoor pool, whirlpool. Airport transportation available. $

## SPECIALTY LODGINGS
### THE MANSION AT ELFINDALE

*1701 S. Fort, Springfield, 417-831-5400, 800-443-0237; www.mansionatelfindale.com*
This inn is housed in a mansion constructed in 1890. 13 rooms. Children over 11 years only. Complimentary full breakfast. $

### WALNUT STREET INN

*900 E. Walnut St., Springfield, 417-864-6346, 800-593-6346; www.walnutstreetinn.com*
This bed and breakfast is located in a Queen Anne-style Victorian house built in 1894. 14 rooms. Complimentary full breakfast. Wireless Internet access. $

## RESTAURANTS
### ★★GEE'S EAST WIND

*2951 E. Sunshine, Springfield, 417-883-4567; www.blueheronpottedsteer.com*
Chinese, American menu. Lunch, dinner. Closed Sunday; last week in June, first week in July. Bar. Children's menu. $$

### ★J. PARRIONO'S PASTA HOUSE

*1550 E. Battlefield, Springfield, 417-882-1808*
Italian menu. Lunch, dinner. Bar. Children's menu. $$

# ST. CHARLES

St. Charles, one of the early settlements on the Missouri River, was the first capital of the state from 1821-1826. Between 1832 and 1870, a wave of German immigrants settled here and developed the town, but St. Louis, by virtue of its location on the

Mississippi, became the state's most important city. Frenchtown, a northern ward of old St. Charles, is home to many antiques shops.

*Information: Convention and Visitors Bureau, 230 S. Main St., 636-946-7776, 800-366-2427; www.historicstcharles.com*

## WHAT TO SEE AND DO
### FIRST MISSOURI STATE CAPITOL STATE HISTORIC SITE
*200-216 S. Main St., St. Charles, 636-940-3322; www.mostateparks.com*

Eleven rooms of the capitol have been restored to their original state; nine rooms have 1820 period furnishings; also restoration of the Peck Brothers General Store and house. Restaurant, shops. Daily. Closed holidays.

### KATY TRAIL STATE PARK
*St. Charles, 660-882-8196, 800-334-6946; www.mostateparks.com*

A 236-mile bicycling and hiking trail across Missouri, this is among the longest of its kind in the United States.

### LEWIS AND CLARK CENTER
*Bishop's Landing, 1050 Riverside, St. Charles, 636-947-3199; www.lewisandclarkcenter.org*

Museum depicts the 1804-1806 expedition from St. Charles to the Pacific Ocean. Hands-on exhibits, life-size models of Sacagawea and the men of the expedition; Mandan and Sioux villages. Daily. Monday-Saturday 10 a.m.-5 p.m., Sunday noon-5 p.m.

## SPECIAL EVENT
### LEWIS AND CLARK HERITAGE DAYS
*Frontier Park, Riverside Drive, St. Charles, 800-366-2427; www.lewisandclarkheritagedays.com*

Reenactment of the explorers' encampment in 1804 prior to embarking on their exploration of the Louisiana Purchase; parade, fife and drum corps. authentic period clothing, children's activities, military encampment, grand parade, music and demonstrations. Mid-May.

## HOTEL
### ★★HOLIDAY INN
*4341 Veteran's Memorial Parkway, St. Peters, 636-928-1500, 800-972-3145; www.holiday-inn.com*

195 rooms. Pets accepted; fee. High-speed Internet access. Restaurant, bar. Fitness room. Indoor pool, outdoor pool, whirlpool. Business center. $

## RESTAURANT
### ★★ST. CHARLES VINTAGE HOUSE
*1219 S. Main St., St. Charles, 636-946-7155; www.stcharlesvintagehouse.com*

American, German, seafood menu. Dinner. Closed Monday. Bar. Children's menu. Outdoor seating. Former winery (1860). $$

**MISSOURI**

# ST. JOSEPH

A historic city with beautiful parks, St. Joseph retains traces of the frontier settlement of the 1840s in its "original town" near the Missouri River. It was founded and named by Joseph Robidoux III, a French fur trader from St. Louis, who established his post in 1826. St. Joseph, the western terminus of the first railroad to cross the state, became the eastern terminus of the Pony Express, whose riders carried mail to and from Sacramento, California, from 1860-1861 using relays of fast ponies. The record trip, which carried copies of President Lincoln's inaugural address, was made in seven days and 17 hours. The telegraph ended the need for the Pony Express.

*Information: Convention and Visitors Bureau, 109 S. Fourth St.,*
*816-233-6688, 800-785-0360; www.stjomo.com*

## WHAT TO SEE AND DO

### ALBRECHT-KEMPER MUSEUM OF ART

*2818 Frederick Blvd., St. Joseph, 816-233-7003, 888-254-2787;*
*www.albrecht-kemper.org*

Exhibits of 18th-, 19th- and 20th-century American paintings, sculpture, graphic art. Formal gardens. Friday 10 a.m.-4 p.m., Saturday and Sunday 1-4 p.m.

### GLORE PSYCHIATRIC MUSEUM

*3408 Frederick Ave., St. Joseph, 816-364-1209, 800-530-8866;*
*www.gloremuseum.org*

Housed in a ward of the original 1874 administration building, the museum displays the evolution of treatment philosophy and techniques over a 400-year period. Daily.

### JESSE JAMES HOME

*1202 Penn St., St. Joseph, 816-232-8206;*
*www.stjoseph.net/ponyexpress*

This is the one-story frame cottage where the outlaw had been living quietly as "Mr. Howard" until he was killed here on, April 3, 1882, by an associate, Robert Ford. Some original furnishings. Daily.

### PATEE HOUSE MUSEUM

*1202 Penn St., St. Joseph, 816-232-8206;*
*www.stjoseph.net/ponyexpress*

Built in 1858 as a hotel, this building once served as headquarters of the Pony Express. Contains pioneer exhibits related to transportation and communication and includes restored an 1860 Buffalo Saloon, wood-burning engine and the original last mail car from the Hannibal and St. Joseph railroad. April-October, daily; January-March and November, weekends.

### PONY EXPRESS MUSEUM

*914 Penn St., St. Joseph, 816-279-5059, 800-530-5930;*
*www.ponyexpress.org*

This museum is located in the old Pikes Peak (Pony Express) Stables, the starting point of the service's first westward ride. Original stables; displays illustrate the creation, operation, management and termination of the famed mail service. Monday-Saturday 9 a.m.-5 p.m., Sunday 1-5 p.m.

★
★
★
★
☆

## PONY EXPRESS REGION TOURIST INFORMATION CENTERS

*502 N. Woodvine Road, St. Joseph, 816-232-1839; www.stjomo.com*

Housed in historic railroad cabooses, centers provide brochures and information on St. Joseph, Northwest Missouri and Northeast Kansas; free maps. Daily.

## ROBIDOUX ROW MUSEUM

*219-227, E. Poulin St., St. Joseph, 816-232-5861*

Built by the city's founder, French fur trader Joseph Robidoux, as temporary housing for newly arrived settlers who had purchased land from him. Authentically restored; some original furnishings. Tours. Tuesday-Sunday.

# HOTELS

### ★DAYS INN

*4312 Frederick Blvd., St. Joseph, 816-279-1671, 800-329-7466; www.daysinn.com*

100 rooms. Complimentary continental breakfast. High-speed Internet access. Bar. Outdoor pool. $

### ★DRURY INN

*4213 Frederick Blvd., St. Joseph, 816-364-4700; www.druryhotels.com*

132 rooms. Pets accepted. Complimentary continental breakfast. High-speed Internet access. Fitness room. Indoor pool. Business center. $

### ★★HOLIDAY INN

*102 S. Third St., St. Joseph, 816-279-8000, 800-824-7402; www.holiday-inn.com*

170 rooms. Pets accepted. High-speed Internet access. Restaurant, bar. Fitness room. Indoor pool, whirlpool. $

# RESTAURANTS

### ★★36TH STREET FOOD & DRINK COMPANY

*501 N. Belt Highway, St. Joseph, 816-364-1565; www.36thstreet.com*

American, Italian menu. Lunch, dinner. Closed Sunday. Bar. $$

### ★BARBOSA'S CASTILLO

*906 Sylvanie St., St. Joseph, 816-233-4970; www.barbosasrestaurant.com*

Mexican menu. Lunch, dinner. Closed Sunday. Bar. Children's menu. Valet parking. $$

# ST. LOUIS

One of the oldest settlements in the Mississippi Valley, St. Louis was founded by Pierre Laclede as a fur trading post and was named for Louis IX of France. Early French settlers, a large German immigration in the mid-1800s and a happy mix of other national strains contribute to the city's cosmopolitan flavor. In 1804, it was the scene of the transfer of Louisiana to the United States, which opened the way to westward expansion. During the Civil War, though divided in sympathy, the city was a base of Union operations. In 1904, the Louisiana Purchase Exposition, known as the St. Louis World's Fair, brought international fame to the city.

For more than 200 years, St. Louis has been the dominant city in the state. It's the home of St. Louis University, the University of Missouri-St. Louis and Washington University. After the steamboat era, St. Louis grew westward away from the river-front, which deteriorated into slums. This original center of the city has now been developed as the Jefferson National Expansion Memorial. Recent redevelopment of downtown and the riverfront is revitalizing the city. Busch Stadium brings St. Louis Cardinals fans into the downtown area and the rehabilitated Union Station offers visitors a vast shopping experience within a restored turn-of-the-century railroad station that was one of the nation's most magnificent.

*Information: Convention and Visitors Commission, 1 Metropolitan Square, 314-421-1023, 800-325-7962; www.explorestlouis.com*

## WHAT TO SEE AND DO
### ANHEUSER-BUSCH BREWERY
*12th and Lynch streets, St. Louis, 314-577-2626; www.budweisertours.com*
Trace the making of Budweiser beer from farm fields to finished product in a tour of the nation's largest brewery. Inside the 150-year-old plant, you'll also experience a historic brewhouse, beechwood aging cellars, a packing facility and Clydesdale stables. Adults can sample Bud products. Daily.

### BUTTERFLY HOUSE AND EDUCATION CENTER
*Faust Park, 15193 Olive Blvd., Chesterfield, 636-530-0076; www.butterflyhouse.org*
A three-story crystal palace conservatory with more than 2,000 butterflies in free flight. Educational programs, films, miracle of metamorphosis display. Memorial Day-Labor Day, daily; rest of year, Tuesday-Sunday.

### CAMPBELL HOUSE MUSEUM
*1508 Locust St., St. Louis, 314-421-0325*
Mansion with original 1840-1880 furnishings. March-December, Wednesday-Sunday.

### CATHEDRAL OF ST. LOUIS
*4431 Lindell Blvd., St. Louis, 314-373-8242; www.cathedralstl.org*
The city's cathedral, built in 1907, is a fine example of Romanesque architecture with Byzantine details. The interior mosaic work is among the most extensive in the world.

### CHRIST CHURCH CATHEDRAL
*1210 Locust St., St. Louis, 314-231-3454*
Founded in 1919, this was the first Episcopal parish west of the Mississippi River. English Gothic sandstone building; altar carved in England from stone taken from a quarry in Caen, France; Tiffany windows on north wall. Occasional concerts. Sunday-Friday. Tours by appointment.

### CLIMATRON
*4344 Shaw Blvd., St. Louis, 314-577-5141; www.mobot.org*
Seventy-foot high, prize-winning geodesic dome—first of its kind to be used as a conservatory—houses a two-level, half-acre tropical rain forest with canopies, rocky

outcrops, waterfalls and mature tree collection; exhibits explain the many facets of a rain forest. Entrance to Climatron through series of sacred lotus and lily pools.

## DELTA QUEEN AND MISSISSIPPI QUEEN
*St. Louis, 800-543-1949; www.deltaqueen.com*
Paddle wheelers offer three- to eight-night cruises on the Ohio, Cumberland, Mississippi and Tennessee rivers.

## EADS BRIDGE
*St. Louis Riverfront area*
Designed in 1874 by engineer James B. Eads, the Eads was the first bridge to span the wide southern section of the Mississippi and the first bridge in which steel and the cantilever were used extensively. The approach ramps are carried on enormous Romanesque stone arches.

## EUGENE FIELD HOUSE AND TOY MUSEUM
*634 S. Broadway, St. Louis, 314-421-4689; www.eugenefieldhouse.org*
This was the birthplace of the famous children's poet. The museum includes mementos, manuscripts and many original furnishings plus antique toys and dolls. Wednesday-Saturday, Sunday afternoons; also by appointment.

## GATEWAY ARCH
*The Gateway Arch Riverfront, St. Louis, 877-982-1410; www.gatewayarch.com*
Eero Saarinen's Gateway Arch is a 630-foot stainless steel arch that symbolizes the starting point of the westward expansion of the United States. Visitor center includes capsule transporter to observation deck. There is often a wait for observation deck capsules. Memorial Day-Labor Day, daily 8 a.m.-10 p.m.; rest of year, daily 9 a.m.-6 p.m.; closed holidays.

★
★
★
★
★

## GRANT'S FARM
*10501 Gravois Road, St. Louis, 314-843-1700; www.grantsfarm.com*
This 281-acre wooded tract contains a log cabin and land once owned by Ulysses S. Grant. Anheuser-Busch Clydesdale barn; carriage house with horse-drawn vehicles, trophy room; deer park where deer, buffalo, longhorn steer and other animals roam freely in their natural habitat. May-September: Tuesday-Sunday; mid-April-May and September-mid-October: Wednesday-Sunday.

## INTERNATIONAL BOWLING MUSEUM AND HALL OF FAME
*111 Stadium Plaza, St. Louis, 314-231-6340; www.bowlingmuseum.com*
View wacky bowling shirts and the sublime Hall of Fame, or bowl a few frames. The museum shares the building with the St. Louis Cardinals Museum, which boasts an outstanding collection of Redbirds memorabilia. April-September, daily 11 a.m-5 p.m.; October-March, Tuesday-Saturday 11 a.m.-4 p.m.

## JAPANESE GARDEN
*4344 Shaw Blvd., St. Louis, 314-577-5100, 800-642-8842; www.mobot.org*
Largest traditional Japanese garden in North America, with lake landscaped with many varieties of water irises, waterfalls, bridges and a teahouse.

### JEFFERSON BARRACKS HISTORICAL PARK

*533 Grant Road, St. Louis, 314-544-5714; www.nps.gov*

This army post was established in 1826 and used through 1946. St. Louis County now maintains 424 acres of the original tract. Restored buildings include a stable, a laborer's house, two powder magazines, ordnance room and visitor center. Picnicking. Buildings: Wednesday-Sunday.

### JEFFERSON NATIONAL EXPANSION MEMORIAL

*11 N. Fourth St., St. Louis, 314-655-1700;*
*www.nps.gov/jeff*

The Jefferson National Expansion Memorial, located along the Mississippi River, pays tribute to Thomas Jefferson and his influence on freedom and democracy.

### OLD COURTHOUSE

*11 N. Fourth St., St. Louis, 314-655-1600; www.nps.gov*

Begun in 1837 and completed in 1862, this building houses five museum galleries on St. Louis history, including various displays, dioramas and films. The first two trials of the Dred Scott case were held in this building. Guided tour. Daily.

### LACLEDE'S LANDING

*720 N. Second St., St. Louis, 314-241-1155; www.lacledeslanding.com*

Early St. Louis commercial district (mid-1800s) includes a nine-block area of renovated pre-Civil War and Victorian buildings that house specialty shops, restaurants and nightclubs.

★
★ ★
★ ★
★ ★
  ★

### MISSOURI BOTANICAL GARDEN

*4344 Shaw Blvd., St. Louis, 314-577-9400, 800-642-8842;*
*www.mobot.org*

This 79-acre park includes rose, woodland and herb gardens; scented garden for the blind; electric tram rides; Butterfly house. Sections of the botanical garden are more than a century old. Daily 9 a.m.-5 p.m.; closed Christmas.

### MISSOURI HISTORY MUSEUM-MISSOURI HISTORICAL SOCIETY

*5700 Lindel Blvd., St. Louis, 314-746-4599; www.mohistory.org*

Exhibits on St. Louis and the American West; artwork, costumes and decorative arts; toys, firearms; 19th-century firefighting equipment; St. Louis history slide show; ragtime-rock 'n' roll music exhibit; 1904 World's Fair and Charles A. Lindbergh collections. Daily.

### MUSEUM OF TRANSPORTATION

*3015 Barrett Station Road, Kirkwood, 314-965-7998;*
*www.transportmuseumassociation.org*

One of the more interesting collections anywhere in the country, the Museum of Transportation houses an extensive collection of passenger and freight train equipment (ranging from elevated cars from Chicago to the last steam locomotive to operate in Missouri), as well as the riverboats and airplanes that local history has helped support. Daily.

## MUSEUM OF WESTWARD EXPANSION

*11 N. Fourth St., St. Louis, 314-655-1700; www.nps.gov*

The Museum of Westward Expansion offers exhibits on the people and events of 19th-century Western America, special exhibits and films on St. Louis, construction of the arch and the westward movement. Daily.

## NASCAR SPEEDPARK

*5555 St. Louis Mills Blvd., Hazelwood, 314-227-5600; www.nascarspeedpark.com*

This mini amusement park is northwest of downtown, and is now one of five now open across North America. The park features everything from an arcade to a rock-climbing wall to a NASCAR merchandise store. But its main draw is its multitude of racetracks. You can climb into a mock stock car and experience centrifugal forces, turns and crash impacts as you "drive" a full-motion NASCAR Silicon Motor Speedway simulator. Monday-Friday 10 a.m.-9:30 p.m., Saturday 10 a.m.-10 p.m., Sunday 11 a.m.-7 p.m.

## OLD CATHEDRAL

*209 Walnut St., St. Louis, 314-231-3250; www.catholic-forum.com*

The 1831 basilica of St. Louis, King of France, is located on the site of the first church built in St. Louis in 1770. The museum on the west side contains the original church bell and other religious artifacts. Daily.

## POWELL SYMPHONY HALL

*718 N. Grand Blvd., St. Louis, 314-534-1700; www.slso.org*

Decorated in ivory and 24-karat gold leaf, the hall, built in 1925 as a movie and vaudeville house, is now home of the St. Louis Symphony Orchestra (mid-September-mid-May). After-concert tours available by appointment.

## SIX FLAGS ST. LOUIS

*I-44 and Six Flags Road, Eureka, 636-938-4800; www.sixflags.com*

This edition of the theme park franchise has rides and attractions for kids and grown-ups, plus live shows throughout summer. Among the two dozen or so rides here are several roller coasters. Mid-May-late August, daily from 10 a.m.; early April-mid-May and late August-Halloween, weekends from 10 a.m.; closing times vary.

## ST. LOUIS ART MUSEUM

*1 Fine Arts Drive, St. Louis, 314-721-0072; www.stlouis.art.museum*

Built for the 1904 World's Fair as the Palace of Fine Arts, this museum has collections of American and European paintings, prints, drawings and decorative arts. Restaurant. Tuesday-Sunday.

## ST. LOUIS BLUES (NHL)

*Scottrade Center, 1401 Clark Ave., St. Louis, 314-241-2500; www.blues.nhl.com*
Professional hockey team.

## ST. LOUIS CARDINALS (MLB)

*Busch Stadium, 250 Stadium Plaza, St. Louis, 314-421-3060; www.cardinals.mlb.com*
Professional baseball team.

### ST. LOUIS RAMS (NFL)
*Edward Jones Dome, 901 N. Broadway, St. Louis, 314-425-8830; www.stlouisrams.com*
Professional football team.

### ST. LOUIS SCIENCE CENTER
*5050 Oakland Ave., St. Louis, 314-289-4444, 800-456-7572; www.slsc.org*
Features three buildings with more than 700 exhibits. Also Omnimax theater, planetarium, children's discovery room. Daily.

### ST. LOUIS UNION STATION
*1820 Market St., St. Louis, 314-421-6655; www.stlouisunionstation.com*
This block-long stone chateauesque railroad station was the world's busiest passenger terminal from 1905 to the late 1940s. After the last train pulled out on October 31, 1978, the station and train shed were restored and redeveloped as a marketplace with more than 100 specialty shops and restaurants, nightclubs and a hotel.

### ST. LOUIS UNIVERSITY
*221 N. Grand, St. Louis, 314-977-8886, 800-758-3678; www.slu.edu*
The oldest university west of the Mississippi River, the campus was opened in 1818 and includes the Pius XII Memorial Library with its Vatican Microfilm Library (the only depository for copies of Vatican documents in the Western Hemisphere). Daily; closed holidays.

### ST. LOUIS ZOO
*1 Government Drive, St. Louis, 314-781-0900, 800-966-8877; www.stlzoo.org*
The St. Louis Zoo is considered one of the best in the country. Lions, cheetahs and giraffes roam in natural African settings while other areas showcase exotic species from the poles to the tropics. Memorial Day-Labor Day, daily 8 a.m.-7 p.m.; rest of year, daily 9 a.m.-5 p.m.

### ULYSSES S. GRANT NATIONAL HISTORIC SITE
*7400 Grant Road, St. Louis, 314-842-3298; www.nps.gov*
The White Haven property was a focal point in Ulysses's and his wife Julia's lives for four decades. Grounds feature more than 50 species of trees and are a haven for a variety of wildlife. Visitors center includes exhibits and information on the Grants and White Haven. Guided tours. Daily.

### WASHINGTON UNIVERSITY
*1 Brookings Drive, St. Louis, 314-935-5959; www.wustl.edu*
Founded in 1853, this prestigious liberal arts institution is home to 11,000 students. The campus of this university includes the Graham Chapel, Edison Theatre and Francis Field, site of the first Olympic Games in the United States.

## SPECIAL EVENTS
### FAIR ST. LOUIS
*Jefferson National Expansion Memorial Park, St. Louis,*
*314-434-3434; www.celebratestlouis.org*
Three-day festival with parade, food, air and water shows, entertainment. July Fourth weekend.

## THE MUNY

*Forest Park, St. Louis, 314-361-1900; www.muny.org*

12,000-seat outdoor theater. Light opera and musical comedy. Mid-June-August.

## ST. LOUIS SYMPHONY ORCHESTRA

*Powell Symphony Hall, 718 N. Grand Blvd., St. Louis, 314-534-1700, 314-533-2500; www.slso.org*

Classical music performances from September-May.

# HOTELS

### ★★★CHASE PARK PLAZA

*212-232 N. Kingshighway Blvd., St. Louis, 314-633-3000; 877-587-2427; www.chaseparkplaza.com*

This historic hotel in St. Louis's Central West End has guest rooms decorated with period furnishings. A resort-like feel pervades the hotel, which has a five-screen movie theater, spa and salon, courtyard with outdoor pool and 24-hour concierge. 250 rooms. High-speed Internet access. Four restaurants, five bars. Fitness room. Spa. Outdoor pool. Business center. **$$**

### ★★CHESHIRE LODGE

*6300 Clayton Road, St. Louis, 314-647-7300, 800-325-7378; www.cheshirelodge.com*

Restaurant, two bars. Fitness room. Indoor pool, outdoor pool. **$**

### ★★★CLAYTON ON THE PARK

*8025 Bonhomme Ave., Clayton, 314-725-9990, 800-323-7500; www.claytononthepark.com*

The suites at this tower are contemporary in design and offer the amenities of an apartment, from fully stocked kitchens to separate living areas with work desks and high-speed Internet access. The onsite Finale restaurant offers creative American cuisines and live music inside or on the rooftop veranda in good weather. 109 rooms, all suites. Pets accepted. Complimentary continental breakfast. High-speed Internet access. Restaurant, bar. Fitness room. **$$**

### ★★COURTYARD ST. LOUIS DOWNTOWN

*2340 Market St., St. Louis, 314-241-9111, 800-321-2211; www.courtyard.com*

151 rooms. Wireless Internet access. Fitness room. Indoor pool, whirlpool. **$**

### ★★DRURY INN

*201 S. 20th St., St. Louis, 314-231-3900; www.druryinn.com*

176 rooms. Pets accepted, some restrictions. Complimentary continental breakfast. Restaurant, bar. Fitness room. Indoor pool, whirlpool. Restored 1907 railroad hotel. **$**

### ★DRURY INN-NATURAL BRIDGE ROAD

*10490 Natural Bridge Road, St. Louis, 314-423-7700, 800-378-7946; www.druryhotels.com*

172 rooms. Pets accepted. Complimentary continental breakfast. High-speed Internet access. Fitness room. Indoor pool, whirlpool. Airport transportation available. **$**

★
★
★
★
★

### ★★★★FOUR SEASONS ST. LOUIS

*999 N. Second St., St. Louis, 314-881-5800; www.fourseasons.com*

St. Louis has not been this exciting since the Cardinals won the World Series in 2006. The arrival of the Four Seasons brings new levels of both energy and luxury to the city's downtown. The airy guest rooms have contemporary furnishings and a light-wood color palette, plus amenities such as a LCD television and an iPod docking station. Just be sure to request a room facing south to get a view of the Gateway Arch—the north view is nothing but empty parking lots and demolished buildings. If you venture out, head for the Vegas-style casino Lumiere Place just at your doorstep. Or if you feel like staying in, retreat to the outdoor pool with hot tub overlooking downtown St. Louis, or make for the spa and indulge in the signature Caviar Serum Facial. Grab a drink or dinner at Italian restaurant Cielo at sunset to capture the striking urban view from the terrace. 186 Rooms, 14 suites. Wireless Internet access. Restaurant, bar. Fitness center. Pool. Spa. Business center. $$$

### ★HAMPTON INN

*2211 Market St., St. Louis, 314-241-3200, 800-426-7866; www.hamptoninn.com*

239 rooms. Pets accepted, some restrictions. Complimentary continental breakfast. Bar. Fitness room. Indoor pool, whirlpool. $

### ★★★HILTON ST. LOUIS AT THE BALLPARK

*1 S. Broadway, St. Louis, 314-421-1776, 800-228-9290; www.hilton.com*

As its name suggests, this hotel is located across the street from the home of the Cardinals, Busch Stadium. The entire space has been recently renovated in a contemporary style, with rooms outfitted with granite bathrooms and duvet-topped beds. 675 rooms. Pets accepted. High-speed Internet access. Two restaurants, bar. Fitness room. Indoor pool, whirlpool. Business center. $$

### ★★★HILTON ST. LOUIS DOWNTOWN

*400 Olive St., St. Louis, 314-436-0002, 800-445-8667; www.hilton.com*

A historic landmark, the Hilton St. Louis occupies the original Merchant Laclede building. All of St. Louis' attractions are within walking distance of this hotel, including the Gateway Arch, Busch Stadium and America's Center. 195 rooms. Pets accepted. Wireless Internet access. Restaurant, bar. Fitness room. Whirlpool. Business center. $

### ★★★HILTON ST. LOUIS FRONTENAC

*1335 S. Lindbergh Blvd., St. Louis, 314-993-1100, 800-325-7800; www.hilton.com*

Located between downtown St. Louis and Lambert International Airport, this hotel is near the St. Louis Zoo, the Science Center, Six Flags Amusement Park and adjacent to the upscale Plaza Frontenac shopping mall. 263 rooms. Pets accepted. Wireless Internet access. Restaurant, bar. Fitness room. Outdoor pool. Airport transportation available. $$

### ★★HOLIDAY INN

*811 N. Ninth St., St. Louis, 314-421-4000, 800-289-8338; www.holiday-inn.com*

295 rooms. Pets accepted. Wireless Internet access. Two restaurants, bar. Fitness room. Indoor pool, whirlpool. $

### ★★★HYATT REGENCY ST. LOUIS

*1 St. Louis Union Station, St. Louis, 314-231-1234, 800-633-7313;*
*www.stlouis.hyatt.com*

Located in the renovated Union Station railroad terminal, the main lobby and lounge of this hotel occupy the Grand Hall. The mall in the station has many stores and restaurants. Décor here is traditional, but contemporary details include an updated fitness center and luxury linens on the beds. 539 rooms. High-speed Internet access. Two restaurants, bar. Fitness room. Outdoor pool. Business center. **$$**

### ★★★MARRIOTT ST. LOUIS AIRPORT

*10700 Pear Tree Lane, St. Louis, 314-423-9700, 877-264-8771; www.marriott.com*

This airport hotel provides complimentary shuttle service and updated business and fitness centers. The Rock River Grill and Rock River Tavern serve a variety of classic American fare. 601 rooms. High-speed Internet access. Restaurant, bar. Fitness room. Indoor pool, outdoor pool, whirlpool. Airport transportation available. Business center. **$$**

### ★★★OMNI MAJESTIC HOTEL

*1019 Pine St., St. Louis, 314-436-2355, 800-843-6664; www.omnihotels.com*

This European-style hotel is located in downtown St. Louis and is listed in the National Register of Historic Buildings. 91 rooms. Pets accepted, some restrictions; fee. Wireless Internet access. Restaurant, bar. Fitness room. Business center. **$$**

### ★★PARKWAY HOTEL

*4550 Forest Park Blvd., St. Louis, 314-256-7777, 866-314-7700;*
*www.theparkwayhotel.com*

220 rooms. High-speed Internet access. Restaurant, bar. Fitness room. Business center. **$**

### ★★RADISSON HOTEL AND SUITES

*200 N. Fourth St., St. Louis, 314-621-8200, 800-333-3333;*
*www.radisson.com/stlouismo*

440 rooms. High-speed Internet access. Restaurant, bar. Fitness room. Outdoor pool. **$$**

### ★★★RENAISSANCE ST. LOUIS GRANDSUITES AND HOTEL

*800 Washington Ave., St. Louis, 314-621-9600, 800-468-3571;*
*www.renaissancehotels.com*

This historic downtown hotel is close to St. Louis' top attractions. There are five onsite restaurants and a full fitness center as well as an indoor pool. 1083 rooms. Pets accepted. High-speed Internet access. Four restaurants, bar. Fitness room. Indoor pool, whirlpool. Airport transportation available. Business center. **$**

### ★★★RENAISSANCE ST. LOUIS HOTEL AIRPORT

*9801 Natural Bridge Road, St. Louis, 314-429-1100, 800-340-2594;*
*www.renaissancehotels.com*

This hotel is adjacent to the Lambert International Airport and has been recently updated with pillow-top mattresses and an onsite Starbucks. 393 rooms. High-speed Internet access. Restaurant, bar. Fitness room. Indoor pool, outdoor pool, whirlpool. Business center. **$$**

★
★
★
★
★

### ★★★★THE RITZ-CARLTON, ST. LOUIS

*100 Carondelet Plaza, Clayton, 314-863-6300, 800-241-3333;*
*www.ritzcarlton.com*

This sophisticated hotel features spacious and plush guest rooms, all with private balconies with views of the city skyline. A comprehensive fitness center includes lap and hydrotherapy pools. The Wine Room is a unique spot for sampling one of the hotel's more than 7,000 bottles of wine while the restaurant offers a fine dining experience. 301 rooms. Pets accepted; fee. Wireless Internet access. Two restaurants, bar. Fitness room. Indoor pool, whirlpool. Airport transportation available. Business center. $$$$

### ★★★SEVEN GABLES INN

*26 N. Meramec Ave., Clayton, 314-863-8400, 800-433-6590;*
*www.sevengablesinn.com*

Surrounded by upscale shops, galleries and restaurants, this inn offers a blend of old world charm and modern conveniences. The inn was inspired by sketches in Nathaniel Hawthorne's novel *The House of Seven Gables*. 32 rooms. Complimentary continental breakfast. Restaurant, bar. Airport transportation available. $

### ★★★SHERATON CLAYTON PLAZA

*7730 Bonhomme Ave., Clayton, 314-863-0400, 800-325-3535;*
*www.sheraton.com/clayton*

This hotel, located in Clayton just outside St. Louis, is loaded with amenities from an indoor pool to an onsite Enterprise car rental desk, sundeck and fitness center. 259 rooms. Pets accepted, some restrictions. High-speed Internet access. Two restaurants, bar. Fitness room. Indoor pool, whirlpool. Airport transportation available. Business center. $$

### ★★★SHERATON ST. LOUIS CITY CENTER HOTEL AND SUITES

*400 S. 14th St., St. Louis, 314-231-5007, 800-325-3535;*
*www.sheraton.com*

This downtown hotel has oversized rooms with queen-size sleeper sofas for extra guests. Other amenities include a fitness center, indoor pool and onsite sports bar. 288 rooms. Pets accepted, some restrictions. Restaurant, bar. Fitness room. Indoor pool. Business center. $$

### ★STAYBRIDGE SUITES

*1855 Craigshire Road, St. Louis, 314-878-1555, 800-238-8000;*
*www.staybridgesuites.com*

106 rooms, all suites. Pets accepted; fee. Complimentary continental breakfast. High-speed Internet access. Outdoor pool, whirlpool. Airport transportation available. $

### ★★★THE WESTIN ST. LOUIS

*811 Spruce St., St. Louis, 314-621-2000, 800-228-3000;*
*www.westin.com/stlouis*

Adjacent to Busch Stadium and convenient to shopping and restaurants, this contemporary hotel has a spa, health club and an acclaimed restaurant and bar. 255 rooms. Pets accepted, some restrictions; fee. High-speed Internet access. Restaurant, bar. Fitness room, spa. Business center. $$

# RESTAURANTS

## ★★BIG SKY CAFÉ

*47 S. Old Orchard, Webster Groves, 314-962-5757; www.allgreatrestaurants.com, www.bigskycafe.net*

American menu. Dinner. Bar. Outdoor seating. **$$**

## ★BLUEBERRY HILL

*6504 Delmar Blvd., St. Louis, 314-727-4444; www.blueberryhill.com*

American menu. Lunch, dinner, late-night. Bar. Casual attire. Outdoor seating. Live music. **$**

## ★BRISTOL SEAFOOD GRILL

*11801 Olive Blvd., Creve Coeur, 314-567-0272; www.bristolseafoodgrill.com*

Seafood menu. Lunch, dinner, Sunday brunch. Bar. Children's menu. **$$$**

## ★BROADWAY OYSTER BAR

*736 S. Broadway, St. Louis, 314-621-8811; www.broadwayoysterbar.com*

Cajun/Creole menu. Lunch, dinner, late-night. Bar. Casual attire. Outdoor seating. **$$**

## ★CAFÉ NAPOLI

*7754 Forsyth Blvd., Clayton, 314-863-5731; www.cafenapoli.com*

Italian menu. Lunch, dinner. Bar. Valet parking. **$$$**

## ★★CARDWELL'S AT THE PLAZA

*94 Plaza Frontenac, St. Louis, 314-997-8885; www.cardwellsattheplaza.com*

International menu. Lunch, dinner. Bar. Children's menu. Business casual attire. Reservations recommended. Outdoor seating. **$$**

## ★★★CARDWELL'S IN CLAYTON

*8100 Maryland, Clayton, 314-726-5055; www.cardwellsinclayton.com*

This restaurant's celebrity chefs dish up an innovative American-style menu in a modern dining room. Seafood menu. Lunch, dinner. Closed Sunday. Bar. Children's menu. Outdoor seating. **$$**

## ★CHARLIE GITTO'S

*207 N. Sixth St., St. Louis, 314-436-2828; www.charliegittos.com*

American, Italian menu. Lunch, dinner. Closed Sunday. Bar. Children's menu. Casual attire. **$$**

## ★CICERO'S

*6691 Delmar Blvd., University City, 314-862-0009; www.ciceros-stl.com*

American, Italian menu. Lunch, dinner, late-night. Bar. Children's menu. Outdoor seating. **$$**

## ★CRAVINGS

*8149 Big Bend Blvd., Webster Groves, 314-961-3534; www.cravingsonline.com*

American menu. Lunch, dinner. Closed Sunday-Monday. Valet parking. **$$**

**MISSOURI**

★
★
★
★
★

### ★CROWN CANDY KITCHEN

*1401 St. Louis Ave., St. Louis, 314-621-9650; www.crowncandykitchen.net*
American menu. Lunch, dinner. $

### ★★CUNETTO HOUSE OF PASTA

*5453 Magnolia Ave., St. Louis, 314-781-1135; www.cunetto.com*
Italian menu. Lunch, dinner. Closed Sunday. Bar. Casual attire. Outdoor seating. $$

### ★★DIERDORF & HART'S STEAK HOUSE

*701 E. Market St., St. Louis, 314-878-1801; www.dierdorfharts.com*
Steak menu. Dinner. Bar. Business casual attire. Reservations recommended. $$$

### ★★★DOMINIC'S RESTAURANT

*5101 Wilson Ave., St. Louis, 314-771-1632; www.dominicsrestaurant.com*
Friendly service and a menu of well-crafted, traditional Italian cuisine have earned this restaurant a loyal following since it opened in 1971. Entrées include breast of chicken alla Romano, lobster picante and veal T-bone chop with truffle sauce. Pasta dishes range from pappardelle with mushrooms to risotto with lobster. The wine list is Italian-focused with many exceptional vintages. Italian menu. Dinner. Closed Sunday. Bar. Children's menu. Business casual attire. Reservations recommended. Valet parking. $$$

### ★★FRANK PAPA'S RISTORANTE

*2241 S. Brentwood Blvd., Brentwood, 314-961-3344; www.frankpapas.com*
Italian menu. Dinner. Closed Sunday. Bar. $$$

### ★FRAZER'S RESTAURANT AND LOUNGE

*1811 Pestalozzi St., St. Louis, 314-773-8646; www.frazergoodeats.com*
International menu. Dinner. Closed Sunday. Bar. Outdoor seating. $$

### ★★★THE GARDENS AT MALMAISON

*3519 St. Albans Road, St. Albans, 636-458-0131; www.gardensmalmaison.com*
A rustic replica of a French inn tucked away in the countryside outside of St. Louis, this restaurant offers a small, fresh seasonal menu. French menu. Dinner. Closed Tuesday-Wednesday. Bar. Jacket required. Outdoor seating. $$$

### ★GINO'S RESTAURANT

*4502 Hampton Ave., St. Louis, 314-351-4187*
Italian menu. Dinner. Closed Monday. Bar. Children's menu. Casual attire. Reservations recommended. Outdoor seating. $$

### ★★★GIOVANNI'S

*5201 Shaw Ave., St. Louis, 314-772-5958; www.giovannisonthehill.com*
This restaurant is best described as timeless Italian. The highlight is its focus on fresh seafood, which is flown in daily. The veal and beef dishes are also superlative. Italian menu. Dinner. Closed Sunday. Bar. Business casual attire. Reservations recommended. Valet parking. $$$

## ★★GIUSEPPE'S

*4141 S. Grand Blvd., St. Louis, 314-832-3779; www.giuseppesongrand.com*
Italian menu. Lunch, dinner. Closed Monday. Bar. **$$**

## ★★★THE GRILL

*100 Carondelet Plaza, Clayton, 314-863-6300, 800-241-3333; www.ritzcarlton.com*
Located in the Ritz-Carlton St. Louis hotel, this upscale dining room serves up
contemporary interpretations of American classics. The décor includes extensive
mahogany paneling and woodwork, overstuffed leather banquettes, dramatic lighting
and a marble fireplace. Nightly entertainment is featured (piano or acoustic gui-
tar), and on weekends, there's live music (jazz, blues, or swing) in the hotel lounge.
American menu. Dinner. Bar. Business casual attire. Reservations recommended.
Valet parking. **$$$**

## ★★★HACIENDA

*9748 Manchester Road, Rock Hill, 314-962-7100; www.hacienda-stl.com*
Built as a residence for a steamboat captain in 1861, this rambling, casual restau-
rant consistently delivers in its preparation of the Mexican favorites. Mexican menu.
Lunch, dinner. Bar. Outdoor seating. **$$**

## ★HAMMERSTONE'S

*2028 S. Ninth, St. Louis, 314-773-5565; www.hammerstones.net*
American menu. Breakfast, lunch, dinner. Bar. Children's menu. Casual attire. Out-
door seating. **$$**

## ★HANNEGAN'S

*719 N. Second St., St. Louis, 314-241-8877; www.hannegans.admitonevip.com*
American menu. Lunch, dinner. Bar. Children's menu. Casual attire. Outdoor seat-
ing. **$$**

## ★★HARRY'S

*2144 Market St., St. Louis, 314-421-6969; www.harrysrestaurantandbar.com*
American menu. Lunch, dinner, late-night. Bar. Casual attire. Reservations recom-
mended. Valet parking. Outdoor seating. **$$$**

## ★★HARVEST

*1059 S. Big Bend Road, St. Louis, 314-645-3522; www.harveststlouis.com*
International menu. Dinner. Closed Monday. Bar. Business casual attire. Reservations
recommended. **$$$**

## ★HOUSE OF INDIA

*8501 Delmar Blvd., St. Louis, 314-567-6850; www.hoistl.com*
Indian menu. Lunch, dinner. Casual attire. Reservations recommended. **$$**

## ★★J. F. SANFILIPPO'S

*705 N. Broadway, St. Louis, 314-621-7213; www.jfsanfilippos.com*
Italian menu. Lunch, dinner. Closed Sunday (except during football season). Bar.
Children's menu. Casual attire. **$$**

### ★JOHN D. MCGURK'S

*1200 Russell Blvd., St. Louis, 314-776-8309; www.mcgurks.com*

American, Irish menu. Lunch, dinner. Bar. Casual attire. **$$**

### ★★★JOHN MINEO'S

*13490 Clayton Road, Town and Country, 314-434-5244; www.johnmineos.com*

For decades, this Italian-continental restaurant has lured diners with dishes such as Dover sole and veal chop, as well as daily fresh fish specials and house-made pasta. Italian menu. Dinner. Bar. Jacket required. **$$$**

### ★★JOSEPH'S ITALIAN CAFÉ

*107 N. Sixth St., St. Louis, 314-421-6366; www.josephsofstlouis.com*

Italian menu. Lunch, dinner. Closed Sunday. Bar. Children's menu. Casual attire. Outdoor seating. **$$**

### ★★★KEMOLL'S

*1 Metropolitan Square, St. Louis, 314-421-0555; www.kemolls.com*

Since 1927, this downtown landmark restaurant has served classic specialties in an elegant atmosphere. The name was originally shortened from the Sicilian name Camuglia, and the restaurant is run by fourth-generation family members. Italian menu. Dinner. Closed Sunday. Business casual attire. Reservations recommended. **$$$**

### ★KING & I

*3157 S. Grand Blvd., St. Louis, 314-771-1777; www.thaispicy.com*

Thai menu. Lunch, dinner. Closed Monday. Bar. **$$**

### ★★★KREIS'S

*535 S. Lindbergh Blvd., St. Louis, 314-993-0735; www.kreisrestaurant.com*

This German-influenced steakhouse (think meat and potatoes) has been at the same location more than 50 years. It's housed in a renovated 1930s brick house with beamed ceilings. Steak menu. Dinner. Bar. **$$**

### ★★LOMBARDO'S

*10488 Natural Bridge Road, St. Louis, 314-429-5151; www.lombardosrestaurants.com*

Italian menu. Lunch, dinner. Closed Sunday. Bar. Casual attire. Reservations recommended. **$$**

### ★★★LOMBARDO'S TRATTORIA

*201 S. 20th St., St. Louis, 314-621-0666; www.lombardosrestaurants.com*

Family-owned and operated for three generations, this restaurant is located in a converted hotel. The menu lists family classics as well as creative seasonal entrées. Italian menu. Lunch, dinner. Closed Sunday. Bar. Business casual attire. Reservations recommended. Valet parking. **$$**

### ★★LORUSSO'S CUCINA

*3121 Watson Road, St. Louis, 314-647-6222; www.lorussos.com*

Italian menu. Lunch, dinner. Closed Monday. Bar. Children's menu. Business casual attire. Reservations recommended. **$$**

**MISSOURI**

★
★
★
★

### ★MAGGIE O'BRIEN'S

*2000 Market St., St. Louis, 314-421-1388; www.maggieobriens.com*

American, Irish menu. Lunch, dinner. Bar. Children's menu. Casual attire. Valet parking. Outdoor seating. $$

### ★MARCIANO'S

*333 Westport Plaza, St. Louis, 314-878-8180*

Italian menu. Lunch, dinner. Closed holidays. Bar. Children's menu. Business casual attire. Outdoor seating. $$

### ★★MIKE SHANNON'S

*100 N. Seventh St., St. Louis, 314-421-1540; www.shannonsteak.com*

Steak menu. Lunch, dinner. Bar. Children's menu. Business casual attire. Reservations recommended. Outdoor seating. $$

### ★★PORTABELLA

*15 N. Central Ave., Clayton, 314-725-6588; www.portabellarestaurant.com*

Mediterranean menu. Lunch, dinner. Bar. $$$

### ★★REMY'S

*222 S. Bemiston, Clayton, 314-726-5757; www.allgreatrestaurants.com*

Mediterranean menu. Lunch, dinner, late-night. Bar. Outdoor seating. $$

### ★RIDDLE PENULTIMATE

*6307 Delmar Blvd., University City, 314-725-6985; www.riddlescafe.com*

International menu. Dinner, late-night. Closed Monday. Bar. Outdoor seating. $$

### ★SALEEM'S LEBANESE CUISINE

*6501 Delmar Blvd., St. Louis, 314-721-7947*

Middle Eastern menu. Lunch, dinner. Closed Sunday. Bar. Casual attire. Outdoor seating. $$

★
★★
★★
★★
★

## WARM AND TOASTY

Ravioli: Classic Italian dish consisting of pasta squared around a filling of meat or cheese, boiled and topped with a sauce. In most places, yes, but in St. Louis, the near-mandatory appetizer in classic Italian joints takes a twist on the recipe. In the Hill District that is home to many old-time Italian dining spots—as well in just about any of the many excellent strip-mall Italian restaurants in the suburbs—the ravioli takes a detour into some breading and then to the deep-fryer before it reaches the plate.

Many establishments claim to have invented the dish. Among the more legitimate contenders is Charlie Gitto's (originally called Angelo's). The story goes that a chef accidentally dropped some raviolis into bread crumbs and decided to deep-fry them for the heck of it. A tradition was born.

Whatever the truth is, toasted ravioli—which is generally a concoction encasing savory beef or veal, topped with marina sauce and sprinkled with Parmesan cheese—is a St. Louis original and a comforting opener to any dinner.

### ★★SCHLAFLY TAP ROOM

*2100 Locust St., St. Louis, 314-241-2337; www.schlafly.com*

American menu. Lunch, dinner. Bar. Casual attire. Outdoor seating. $$

### ★★★SCHNEITHORST'S HOFAMBERG INN

*1600 S. Lindbergh Blvd., Ladue, 314-993-4100;*
*www.schneithorst.com*

Unusual ethnic influences give traditional German cuisine an unexpected new face on this menu. Atlantic salmon with rain forest fruit relish and seafood strudel Johann Strauss are a few examples. In true German fashion, 33 specialty beers are also available on tap. German, American menu. Breakfast, lunch, dinner. Bar. Children's menu. Outdoor seating. $$

### ★★SIDNEY STREET CAFÉ

*2000 Sidney St., St. Louis, 314-771-5777; www.sidneystreetcafe.com*

American menu. Dinner. Closed Sunday-Monday. Bar. Children's menu. Casual attire. Reservations recommended. $$

### ★SPIRO'S

*3122 Watson Road, St. Louis, 314-645-8383; www.spiros-restaurant.com*

American menu. Lunch, dinner. Closed Monday. Children's menu. Reservations recommended. $$

### ★THAI CAFÉ

*6170 Delmar Blvd., St. Louis, 314-862-6868; www.thaicuisine.com*

Thai menu. Lunch, dinner. Casual attire. $$

### ★★★★TONY'S

*410 Market St., St.Louis, 314-231-7007; www.tonysstlouis.com*

Italian food may bring to mind images of pasta with red sauce, but at Tony's you'll find a menu of authentic Italian fare prepared with a measured and sophisticated hand. Expect appetizers like smoked salmon with mascarpone cheese and asparagus and Belgian endive and entrées like tenderloin of beef with foie gras in a port wine demi-glaze. The room has an urban, postmodern style, with sleek low lighting, linen-topped tables and glossy, wood-paneled walls. The chef's tasting menu is a nice choice for gourmands with healthy appetites. Italian menu. Dinner. Closed Sunday; also first week of January and first week of July. Bar. Jacket required. Reservations recommended. Valet parking. $$$

### ★★TRATTORIA MARCELLA

*3600 Watson Road, St. Louis, 314-352-7706;*
*www.trattoriamarcella.com*

Italian menu. Dinner. Closed Sunday-Monday. Bar. Casual attire. Reservations recommended. $$

### ★YACOVELLI'S

*407 Dunn Road, Florissant, 314-839-1000; www.yacovellis.com*

Italian menu. Dinner, brunch. Closed Monday-Tuesday. Bar. Children's menu. $$

**MISSOURI**

★
★★
★★
★

## ★★YEMANJA BRASIL

*2900 Missouri Ave., St. Louis, 314-771-7457; www.brazildining.com*

Brazilian menu. Dinner. Bar. Outdoor seating. **$$**

## ★ZIA'S

*5256 Wilson Ave., St. Louis, 314-776-0020; www.zias.com*

Italian menu. Lunch, dinner. Closed Sunday. Bar. Casual attire. Outdoor seating. **$$**

# ST. GENEVIEVE

Sainte Genevieve, the first permanent settlement in Missouri, developed on the banks of the Mississippi River early in the 18th century when Frenchmen began mining lead in the region. After a flood in 1785, the village was moved to higher ground. Once St. Louis's chief rival, Sainte Genevieve preserves its French heritage in its festivals, old houses and massive redbrick church.

*Information: Great River Road, Interpretive Center, 66 S. Main.,*
*573-883-7097, 800-373-7007; www.ste-genevieve.com*

## WHAT TO SEE AND DO

### BOLDUC HOUSE MUSEUM

*125 S. Main St., Ste. Genevieve, 573-883-3105; www.bolduchouse.com*

This restored French house with walls of upright heavy oak logs features period furnishings, orchard and a herb garden. April-November, daily.

### FELIX VALLE HOME STATE HISTORIC SITE

*198 Merchant St., Ste. Genevieve, 573-883-7102;*
*www.mostateparks.com/felixvalle.htm*

A restored and furnished Federal-style stone house of an early fur trader. Guided tours are available. Daily.

### GUIBOURD-VALLE HOUSE

*1 N. Fourth St., Ste. Genevieve, 573-883-7544*

Late 18th-century restored vertical log house on a stone foundation; French heirlooms. Attic with Norman truss and hand-hewn oak beams secured by wooden pegs. Courtyard; rose garden; stone well; costumed guides. April-October, daily; March and November, weekends.

### SAINTE GENEVIEVE MUSEUM

*Merchant Street and DuBourg Place, Ste. Genevieve, 573-883-3461;*
*www.greatriverroad.com/stegen/sgattract/sgmuseum.htm*

Display of salt manufacturing, the state's first industry. Scale model of rail car transfer boat, *Ste. Genevieve*, which carried trains across the Mississippi. Native American artifacts; local mementos. Daily; closed holidays.

## SPECIALTY LODGINGS

### SOUTHERN HOTEL BED AND BREAKFAST

*146 S. Third St., Ste. Genevieve, 573-883-3493, 800-275-1412;*
*www.southernhotelbb.com*

Eight rooms. Children over 12 years only. Complimentary full breakfast. Built in 1791. **$**

**MISSOURI**

★
★
★
★
★

## RESTAURANTS
### ★ANVIL SALOON
*46 S. Third St., Ste. Genevieve, 573-883-7323*

German, American menu. Lunch, dinner. Closed holidays. Bar. Oldest commercially operated building in the city (circa 1850); early Western saloon décor. **$$**

### ★OLD BRICK HOUSE
*90 S. Market St., Ste. Genevieve, 573-883-2724*

American menu. Breakfast, lunch, dinner. Bar. Children's menu. One of the first brick buildings (1785) west of the Mississippi. **$$**

# WENTZVILLE

Daniel Boone and his family were the first to settle in the area around Wentzville, which was named after Erasmus L. Wentz, principal engineer of the North Missouri Railroad. From 1850-1880 the area was devoted to growing tobacco. The original Liggett and Myers Tobacco Company factory still stands in Wentzville.

*Information: Chamber of Commerce, 5 W. Pearce,*
*636-327-6914; www.wentzvillemo.org*

## WHAT TO SEE AND DO
### CUIVRE RIVER STATE PARK
*678 St. Route 147, Troy, 636-528-7247; www.mostateparks.com/cuivre.htm*

One of the state's largest and most natural parks, this 6,251-acre area contains rugged, wooded terrain, native prairie and an 88-acre lake. Daily.

### DANIEL BOONE HOME
*County Z, Wentzville, 636-987-2221*

Built by Boone and his son Nathan around 1803, this stone house is where Boone died in 1820; restored and authentically furnished; museum. Mid-March-mid-December, daily; rest of year, weekends.

## HOTEL
### ★★HOLIDAY INN
*900 Corporate Parkway, Wentzville, 636-327-7001, 800-465-4329;*
*www.holidayinn.com*

139 rooms. Pets accepted, some restrictions. Restaurant, bar. Outdoor pool. Business center. **$**

# WESTON

Before the Civil War, Weston was at its peak. Founded on whiskey, hemp and tobacco, it rivaled St. Louis as a commercial trade center and promised to become a major U.S. city. But disasters—fire, floods and the Civil War—ruined Weston's urban future. Today Weston, the first "district" west of the Mississippi entered into the National Register of Historic Sites, is a quiet town with more than 100 antebellum houses and other buildings.

*Information: Information Center, 502 Main St., 816-640-2909; www.ci.weston.mo.us*

## WHAT TO SEE AND DO
### HISTORICAL MUSEUM
*601 Main St., Weston, 816-640-2977; www.westonhistoricalmuseum.org*
On the site of the International Hotel built by stagecoach king and distillery founder Benjamin Holladay. Mid-March-mid-December, Tuesday-Sunday.

### SNOW CREEK SKI AREA
*1 Snow Creek Drive, Weston, 816-386-2200; www.skisnowcreek.com*
Two triple and one double chairlift, rope tow; nine intermediate trails. Rentals; ski school, snow-making. Lodge, restaurant. Vertical drop 300 feet. Mid-December-mid-March, daily.

## SPECIALTY LODGING
### INN AT WESTON LANDING
*526 Welt St., Weston, 816-640-5788; www.innatwestonlanding.com*
Built atop the cellars of a former brewery, this inn has an Irish atmosphere and each room is individually decorated. Four rooms. Complimentary full breakfast. Restaurant. $

## RESTAURANT
### ★★AMERICA BOWMAN
*500 Welt St., Weston, 816-640-5235; www.westonirish.com/AMERICANBOWMAN.html*
American, Irish menu. Lunch, dinner. Closed Monday. Bar. Mid-19th-century Irish pub atmosphere. $$

**137**

**MISSOURI**

★
★
★
★

# NEBRASKA

IN LITTLE MORE THAN A CENTURY, NEBRASKA—PART OF WHAT WAS ONCE CALLED THE "great American desert"—has evolved from a vast prairie occupied by Native Americans and buffalo to a farming, ranching and manufacturing mainstay of America, with an enticing array of recreational and cultural attractions.

Spaniards visited the region first, but it was on the basis of explorations by Father Marquette and Louis Jolliet in 1673 that French fur traders and missionaries swept over the land, and France claimed it. Nevertheless, it was recognized as Spanish land until 1800, when it became a plaything of European politics and was sold by Napoleon to the United States as part of the Louisiana Purchase in 1803. Famous pathfinders like John C. Fremont, Kit Carson and the men who trapped for John Jacob Astor thought the land was unfit for cultivation.

Today, Nebraska is a "breadbasket" state, with an economy rooted in agriculture. But for the visitor, there is much more than corn, wheat and cows. As with Kansas to the south and South Dakota to the north, to traverse Nebraska from east to west is to trace a transition of terrain, climate and culture—from the tidy farms, sticky summers and small towns, along with the occasional big city, to a more unbridled landscape. Cattle graze on vast tracts of rangeland patrolled by actual cowboys, counties are bigger than some Northeastern states, the air dries out and the wind is almost always blowing as the land gradually slopes upward and becomes the high country stretching to the Rocky Mountains and the West.

At the eastern edge, by the Missouri River, is Omaha, the state's largest city. As one might expect in cattle country, it's a place to find a good steak, but if you're hunting for more adventurous cuisine, you'll find it. Home to a number of Fortune 500 companies as well as a major branch of the state university and the highly regarded Creighton University, Omaha offers its share of big-city sophistication.

Heading west on the interstate, you'll come to Lincoln, the state capital and site of the University of Nebraska main campus and the fabled Cornhuskers football team. A rabid army of red-clad fans chew over the fortunes of their squad year-round.

Farther out, if you are traveling by Kearney on Interstate 80, one attraction you literally can't miss is the Great Platte River Road Archway, a structure that spans 300 feet over the highway and houses a multimedia exhibit that salutes Nebraska's pioneer spirit along with the state's progression into modern times. In the movie *As Good as It Gets,* Jack Nicholson's character pays a visit here.

Wherever you are in Nebraska, the history, whether of the Native population, the settlers from the East, or some of the tragic clashes between the two, is rich The landscape, whether bleak or lush, can be beautiful and is easily explored by car, bike, horse or foot.

★ **FUN FACTS**

Nebraska is the birthplace of the Reuben sandwich.

Nebraska has more miles of river than any other state.

## FROM CRAZY HORSE TO CARHENGE

Vast, lightly populated and filled with raw beauty, the Sandhills country of western Nebraska takes visitors by surprise. Start in North Platte with a visit to Buffalo Bill Ranch State Historical Park, which preserves the Western icon's home on the range. Head north on Highway 83 to the Nebraska National Forest. At 90,000 acres, it's the largest hand-planted forest in the country. Continue north to Valentine, set along the Niobrara River, a favorite for canoeing. Drive west on Highway 20 to Merriman, site of the Sandhills Ranch State Historical Park (still a working ranch despite its name), then on to Chadron to visit the Museum of the Fur Trade. Continue west to Fort Robinson State Park, where Crazy Horse died. The nearby Pine Ridge and Oglala National Grassland are great spots for horseback riding, mountain biking and hiking. To return to civilization, take Highway 2 south from Crawford to Alliance, home to the famous Carhenge, a variation on England's Stonehenge. From Alliance, head south on Highway 385 to pick up the Oregon Trail route at Bridgeport or return to North Platte on Highway 2 east and Highway 83 south. Approximately 550 miles.

# AUBURN

## WHAT TO SEE AND DO

### BROWNVILLE
*Highway 136, Auburn*

Restored riverboat town of the 1800s. More than 30 buildings, many of which are open to the public.

### INDIAN CAVE STATE PARK
*RR 1, Shubert, 402-883-2575*

On approximately 3,400 acres, this park includes oak-covered Missouri River bluffs and the old St. Deroin town site, which has been partially reconstructed. Also here are ancient petroglyphs in Indian Cave; scenic overlooks of the river. Redbud trees bloom in profusion during spring.

### MISSOURI RIVER HISTORY MUSEUM
*Highway 136, Auburn, 402-825-3341*

Located aboard the *Captain Meriwether Lewis,* a former Corps of Engineers dredge, this museum contains exhibits on river history. Memorial Day-Labor Day, daily; rest of year, weekends.

### NEMAHA VALLEY MUSEUM
*1423 19th St., Auburn, 402-274-3203*

Exhibits trace history of Nemaha County; period rooms; farm equipment. Tuesday-Sunday afternoons.

## HOTELS

### ★AUBURN INN
*517 J St., Auburn, 402-274-3143, 800-272-3143*

36 rooms. Pets accepted, some restrictions. $

**NEBRASKA**

★★★★★

*1918 J St., Auburn, 402-274-3193, 800-272-3143*
22 rooms. Pets accepted, some restrictions; fee. **$**

## RESTAURANT
### ★WHEELER INN
*1905 J St., Auburn, 402-274-4931*
American menu. Dinner. Closed Sunday; holidays. Bar. Casual attire. **$$**

# CHADRON
The starting point of a sensational 1,000-mile horse race to Chicago in 1893, Chadron saw nine men leave in competition for a $1,000 prize. Doc Middleton, a former outlaw, was one of the starters, but John Berry beat him to the door of Buffalo Bill's Wild West Show in 13 days and 16 hours. The headquarters and a Ranger District office of the Nebraska National Forest and headquarters of the Oglala National Grasslands are located here.
*Information: Chamber of Commerce, 706 W. Third St.,*
*308-432-4401, 800-603-2937; www.chadron.com*

## WHAT TO SEE AND DO
### CHADRON STATE PARK
*15951 Highway 385, Chadron, 308-432-6167;*
*www.chadron.com*
A park with approximately 950 acres. Paddleboats, hiking, horseback riding, cross-country skiing and camping are available.

### MUSEUM OF THE FUR TRADE
*6321 Highway 20, Chadron, 308-432-3843; www.furtrade.org*
Displays depict the history of the North American fur trade from 1500-1900. Restored trading post and storehouse used by James Bordeaux, a French trader. Memorial Day-September, daily; rest of year, by appointment.

**140**

**NEBRASKA**

★
★ ★
★ ★
★ ★
★

## HOMESTEADING ALONG THE MISSOURI RIVER
Wooded river bluffs, historic towns and Homestead National Monument are among the attractions of this drive through southeast Nebraska. Take Highway 77 from Lincoln south to Beatrice, the first of several charming small towns on this route. A few miles west of town, Homestead National Monument showcases a restored tallgrass prairie and explains the Homestead Act of 1862, which led to widespread settlement in the Western United States. From Beatrice, drive east through the farmlands along Highway 136 to Auburn, a town known for its antique stores. Continue on to Brownville, which features a Missouri River History Museum aboard the dry-docked *Captain Meriwether Lewis* and riverboat cruises aboard the *Spirit of Brownville*. From Brownville, backtrack to Auburn and head north on Highway 75 to Nebraska City, the birthplace of Arbor Day. Head west on Highway 34 north of Nebraska City to return to Lincoln. Approximately 180 miles.

## HOTELS

### ★BEST WESTERN WEST HILLS INN

*1100 W. 10th St., Chadron, 308-432-3305, 877-432-3305; www.bestwestern.com*

67 rooms. Pets accepted, some restrictions; fee. Complimentary continental breakfast. High-speed Internet access. Fitness room. Indoor pool, whirlpool. Business center. **$**

### ★SUPER 8

*840 W. Highway 20, Chadron, 308-432-4471; www.super8.com*

45 rooms. Pets accepted. Complimentary continental breakfast. High-speed Internet access. Indoor pool, whirlpool. **$**

# COLUMBUS

Named by its founders for Ohio's capital, Columbus has become a center of industry, agriculture and statewide electrical power.

*Information: Chamber of Commerce, 764 33rd Ave.,*
*402-564-2769; www.ci.columbus.ne.us*

### PAWNEE PARK

*Highway 30, Columbus, 402-564-0914*

Swimming pool. Ball fields, tennis. Picnicking facilities, playground on 130 acres along Loup River. Quincentenary bell tower dedicated to Columbus's voyage to the new world.

### PLATTE COUNTY HISTORICAL SOCIETY

*2916 16th St., Columbus, 402-564-1856; www.megavision.net/museum*

See exhibits on local history, a period schoolroom, barbershop, research library and cultural center. April-mid-October, Friday-Sunday.

## HOTELS

### ★★NEW WORLD INN AND CONFERENCE CENTER

*265 33rd Ave., Columbus, 402-564-1492, 800-433-1492; www.newworldinn.com*

140 rooms. Restaurant, bar. Indoor pool, whirlpool. Airport transportation available. Indoor courtyard. **$**

### ★SUPER 8

*3324 20th St., Columbus, 402-563-3456; www.super8.com*

63 rooms. Pets accepted, some restrictions; fee. Complimentary continental breakfast. High-speed Internet access. **$**

# COZAD

Cozad is headquarters for a number of industries, as well as a shipping and agricultural center known for the production of alfalfa.

*Information: Chamber of Commerce,*
*135 W. Eighth St., 308-784-3930; www.ci.cozad.ne.us*

## WHAT TO SEE AND DO
### GALLAGHER CANYON STATE RECREATION AREA
*Highways 751 and 424, Cozad, 308-784-3907*
Approximately 20 acres of park surround 400 acres of water. Fishing, boating, hiking, picnicking, camping.

### ROBERT HENRI MUSEUM AND HISTORICAL WALKWAY
*112 E. Eighth St., Cozad, 308-784-4154*
This museum occupies the childhood home of artist Robert Henri, founder of the Ash Can School, as well as a former hotel built by Henri's father. Other historic buildings along the walkway include an original Pony Express station, a pioneer school and an early 20th-century church. Memorial Day-September, Tuesday-Saturday, also by appointment.

## HOTEL
### ★★CIRCLE S BEST VALUE INN
*440 S. Meridian St., Cozad, 308-784-2290, 888-315-2378;*
*www.bestvalueinn.com*
49 rooms. Pets accepted, some restrictions; fee. Restaurant. Outdoor pool. $

# CRAWFORD
The area around this community is rich in fossil beds. The Hudson-Meng Bison Kill Site is loaded with animal bones and other artifacts more than 10,000 years old.

*Information: Chamber of Commerce, 308-665-1817; www.crawfordnebraska.com*

## FORT ROBINSON'S WORLD WAR II HISTORY
Nebraska might seem an unlikely place to encounter World War II history, but out in the northwestern corner of the state you can visit a fort that, having originally stood as an important outpost in the Indian Wars, served as camp for German and Axis prisoners of war in 1943.

The fort compound had already come into wartime use as a K-9 Dogs for Defense training center. But as prisoner capacity in Great Britain became squeezed, Fort Robinson, located far from any city but alongside mainline railways and with opportunities for needed labor, was picked as a spot to hold captured enemy soldiers. The first to arrive in the facility, built to accommodate 3,000 men, were soldiers captured from Rommel's Tenth Panzer Division in North Africa. They traveled by train from Virginia. When they arrived at the camp, the men were searched for contraband; items such as maps, cameras and binoculars were confiscated. Somehow one German soldier had managed to travel with a chihuahua in his coat pocket.

The prisoners worked at a variety of camp-based jobs and were paid 80 cents an hour, as mandated by the Geneva Conventions. But even though the war had caused a labor shortage in agriculture, the Fort Robinson prisoners were not pressed into farm work, whereas at Camp Scottsbluff, approximately 80 miles to the south, German and Italian POWs worked in sugar beet and bean fields.

## WHAT TO SEE AND DO

### FORT ROBINSON MUSEUM
*3200 W. Highway 20, Crawford, 308-665-2919*

The museum is located in the former fort headquarters building and displays authentic costumes and weapons of Native Americans and soldiers. Other exhibit buildings include guardhouse, a harness repair, blacksmith wheelwright shops, an adobe officer quarters and a veterinary hospital. Site of Red Cloud Indian Agency. Guided tours, Memorial Day-Labor Day. Museum, Memorial Day-Labor Day, daily; rest of the year, Monday-Friday.

### FORT ROBINSON STATE PARK
*3200 Highway 20, Crawford, 308-665-2660; www.stateparks.com/fort_robinson.html*

This fort was established in 1874 in the midst of Native American fighting (the Sioux leader, Crazy Horse, was killed here). Displays herds of buffalo. Park entry permit required.

### OGLALA NATIONAL GRASSLAND
*16524 Highway 385, Chadron, 308-432-4475*

This area includes nearly 95,000 acres of prairie grasses in the badlands of Northwestern Nebraska, popular for hunting (in season), hiking and backpacking.

### TRAILSIDE MUSEUM
*Main Street, Crawford, 308-665-2929; www.trailside.unl.edu*

The newest exhibit at this museum features the fossils of two mammoths discovered in the nearby Little Badlands. The creatures locked tusks in battle and died intertwined. The museum also features exhibits of natural history from the Fort Robinson area and daily science field trips to Toadstool Park and fossil sites. Memorial Day-Labor Day, daily; May, Wednesday-Sunday.

## HOTEL

### ★★FORT ROBINSON LODGE
*Crawford, 308-665-2900*

53 rooms. Closed late November-mid-April. Restaurant. Indoor pool. Tennis. Access to facilities of state park. $

# FREMONT

This town was named for John C. Fremont, a Union general in the Civil War who ran for president of the United States. In the town's early days, the crops were so bad that lots sold for 75 cents each. Finally, travelers on the Overland Trail brought with them enough trade that the town began to prosper and grow. Midland Lutheran College gives a collegiate atmosphere to an otherwise industrial town.

*Information: Fremont Area Chamber of Commerce and Dodge County Convention and Visitors Bureau,1420 East Military Ave., 402-753-6414, 800-727-8323; www.visitdodgecountyne.org*

## WHAT TO SEE AND DO
### FREMONT AND ELKHORN VALLEY RAILROAD
*1835 N. Somers Ave., Fremont, 402-727-0615, 800-942-7245;*
*www.fremontrailroad.com*
Train rides to Nickerson and Hooper aboard vintage rail cars. Reservations recommended. Schedule varies.

### FREMONT DINNER TRAIN
*1835 N. Somers Ave., Fremont, 402-727-8321; www.fremontrailroad.com*
Two restored 1940s rail cars make 30-mile round trips through the Elkhorn Valley. Dinner and varied entertainment. Weekends, some holidays.

### LOUIS E. MAY HISTORICAL MUSEUM
*1643 N. Nye Ave., Fremont, 402-721-4515*
The 25-room house of Fremont's first mayor, built in 1874, features oak and mahogany paneling, art glass windows and rooms furnished in late 19th-century style. May-August and December, Wednesday-Sunday; April and September-October, Wednesday-Saturday; closed holidays.

## HOTELS
### ★AMERICA'S BEST VALUE INN
*1649 E. 23rd St., Fremont, 402-721-1109; www.bestvalueinn.com*
48 rooms. Pets accepted; fee. Complimentary continental breakfast. Indoor pool, whirlpool. $

### ★★WILDERNESS LODGE AND COMFORT CENTER
*1220 E. 23rd Ave., Fremont, 402-727-1110, 800-743-7666;*
*www.wildernesslodgecc.com*
100 rooms. Pets accepted, some restrictions; fee. Restaurant, bar. Fitness room. Indoor pool, whirlpool. $

# GRAND ISLAND
Named by French trappers for a large island in the Platte River, the town was moved five miles north in 1869 to its present location on the Union Pacific Railroad, which dominated Grand Island's early existence. Traditionally a trade center for a rich irrigated agriculture and livestock region, the city now has diversified industry, including meat and food processing, agricultural and irrigation equipment and mobile homes.
*Information: Grand Island/Hall County Convention and Visitors Bureau,*
*309 W. Second St., 308-382-4400, 800-658-3178; www.visitgrandisland.com*

## WHAT TO SEE AND DO
### CRANE MEADOWS NATURE CENTER
*9325 S. Alda Road, Wood River, 308-382-1820*
Educational center features exhibits and programs about the Platte River habitat. Five miles of public nature trails. Daily; closed holidays.

### MORMON ISLAND STATE RECREATION AREA
*7425 S. Highway 281, Grand Island, 308-385-6211*
Approximately 90 acres with 61 water acres on the Mormon Trail. Swimming, fishing, boating, picnicking. Tent and trailer sites.

### RAILROAD TOWN ANTIQUE MALL
*319 W. Third St., Grand Island, 308-398-2222*
Turn-of-the-century outdoor museum contains 60 original buildings, including three houses, the cottage where Henry Fonda was born, schoolhouse, newspaper office, bank, post office, hotel, country church and more. May-mid-October, daily.

### STUHR MUSEUM OF THE PRAIRIE PIONEER
*3133 W. Highway 34, Grand Island, 308-385-5316; www.stuhrmuseum.org*
This museum situated on an island surrounded by a man-made lake, was designed by Edward Durell Stone. Daily; closed holidays.

## SPECIAL EVENT
### HUSKER HARVEST DAYS
*Cornhusker Army Ammunition Plant, 309 W. Second St.,*
*Grand Island, www.huskerharvestdays.com*
Agricultural exhibits, techniques, and equipment used in irrigation. Mid-September.

## HOTELS
### ★DAYS INN
*2620 N. Diers Ave., Grand Island, 308-384-8624, 800-329-7466; www.daysinn.com*
63 rooms. Pets accepted; fee. Complimentary continental breakfast. High-speed Internet access. $

### ★★HOLIDAY INN
*2503 S. Locust St., Grand Island, 308-384-1330, 800-548-5542; www.holiday-inn.com*
197 rooms. High-speed Internet access. Restaurant, bar. Children's pool, whirlpool. Business center. $

### ★★HOWARD JOHNSON
*3333 Ramada Road, Grand Island, 308-384-5150, 800-446-4656; www.hojo.com*
181 rooms. Pets accepted; fee. Complimentary continental breakfast. High-speed Internet access. Restaurant, bar. Indoor pool, whirlpool. $

## RESTAURANT
### ★HUNAN
*2249 N. Webb Road, Grand Island, 308-384-6964*
Chinese menu. Lunch, dinner. Closed holidays. Bar. $$

★
★
★
★
★

# HASTINGS

Hastings came into being almost overnight when two railroad lines crossed. Within eight years of its founding, its population swelled to almost 3,000. After 75 years as a depot and supply center, the town turned out large quantities of ammunition during World War II and the Korean War.

*Information: Convention and Visitors Bureau, 100 N. Shore Drive,*
*402-461-2370, 800-967-2189; www.visithastingsnebraska.com*

## WHAT TO SEE AND DO
### HASTINGS MUSEUM

*1330 N. Burlington Ave., Hastings, 402-461-2399; www.hastingsmuseum.org*
Includes natural science, pioneer history, Native American lore and historical displays. Daily; closed holidays. J. M. McDonald Planetarium, sky shows daily.

### WILLA CATHER STATE HISTORIC SITE

*413 N. Webster St., Red Cloud, 402-746-2653*
Author Willa Cather grew up in Red Cloud, and her childhood home has been converted into a museum. Included are her letters, first editions of her books, photos and Cather family memorabilia. Other buildings include the Red Cloud depot, St. Juliana Falconieri Catholic Church, Grace Episcopal Church and *My Ántonia* farmhouse. Tours of properties four times daily. Daily; closed holidays.

## HOTELS

### ★★QUALITY HOTEL AND CONVENTION CENTER

*2205 Osborne Drive E., Hastings, 402-463-6721, 888-465-4329;*
*www.choicehotels.com*
101 rooms. Pets accepted. Wireless Internet access. Restaurant, bar. Indoor pool, whirlpool. $

### ★SUPER 8

*2200 N. Kansas Ave., Hastings, 402-463-8888; www.super8.com*
50 rooms. Pets accepted, some restrictions; fee. Complimentary continental breakfast. High-speed Internet access. $

## RESTAURANTS
### ★BERNARDO'S STEAK HOUSE

*1109 S. Baltimore, Hastings, 402-463-4666*
Steak menu. Lunch, dinner. Closed holidays. Bar. Children's menu. $

### ★★TAYLOR'S STEAKHOUSE

*1609 N. Kansas, Hastings, 402-462-8000; www.taylorssteakhouseandcatering.com*
Steak menu. Dinner. Closed Sunday; holidays. Bar. Children's menu. $$$

# KEARNEY

Kearney (CAR-nee) is named for the frontier outpost Fort Kearny. It is one of the largest migratory bird flyways in the world, a temporary home for millions of species.
*Information: Visitors Bureau, 1007 Second Ave.,*
*308-237-3101, 800-652-9435; www.kearneycoc.org*

## WHAT TO SEE AND DO
### FORT KEARNY STATE HISTORICAL PARK
*1020 V Road, Kearney, 308-865-5305*

The first Fort Kearny was erected at Nebraska City in 1846; it was moved here in 1848 to protect the Oregon Trail. In the park are a restored 1864 stockade, a sod blacksmith-carpenter shop, museum and interpretive center. Memorial Day-Labor Day, daily.

### GEORGE W. FRANK HOUSE
*West Highway 30, Kearney, 308-865-8284; www.unk.edu*

This three-story mansion, built in 1889, has a Tiffany window. June-August, Tuesday-Sunday.

### MUSEUM OF NEBRASKA ART
*2401 Central Ave., Kearney, 308-865-8559*

Collection of paintings, sculptures, drawings and prints created by Nebraskans or with Nebraska as the subject. Tuesday-Saturday, Sunday afternoons; closed holidays.

### TRAILS AND RAILS MUSEUM
*710 W. 11th St., Kearney, 308-234-3041; www.bchs.kearney.net/museum.html*

Visit a restored 1898 depot, 1880s freighters' hotel and 1871 country schoolhouse. Includes displays of pioneer trails and rails, steam engines and more. Memorial Day-Labor Day, daily; rest of year by appointment.

### UNIVERSITY OF NEBRASKA AT KEARNEY
*905 W. 25th St., Kearney, 308-865-8441; www.unk.edu*

This branch of the state university offers undergraduate, graduate and specialist degrees. Two art galleries and a planetarium are located on campus.

## HOTELS
### ★★BEST WESTERN INN OF KEARNEY
*1010 Third Ave., Kearney, 308-237-5185, 800-641-5437; www.bestwestern.com*

61 rooms. Pets accepted, some restrictions; fee. Complimentary full breakfast. High-speed Internet access. Restaurant. Fitness room. Outdoor pool, children's pool, whirlpool. $

### ★★HOLIDAY INN
*110 S. Second Ave., Kearney, 308-237-5971; www.holiday-inn.com*

163 rooms. High-speed Internet access. Restaurant, bar. Fitness room. Indoor pool, whirlpool. $

### ★★RAMADA INN
*301 Second Ave., Kearney, 308-237-3141, 800-652-1909; www.ramada.com*

209 rooms. Pets accepted; fee. Complimentary continental breakfast. Restaurant, bar. Indoor pool, children's pool, whirlpool. $

★
★
★
★
★

## RESTAURANTS
### ★★ALLEY ROSE
*2013 Central Ave., Kearney, 308-234-1261; www.alleyrose.com*
Lunch, dinner. Closed Sunday; holidays. Bar. Children's menu. **$$**

### ★★GRANDPA'S STEAK HOUSE
*13 Central Ave., Kearney, 308-237-2882*
Steak menu. Lunch, dinner. Closed holidays. Bar. Children's menu. **$$**

# LEXINGTON
Originally a frontier trading post and settlement along the Oregon Trail, completion of the Union Pacific Railroad brought more settlers to this farmland. Lexington is known as the antiques center of Nebraska.
*Information: Lexington Area Chamber of Commerce, 709 E. Pacific Ave.,*
*308-324-5504, 888-966-0564; www.ci.lexington.ne.us*

## WHAT TO SEE AND DO
### DAWSON COUNTY HISTORICAL MUSEUM
*805 N. Taft St., Lexington, 308-324-5340; www.dchsmuseum.com*
Exhibits include Dawson County history gallery, furnished rural schoolhouse, 1885 Union Pacific depot, 1903 locomotive, farm equipment and 1919 experimental biplane. Collection also includes quilts and prehistoric Native American artifacts. Art gallery and archives. Monday-Saturday, closed holidays.

## SPECIAL EVENT
### ANTIQUE AND CRAFT EXTRAVAGANZA
*Dawson County Fairgrounds, Lexington, 308-324-5504; www.visitlexington.org*
More than 275 antiques, craft and flea market dealers. Labor Day weekend.

## HOTELS
### ★FIRST INTERSTATE INN
*2503 Plum Creek Parkway, Lexington, 308-324-5601, 800-462-4667; www.1stinns.com*
52 rooms. Pets accepted; fee. Complimentary continental breakfast. Outdoor pool. **$**

### ★SUPER 8
*104 E. River Road, Lexington, 308-324-7434, 800-800-8000; www.super8.com*
47 rooms. Complimentary continental breakfast. High-speed Internet access. Fitness room. **$**

# LINCOLN
The second-largest city in Nebraska, Lincoln feuded with Omaha, the territorial seat of government, for the honor of being capital of the new state. When the argument was settled in Lincoln's favor in 1867, books, documents and office furniture were moved in covered wagons late one night to escape the armed band of Omaha boosters. As a young lawyer in the 1890s, William Jennings Bryan went to Congress from Lincoln; in 1896, 1900 and 1908 he ran unsuccessfully for president.

The unicameral (one-house legislature) form of government in Nebraska, which was set up by an amendment to the state constitution in 1934 (mostly by the efforts

★
★
★
★
★

of Nebraska's famous senator, George W. Norris), is of great interest to students of political science. Supporters say it works efficiently and avoids delays and deadlocks common to two-house legislatures.

*Information: Convention and Visitors Bureau, 1135 M St.,*
*402-434-5335, 800-423-8212; www.lincoln.org*

## WHAT TO SEE AND DO

### EXECUTIVE MANSION

*1135 M St., Lincoln, 402-434-5335; www.lincoln.org*
The state governor's mansion features Georgian Colonial architecture. Guided tours. Thursday afternoons; closed holidays.

### FOLSOM CHILDREN'S ZOO

*1222 S. 27th St., Lincoln, 402-475-6741; www.lincolnzoo.org*
Exotic animals, contact areas, botanical gardens. Train and pony rides. April-mid-August, daily.

### GREAT PLAINS ART MUSEUM

*1155 Q St., Lincoln, 402-472-6220; www.unl.edu*
Works by Remington, Russell and other artists are among the nearly 700 pieces in this collection. Also featured are 4,000 volumes of Great Plains and Western Americana. Tuesday-Sunday; closed between exhibits.

### LINCOLN CHILDREN'S MUSEUM

*1420 P St., Lincoln, 402-477-4000; www.lincolnchildrensmuseum.org*
A variety of cultural and scientific exhibits invite exploration and involve the senses. Tuesday-Sunday; closed holidays.

### LINCOLN MONUMENT

*201 N. Seventh St., Lincoln, 402-434-5348*
This standing figure of Abraham Lincoln was designed by the sculptor Daniel Chester French, who also produced the seated statue for Henry Bacon's Lincoln Memorial in Washington, D.C. Architectural setting by Bacon.

### MUSEUM OF NEBRASKA HISTORY

*15th and P streets, Lincoln, 402-471-4754; www.nebraskahistory.org*
History of Nebraska summarized in exhibits covering events from prehistoric times through the 1950s. Native American Gallery, period rooms. Tuesday-Sunday; closed holidays.

### NATIONAL MUSEUM OF ROLLER SKATING

*4730 South St., Lincoln, 402-483-7551; www.rollerskatingmuseum.com*
Skates, costumes and photographs documenting the sport and industry from 1700 to the present; also archives dealing with world and national competitions since 1910. The only museum in the world devoted solely to roller skating. Monday-Friday; closed holidays.

NEBRASKA

★
★
★
★
★

### PIONEERS PARK

*2740 A St., Lincoln, 402-441-7895; www.lincoln.ne.gov*

Hiking, bike trails, bridle path; golf course, picnicking, playgrounds. Nature preserve, outdoor amphitheater. Daily.

### STATE CAPITOL

*1445 K St., Lincoln, 402-471-0448*

Designed by Bertram Goodhue, the most dominant feature of this building is the central tower, which rises 400 feet. Ground was broken in 1922 for this third capitol building at Lincoln and was completed 10 years later. Sculpture by Lee Lawrie includes reliefs and friezes depicting the history of law and justice, great philosophers, symbols of the state and a bronze statue of the Sower (32 feet) atop the tower dome. The great hall, rotunda and legislative chambers are decorated in tile and marble murals, tapestries and wood-inlaid panels. Guided tours. Daily; closed holidays.

### STATEHOOD MEMORIAL—THOMAS P. KENNARD HOUSE

*1627 H St., Lincoln, 402-471-4764; www.nebraskahistory.org*

This 1869 house is the restored residence of Nebraska's first secretary of state. Monday-Friday, by appointment; closed holidays.

### STRATEGIC AIR & SPACE MUSEUM

*28210 W. Park Highway, Ashland, 402-944-3100; www.strategicairandspace.com*

Features a permanent collection of 33 aircrafts and six missiles relating to the history of SAC and its importance in the preservation of world peace. Interactive children's gallery, theater, museum store. Daily; closed holidays.

★
★
★
★
★

### UNIVERSITY OF NEBRASKA

*501 N. 14th St., Lincoln, 402-472-7211; www.unl.edu*

This state university of more than 33,000 students has research-extension divisions throughout the state. Following Cornhuskers football is a treasured state pasttime.

### UNIVERSITY OF NEBRASKA STATE MUSEUM

*307 Morrill Hall, 402-472-2642; www-museum.unl.edu*

Displays of fossils (dinosaurs and mounted elephants), rocks and minerals, ancient life, Nebraska plants and animals. Native American exhibits; changing exhibits. Daily; closed holidays.

## SPECIAL EVENTS

### JULY JAMM

*12 and N streets, Lincoln, 402-434-6900*

Art show, music festival. Late July.

### NEBRASKA STATE FAIR

*1800 State Fair Park Drive, Lincoln, 402-474-5371; www.statefair.org*

Large fair with livestock, food, contests, games. Late August.

# HOTELS

## ★★BEST WESTERN VILLAGER COURTYARD & GARDENS
*5200 O St., Lincoln, 402-464-9111; www.bestwestern.com*
186 rooms. Pets accepted. Complimentary continental breakfast. Restaurant, bar. Fitness room. Outdoor pool, whirlpool. **$**

## ★CHASE SUITE HOTEL
*200 S. 68th Place, Lincoln, 402-483-4900, 888-433-6183; www.chasehotellincoln.com*
120 rooms. Pets accepted; fee. Complimentary full breakfast. High-speed Internet access. Fitness room. Outdoor pool, whirlpool, spa. Business center. Tennis. **$**

## THE CORNHUSKER
*333 S. 13th St., Lincoln, 402-474-7474, 800-793-7474; www.thecornhusker.com*
Continental style meets Midwestern friendliness at Lincoln's luxurious Cornhusker Hotel. A Nebraska landmark since 1926, today's Cornhusker has sophisticated décor, fine dining, exceptional amenities and dedicated service. The tenth-floor Executive Level offers an upgraded experience. Hand-painted murals and fiber-optic starlight help make the Terrace Grille a pleasant setting for continental cuisine. 297 rooms. Restaurant, bar. Wireless Internet access. Fitness room. Indoor pool. Business center. Airport transportation available. **$$**

## ★★HOLIDAY INN
*141 N. Ninth St., Lincoln, 402-475-4011, 800-432-0002; www.holiday-inn.com*
230 rooms. Restaurant, bar. High-speed Internet access. Indoor pool, whirlpool. **$**

# RESTAURANTS

## ★★BILLY'S
*1301 H St., Lincoln, 402-474-0084; www.billysrestaurant.com*
American menu. Lunch Monday-Friday, dinner. Closed Sunday; holidays. Bar. **$$**

## ★YIA YIA
*1423 O St., Lincoln, 402-477-9166*
Pizza. Lunch, dinner. Closed Sunday; holidays. Bar. Outdoor seating. No credit cards accepted. **$**

# MCCOOK

McCook began as the small settlement of Fairview. The Lincoln Land Company and the Burlington & Missouri Railroad gave the town its name and ensured its growth.
*Information: Chamber of Commerce, 107 Norris Ave.,*
*308-345-3200, 800-657-2179; www.aboutmccook.com*

## WHAT TO SEE AND DO

### MUSEUM OF THE HIGH PLAINS
*423 Norris Ave., McCook, 308-345-3661*
Pioneer and Native American artifacts; World War II prisoner of war paintings; apothecary shop; fossils; flour mill; oil industry exhibit; special exhibits. Tuesday-Sunday afternoons; closed holidays.

★
★
★
★
★

### SENATOR GEORGE W. NORRIS STATE HISTORIC SITE

*706 Norris Ave., McCook, 308-345-8484; www.nebraskahistory.org*

Restored house of former senator; original furnishings; museum depicts events in his life. Wednesday-Saturday; closed holidays.

## SPECIAL EVENTS
### HERITAGE DAYS

*Norris Park, McCook, 308-345-3200*

Entertainment, parade, arts and crafts fair, carnival. Last full weekend in September.

### RED WILLOW COUNTY FAIR AND RODEO

*Fairgrounds, W. Fifth and O streets, McCook, 308-345-4650;*
*www.redwillowcountyfair.com*

Late July.

## HOTEL
### ★★CHIEF MOTEL

*612 W. B St., McCook,*
*308-345-3700, 866-641-5437; www.bestwestern.com*

111 rooms. Pets accepted, some restrictions. Complimentary continental breakfast. Restaurant. Fitness room. Outdoor pool, whirlpool. $

# NEBRASKA CITY

Nebraska City began as a trading post but grew larger and wilder as the Missouri River and overland traffic brought bullwhackers, muleskinners and riverboat men with bowie knives and pistols in their belts. Located on the Missouri River, Nebraska City ships grain and agricultural products worldwide.

*Information: Chamber of Commerce, 806 First Ave.,*
*402-873-3000, 800-514-9113; www.nebraskacity.com*

## WHAT TO SEE AND DO
### ARBOR LODGE STATE HISTORICAL PARK

*2300 Second Ave., Nebraska City, 402-873-7222*
*www.ngpc.state.ne.us/nebland/articles/parks/arbor.asp*

More than 72 acres of wooded grounds surround the 52-room, neo-Colonial mansion of J. Sterling Morton (the originator of Arbor Day and the secretary of agriculture under Grover Cleveland) and summer residence of his son Joy Morton (the founder of Morton Salt Company). Picnicking. Mansion, April-December, daily. Park grounds daily.

### MAYHEW CABIN AND HISTORIC VILLAGE FOUNDATION

*2012 Fourth Corso, Nebraska City, 402-873-3115; www.johnbrownscave.com*

Original log cabin and cave where slaves were hidden before and after the Civil War. April-November, Wednesday-Sunday.

### WILDWOOD HISTORIC HOME

*420 S. Steinhart Park Road, Nebraska City, 402-873-6340*

A 10-room 1869 house with mid-Victorian-era furnishings, this home has a formal parlor, antique lamps and fixtures. The original brick barn is now an art gallery. Mid-April-October, Monday-Saturday 10 a.m.-5 p.m., Sunday 1-5 p.m. or by appointment.

## SPECIAL EVENTS
### APPLEJACK FESTIVAL

*Nebraska City, 402-873-3000; www.nebraskacity.com/new/applejack.html*

Celebration of the apple harvest. Parade, antique and craft show, classic car show, football game. Third weekend in September.

### ARBOR DAY CELEBRATION

*2300 Second Ave., Nebraska City, 402-873-3000*

Tree-planting ceremonies in Arbor Lodge State Historical Park; parade, arts festival, fly-in, breakfast. Last weekend in April.

## RESTAURANT
### ★★EMBERS STEAKHOUSE

*1102 Fourth Corso, Nebraska City, 402-873-6416*

Steak menu. Lunch, dinner. Bar. Children's menu. $$

# NORFOLK

German families from Wisconsin were the first to till the rich soil around Norfolk. The town's livestock business and expanding industries have brought prosperity, making Norfolk the chief marketplace of Northeastern Nebraska.

*Information: Madison County Convention and Visitors Bureau,*
*402-371-2932, 888-371-2932; www.norfolk.ne.us*

## WHAT TO SEE AND DO
### COWBOY TRAIL

*Highway 81 and Tahazorika Road, Norfolk, 402-371-4862*

This 321-mile trail follows the former Chicago and Northwestern railroad line from Norfolk to Chadron. Includes 13,878 feet of handrailed bridges. Trail is suitable for hiking and mountain biking, with horseback riding allowed alongside the trail.

## HOTELS
### ★★NORFOLK COUNTRY INN

*1201 S. 13th St., Norfolk, 402-371-4430, 800-233-0733;*
*www.norfolkcountryinn.com*

127 rooms. Pets accepted. Restaurant, bar. High-speed Internet access, Outdoor pool. $

### ★★RAMADA INN

*1227 Omaha Ave., Norfolk, 402-371-7000; www.ramada.com*

98 rooms. Pets accepted; fee. Restaurant, bar. Indoor pool. $

### ★SUPER 8

*1223 W. Omaha Ave., Norfolk, 402-379-2220, 800-800-8000;*
*www.super8.com*

66 rooms. Pets accepted, some restrictions; fee. Complimentary continental breakfast. High-speed Internet access. $

## RESTAURANTS
### ★★BRASS LANTERN

*1018 S. Ninth St., Norfolk, 402-371-2500*

Steak menu. Lunch, dinner. Closed holidays. Bar. Children's menu. $$

### ★★PRENGER'S

*116 E. Norfolk Ave., Norfolk, 402-379-1900; www.prengers.com*

American menu. Lunch, dinner. Closed holidays. Bar. Children's menu. $$

### ★★★THE UPTOWN CAFÉ

*801 10th St., Stanton, 402-439-5100*

Visitors to this restaurant in the middle of the Wild West may be surprised by the refined food and good wine selection. Famed for its support of local artists and musicians, the dining room is filled with paintings and live music. Seafood menu. Lunch, dinner, late-night. Bar. $$

# NORTH PLATTE

North Platte, Buffalo Bill Cody's hometown, is the retail, railroad and agricultural hub of West Central Nebraska.

*Information: North Platte/Lincoln County Convention and Visitors Bureau,*
*211 West Third St., North Platte, 308-535-6724, 800-955-4528;*
*www.ci.north-platte.ne.us*

## WHAT TO SEE AND DO
### BUFFALO BILL RANCH STATE HISTORICAL PARK

*2921 Scouts Rest Ranch Road, North Platte, 308-535-8035; www.visitnebraska.org*

The 18-room house, barn and outbuildings of William F. Cody's ranch include an interpretive film and displays of buffalo. Memorial Day-Labor Day, daily; October-April, Monday-Friday.

### FORT MCPHERSON NATIONAL CEMETERY

*Interstate 80, exit 190, Maxwell*

Soldiers and scouts of Native American and later wars are buried here.

### LINCOLN COUNTY HISTORICAL MUSEUM

*2403 N. Buffalo Bill Ave., North Platte, 308-534-5640; www.lincolncountymuseum.org*

Several authentically furnished rooms and exhibits, including a World War II canteen, depict the life and history of Lincoln County. In back is the re-creation of a railroad village with a restored depot, house, church, schoolhouse, log house and barn. Memorial Day-Labor Day, daily; rest of year by appointment.

## SPECIAL EVENT
### NEBRASKALAND DAYS CELEBRATION
*509 E. Fourth St., North Platte, 308-532-7939; www.nebraskalanddays.com*
Parades, entertainment, food, and the famous PRCA Rodeo. Mid-late June.

## HOTELS
### ★HAMPTON INN
*200 Platte Oasis Parkway, North Platte, 308-534-6000, 800-426-7866;*
*www.hamptoninn.com*
110 rooms. Complimentary continental breakfast. High-speed Internet access. Indoor pool, whirlpool. Business center. **$**

### RODEWAY INN
*920 N. Jeffers St., North Platte, 308-532-2313, 877-424-6423; www.bestwestern.com*
38 rooms. Pets accepted; fee. Complimentary continental breakfast. Wireless Internet access. Outdoor pool. **$**

### ★★ROYAL COLONIAL INN
*1402 S. Jeffers St., North Platte, 308-534-3630, 800-624-4643;*
*www.royalcolonialinn.com*
140 rooms. Pets accepted, some restrictions; fee. Complimentary continental breakfast. Restaurant, bar. Outdoor pool. **$**

### ★SUPER 8
*220 Eugene Ave., North Platte, 308-532-4224, 800-800-8000; www.super8.com*
113 rooms. Pets accepted, some restrictions; fee. Complimentary continental breakfast. High-speed Internet access. Fitness room. **$**

## RESTAURANT
### ★GOLDEN DRAGON
*120 W. Leota St., North Platte, 308-532-5588*
Chinese menu. Lunch, dinner. Closed holidays. **$$**

# OGALLALA
Developed as a shipping point on the Union Pacific Railroad for the great Western cattle herds, Ogallala was the goal of the cattle-driving cowboys who rode day and night with their "eyelids pasted open with tobacco." Many of them are buried in a genuine Boot Hill Cemetery, between 11th and 12th streets on a 100-foot rise above the South Platte River, where there have been no burials since the 1880s.
*Information: Chamber of Commerce, 204 E. A St.,*
*308-284-4066, 800-658-4390; www.ogallala.com*

## WHAT TO SEE AND DO
### ASH HOLLOW STATE HISTORICAL PARK
*Highway 26, Ogallala, 308-778-5651*
Approximately 1,000 acres on the Oregon Trail. The hills, caves and springs of Ash Hollow have sustained humans from prehistoric times through the pioneer days. Hiking, picnicking. Interpretive center, restored school.

★
★
★
★
★

### CRESCENT LAKE NATIONAL WILDLIFE REFUGE

*10630 Road 181, Oshkosh, 308-762-4893; www.fws.gov*

A nesting and migratory bird refuge comprising more than 45,000 acres with numerous pothole lakes. Birds found in the refuge include Canadian geese, great blue herons, American bitterns, prairie chickens, prairie falcons and long-billed curlews.

### FRONT STREET

*519 E. First St., Ogallala, 308-284-6000; www.megavision.net/frontstreet*

Cowboy museum, general store, saloon, arcade, restaurant. Nightly shows in Crystal Palace during summer.

### LAKE MCCONAUGHY STATE RECREATION AREA

*1500 Highway 61 N., Ogallala, 308-284-3542*

Approximately 5,500 acres on Nebraska's largest lake. Swimming, fishing, boating, picnicking, camping.

### LAKE OGALLALA STATE RECREATION AREA

*1500 Highway 61 N., Ogallala, 308-284-3542*

Approximately 300 acres on a 320-acre lake. Fishing; boating, camping. Standard fees.

### MANSION ON THE HILL

*1004 N. Spruce St., Ogallala*

This 1890s mansion contains period furniture, pioneer household items. Memorial Day-Labor Day, daily.

## HOTELS

### ★★BEST WESTERN STAGECOACH INN

*201 Stagecoach Trail, Ogallala, 308-284-3656, 800-662-2993;*
*www.bestwestern.com*

100 rooms. Pets accepted; fee. Complimentary continental breakfast. High-speed Internet access. Restaurant, bar. Indoor pool, outdoor pool, children's pool, whirlpool. Fitness center. Airport transportation available. $

### ★COMFORT INN

*110 Pony Express Lane, Ogallala, 308-284-4028, 877-424-6423; www.comfortinn.com*

49 rooms. Complimentary continental breakfast. Wireless Internet access. Indoor pool, whirlpool. $

## RESTAURANT

### ★★HILL TOP INN

*197 Kingsley Drive, Ogallala, 308-284-4534*

Dinner. Closed Monday; holidays. Bar. Children's menu. $$

# OMAHA

The largest city in Nebraska, Omaha is named for the Native Americans who lived here until they signed a treaty with the federal government on June 24, 1854. Opportunists across the Missouri River in Council Bluffs, Iowa, who had been waiting for the new territory to open, rushed to stake out property, triggering a real estate boom. Omaha also saw the trial of Standing Bear, chief of the Ponca Tribe, which established the precedent that Native Americans were entitled to constitutional rights and protections.

During early boom times, steamboats docked in Omaha daily, bringing gold-seekers and emigrants to be outfitted for the long journey west. Local merchants further prospered when Omaha was named the eastern terminus for the Union Pacific. The first rail was laid in 1865. Public buildings rose on the prairie; schools, plants and stockyards flourished in the 1870s and 1880s. Fighting tornadoes, grasshopper plagues, floods and drought, the people built one of the farm belt's great commercial and industrial cities.

Today, Omaha continues to be a major transportation and agribusiness center but is also a recognized leader in telecommunications, insurance and manufacturing as well as the home of five Fortune 500 companies. Omaha is also the headquarters of STRATCOM, the Strategic Air Command, one of the vital links in the national defense chain.

*Information: Greater Omaha Convention and Visitors Bureau,*
*6800 Mercy Road, 402-444-4660, 866-937-6624; www.visitomaha.com*

## WHAT TO SEE AND DO

### AK-SAR-BEN AQUARIUM
*21502 W. Highway 31, Gretna, 402-332-3901*
This modern facility features more than 50 species of fish native to Nebraska, as well as a terrarium, the World Herald Auditorium, a natural history classroom and orientation and display areas.

### DURHAM WESTERN HERITAGE MUSEUM
*Omaha Union Station, 801 S. 10th St., Omaha, 402-444-5071;*
*www.durhammuseum.org*
Restored Art Deco railroad depot is now a history museum. Exhibits on Omaha history from 1880 to 1954; Byron Reed coin collection; traveling temporary exhibits. Tuesday-Sunday; closed holidays.

### GENERAL CROOK HOUSE
*5730 N. 30th St., Omaha, 402-455-9990; www.omahahistory.org*
Built in 1878 to serve as the residence of the commander of the Department of the Platte. Originally called Quarters I, Fort Omaha, the house soon came to be known by the name of its first occupant, General George Crook. Italianate architecture; many antiques from the Victorian era; Victorian garden in summer. Guided tours by appointment. Daily; closed holidays.

★
★
★
★
★

### GERALD FORD BIRTH SITE
*32nd and Woolworth Avenues, Omaha, 402-444-5955; www.nebraskahistory.org*
Model of the original house and White House memorabilia. Betty Ford Memorial Rose Garden. Daily.

## GREAT PLAINS BLACK HISTORY MUSEUM

*2213 Lake St., Omaha, 402-345-2212*

Housed in a building designed in 1907 by prominent Nebraska architect Thomas R. Kimball, the museum preserves the history of African-Americans and their part in the heritage of Omaha and Nebraska since the territorial period of the 1850s. Includes rare photographs, relics, historical displays and films. Monday-Friday.

## HEARTLAND OF AMERICA PARK

*Eighth and Douglas streets, Omaha, 402-444-5920*

This 31-acre site features picnic facilities, arbors and waterfalls. The park's 15-acre lake has a computer-driven fountain that has a colored light show at night. Excursion boat rides on *The General Marion:* Memorial Day-Labor Day, Wednesday-Sunday Gene Leahy Mall, bounded by Douglas and Farnam, 10th and 14th streets N. P. Dodge Memorial Park, John Pershing Drive, Elmwood Park, Dodge and 60th streets. Memorial Park, Dodge and 63rd streets across street from Elmwood Park. World War II Memorial, rose garden, walking and jogging paths.

## HENRY DOORLY ZOO

*3701 S. 10th St., Omaha, 402-733-8401; www.omahazoo.org*

More than 18,500 animals, many rare, are on display in a 110-acre park. Exhibits include an aquarium, indoor rainforest, walk-through aviary, white tigers and polar bears. Daily, closed holidays.

## HISTORIC BELLEVUE

*112 W. Mission Ave., Bellevue, 402-293-3080, 800-467-2779*

Restored buildings include the first church in the Nebraska territory; old depot; settlers' log cabin; and Fontenelle Bank. Sarpy County Historical Museum (2402 SAC Place) has displays concerning the history of the county and changing exhibits Tuesday-Sunday; closed holidays.

## JOSLYN ART MUSEUM

*2200 Dodge St., Omaha, 402-342-3300; www.joslyn.org*

Museum building of Art Deco design with collections of art, ancient to modern, including European and American paintings, sculpture; art of the Western frontier, Native American art; traveling exhibitions. Guided tours, lectures, workshops, films, gallery talks, concerts. A 30,000-volume art reference library; museum shop. Tuesday-Sunday; closed holidays.

## KOUNTZE PLANETARIUM

*66th and Dodge streets, Omaha, 402-554-3722; www.physics.unomaha.edu*

Planetarium shows display galaxies, stars, planets and other celestial phenomena. Observatory, first Friday, Saturday each month.

## MORMON TRAIL CENTER AT WINTER QUARTERS

*3215 State St., Omaha, 402-453-9372; www.lds.org*

The winter of 1846-1847 took the lives of more than 600 Mormon emigrants who camped near here. A monument commemorates their hardship. Films and pioneer exhibits in visitor center.

# OMAHA'S OLD MARKET

One of the few downtown areas that preserves Omaha's original Victorian-era architecture, the Old Market Area is a five-square-block shopping, dining and gallery district that's the heart and soul of the city center. Window-shop, stop for coffee, pop into art-filled boutiques—this neighborhood is made for strolling. Bounded by Farnam and Jones streets and 10th and 13th streets, the Old Market Area was originally the food-processing center for the region: Swanson Food, Anheuser-Busch and other stalwarts of the food and beverage industry once occupied these buildings. Food is still one of the finest reasons to visit the Old Market Area. Find provisions for a picnic at one of Omaha's best bakeries, Delice European Bakery and Coffee Bar (1206 Howard), and pick up cheese and wine at La Buvette Wine and Grocery (511 S. 11th St.). On Wednesdays and Saturdays in summer and fall, stop for fresh local produce at the farmer's market, held on 11th Street between Jackson and Howard.

Directly south of the Old Market Area on 10th Street is the Durham Western Heritage Museum (801 S. 10th St.), housed in the architecturally stunning Union Station, an Art Deco gem from Omaha's past. The museum has vintage cars and railroad equipment, and a period soda fountain is still in operation.

Walk north on 10th Street five blocks to reach Gene Leahy Mall, a 10-acre park with a lake that serves as a reflecting pond for the modern high-rise architecture of Omaha. Trails wind through the park, linking formal flower gardens, a playground for children, a bandstand and public art displays. To the east, the Leahy Mall connects to Heartland of America Park and Fountain, which is bounded by Eighth Street and the Missouri River. The highlight of the park is its lake, with a fountain that shoots streams of water 300 feet into the air. The *General Marion* tour boat navigates the lake to take visitors closer to the fountain. At night, the water display is accompanied by pulsing lights.

Return to the Leahy Mall along Douglas Street, which leads into the modern city center. At 24th Street, turn north one block to the Joslyn Art Museum (2200 Dodge St.), Nebraska's premier center for the visual arts. The museum building is itself a work of art, a fanciful Art Deco structure faced with shimmering pink marble. The permanent collection consists of American and European art from the 19th and 20th centuries. A highlight is the cache of works from Karl Bodmer, a German watercolorist who traveled up the Missouri River in the 1830s, capturing the pristine landscapes, Native Americans and wildlife before white pioneer settlement.

★
★
★
★
★

## OLD MARKET

*11th and Howard streets, extending to 10th St. and west to 13th,*
*Omaha, 402-341-1877*

Art galleries, antique shops, restaurants. Revitalization of old warehouse district; some of Omaha's oldest commercial buildings line the market's brick-paved streets.

### OMAHA CHILDREN'S MUSEUM
*500 S. 20th St., Omaha, 402-342-6163; www.ocm.org*
Self-directed exploration and play for children and families; constantly changing series of hands-on exhibits in science, the arts and humanities, health and creative play. Tuesday-Sunday; closed holidays.

### PLATTE RIVER STATE PARK
*14421 346th St., Louisville, 402-234-2217*
These 413 acres are located on rolling bluffs overlooking the Platte River. Swimming pool; paddleboats. Hiking, horseback riding; tennis courts, archery range, recreational fields. Cross-country skiing.

### TWO RIVERS STATE RECREATION AREA
*27702 F St., Waterloo, 402-359-5165; www.ngpc.state.ne.us*
More than 600 acres with a water area of 320 acres. Swimming; trout fishing, boating. Picnicking, concession. Camping late April-October.

## SPECIAL EVENT
### RIVER CITY ROUND-UP
*Fairgrounds, 302 S. 36th St., Omaha, 402-554-9600; www.rivercityroundup.org*
Celebration of agriculture and Western heritage includes parade, barbecues, trail rides. Late September.

## HOTELS

★★★
★★

### ★★BEST WESTERN REDICK PLAZA HOTEL
*1504 Harney St., Omaha, 402-342-1500, 888-342-5339; www.bestwestern.com*
89 rooms. Complimentary full breakfast. Restaurant, bar. Fitness room. Airport transportation available. $

### ★★DOUBLETREE GUEST SUITES OMAHA
*7270 Cedar St., Omaha, 402-397-5141, 800-222-8733; www.doubletree.com*
187 rooms, all suites. Pets accepted. Restaurant. High-speed Internet access. Fitness room. Indoor pool, whirlpool. Fitness center. Business center. Airport transportation available. $

### ★★DOUBLETREE HOTEL
*1616 Dodge St., Omaha, 402-346-7600, 800-222-8733; www.doubletree.com*
414 rooms. Restaurant, bar. High-speed Internet access. Fitness room. Indoor pool, whirlpool. Airport transportation available. Business center. $

### ★★EMBASSY SUITES
*555 S. 10th St., Omaha, 402-346-9000, 800-362-2779;*
*www.embassysuitesomaha.com*
249 rooms, all suites. Pets accepted, some restrictions; fee. Complimentary continental breakfast. High-speed Internet access. Restaurant, bar. Fitness room. Indoor pool, whirlpool. $$

### ★★GREAT ADVENTURE

*1811 Hillcrest Drive, Bellevue, 402-292-3800, 800-292-7277*

126 rooms. Pets accepted; fee. Complimentary full breakfast. High-speed Internet access. Restaurant, bar. Children's pool, whirlpool. **$**


### ★HAMPTON INN

*9720 W. Dodge Road, Omaha, 402-391-5300; www.hamptoninn.com*

128 rooms. Complimentary continental breakfast. Fitness room. Business center. **$**


### ★★HILTON GARDEN INN

*1005 Dodge St., Omaha, 402-341-4400, 800-445-8667; www.hiltongardeninn.com*

178 rooms. Restaurant. High-speed Internet access. Fitness room. Indoor pool, whirlpool. Business center. **$**


### ★LA QUINTA INN

*3330 N. 104th Ave., Omaha, 402-493-1900; www.laquinta.com*

133 rooms. Pets accepted. High-speed Internet access. Outdoor pool. **$**


### ★★★MARRIOTT OMAHA

*10220 Regency Circle, Omaha, 402-399-9000; www.marriott.com*

This hotel offers two restaurants, a lounge, an indoor and outdoor pool, health club, and many more amenities. It is located near the Joslyn Art Museum, Old Market, golf courses and tennis facilities. 301 rooms. Restaurant, bar. High-speed Internet access. Fitness room. Indoor pool, outdoor pool, whirlpool. **$**

## RESTAURANTS

### ★BOHEMIAN CAFÉ

*106 S. 13th St., Omaha, 402-342-9838; www.bohemiancafe.net*

American, Eastern European menu. Lunch, dinner. Closed holidays. **$$**


### ★★BUSTY LE DOUX'S

*1014 Howard St., Omaha, 402-346-5100*

Cajun menu. Lunch, dinner. Closed holidays. Bar. Outdoor seating. **$$**


### ★★★CAFÉ DE PARIS

*1228 S. Sixth St., Omaha, 402-344-0227*

As the name suggests, this is an exceptional French bistro with a menu that does not stray from the classics. A knowledgeable staff and sommelier add to the experience. French menu. Dinner. Closed Sunday-Monday; holidays. Bar. Jacket required. Reservations recommended. **$$$**


### ★★★FRENCH CAFÉ

*1017 Howard St., Omaha, 402-341-3547; www.frenchcafe.com*

Elegant French dishes, continually refreshed with contemporary ingredients, have earned this restaurant a good reputation. Pepper steak is a signature dish, and the roasted rack of pork is popular. The wine cellar is substantial. American, French menu. Lunch, dinner, Sunday brunch. Closed Monday; holidays. Bar. **$$$**

### ★★★GORAT'S STEAK HOUSE

*4917 Center St., Omaha, 402-551-3733; www.goratssteakhouse.com*

An Omaha landmark for more than 60 years, this steakhouse specializes in classics with thick cuts of filet mignon and more. Enhance the old-school experience with a traditional side dish such as escargot doused in butter or chilled shrimp cocktail. Steak menu. Lunch, dinner. Closed Sunday; holidays. Bar. Children's menu. Reservations recommended. **$$$**

### ★★INDIAN OVEN

*1010 Howard St., Omaha, 402-342-4856*

Northern Indian menu. Lunch, dinner. Closed Sunday; holidays. Bar. Reservations recommended. Outdoor seating. **$$**

### ★JOHNNY'S CAFÉ

*4702 S. 27th St., Omaha, 402-731-4774; www.johnnyscafe.com*

Steak menu. Lunch, dinner. Closed Sunday; holidays. Bar. Children's menu. **$$**

### ★MCFOSTER'S NATURAL KIND CAFÉ

*302 S. 38th St., Omaha, 402-345-7477; www.mcfosters.com*

American, seafood menu with natural-foods emphasis. Lunch, dinner. Closed holidays. Bar. Children's menu. Casual attire. Outdoor seating. **$$**

### ★★★SIGNATURES

*1616 Dodge St., Omaha, 402-346-7600*

Located at the top of the Doubletree Hotel, this restaurant offers a panoramic view of the city's skyline. A continental concept, the menu draws on influences from all over the world. Seafood menu. Breakfast, lunch, dinner, late-night. Bar. **$$**

### ★TRINI'S

*1020 Howard St., Omaha, 402-346-8400*

Mexican, seafood menu. Lunch, dinner. Closed Sunday; holidays. **$**

### ★★★V. MERTZ

*1022 Howard St., Omaha, 402-345-8980; www.vmertz.com*

Located just off the brick-walled Old Market Passageway, this cozy restaurant offers a quiet atmosphere. The menu, consisting of continental dishes, changes weekly; extensive wine list. Jacket and tie are recommended for men. American menu. Lunch, dinner. Bar. **$$**

## SCOTTSBLUFF

Scottsbluff is the trading center for a large area of western Nebraska and eastern Wyoming.

*Information: Scottsbluff-Gering United Chamber of Commerce,*
*1517 Broadway, 308-632-2133, 800-788-9475; www.scottsbluffgering.net*

# WHAT TO SEE AND DO
## AGATE FOSSIL BEDS NATIONAL MONUMENT
*301 River Road, Harrison, 308-668-2211*

An approximately 2,700-acre area with two self-guided nature trails, a visitor center with exhibits of the fossils of animals that roamed the area between 19 and 21 million years ago, and exhibits of Plains Native Americans. Visitor center, daily; closed holidays. Park all year.

## CHIMNEY ROCK NATIONAL HISTORIC SITE
*Highway 26, Bridgeport, 308-586-2581; www.nps.gov/chro*

A landmark of the Oregon Trail, Chimney Rock rises almost 500 feet above the south bank of the North Platte River. Starting as a cone-shaped mound, it becomes a narrow 150-foot column towering above the landscape. For early travelers, many of whom sketched and described it in their journals, Chimney Rock marked the end of the prairies. It became a National Historic Site in 1956.

## RIVERSIDE ZOO
*1600 S. Beltline W., Scottsbluff, 308-630-6236; www.riversidezoo.org*

More than 97 species of both native and exotic animals in a lush park setting. Walk-through aviary, white tiger, moose. Daily, weather permitting.

## SCOTTS BLUFF NATIONAL MONUMENT
*190276 Highway 92 W., Gering, 308-436-9700; www.nps.gov/scbl*

This 800-foot bluff in western Nebraska was a landmark to pioneers who traveled the California/Oregon Trail by wagon trains. Historians often speak of this natural promontory in the North Platte Valley, which was originally named me-a-pa-te, "hill that is hard to go around," by the Plains Native Americans. Many people, including fur traders, Mormons and gold seekers, came this way. Westward-bound pioneers, Pony Express riders and the first transcontinental telegraph all passed through Mitchell Pass (within Monument boundaries) to skirt this pine-studded bluff. The Oregon Trail Museum at the monument's visitor center (daily; closed Christmas) depicts the story of westward migration along the trail. A paved road and hiking trail provide access to the summit for a view of the North Platte Valley and other landmarks such as Chimney Rock.

## WEST NEBRASKA ARTS CENTER
*106 E. 18th St., Scottsbluff, 308-632-2226; www.nebraskarts.com*

Changing gallery shows in all media throughout the year showcasing the finest artists in the region. Daily; closed holidays.

# HOTELS
## ★CANDLELIGHT INN
*1822 E. 20th Place, Scottsbluff, 308-635-3751, 800-424-2305;*
*www.candlelightscottsbluff.com*

56 rooms. Complimentary continental breakfast. Fitness room. Airport transportation available. $

163

NEBRASKA

★
★
★
★
★

### ★COMFORT INN

*1902 21st Ave., Scottsbluff, 308-632-7510, 877-424-6423; www.comfortinn.com*
49 rooms. Pets accepted; fee. Complimentary continental breakfast. High-speed Internet access. Fitness room. Indoor pool, whirlpool. **$**

# SIDNEY

In 1867, Sidney was established as a division point on the Union Pacific Railroad. Fort Sidney was established shortly thereafter, providing military protection for railroad workers and immigrants. Many relics of the Fort Sidney era remain and have been restored. Sidney, the seat of Cheyenne County, is also a peaceful farm, trading and industrial center.

*Information: Cheyenne County Chamber of Commerce,*
*740 Illinois St., 308-254-5851, 800-421-4769; www.sidney-nebraska.com*

## WHAT TO SEE AND DO
### CABELA'S

*115 Cabela Drive, Sidney, 308-254-5505; www.cabelas.com*
Sidney is the corporate headquarters for one of the world's largest outdoor gear outfitters. The 73,000-square-foot building displays more than 60,000 products as well as 500 wildlife mounts. Other attractions in the showroom include an 8,000-gallon aquarium, art gallery, gun library, restaurant and "Royal Challenge," a twice-life-size bronze sculpture of two battling elk. Daily.

### FORT SIDNEY POST COMMANDER'S HOME

*1108 Sixth Ave., Sidney, 308-254-2150*
One of the original buildings of old Fort Sidney, this house was used in the 19th century to protect railroad workers during the Native American wars and has been authentically restored. Memorial Day-Labor Day, daily, afternoons.

## HOTELS
### ★COMFORT INN

*730 E. Jennifer Lane, Sidney, 308-254-5011; www.comfortinn.com*
55 rooms. Complimentary continental breakfast. **$**

### ★DAYS INN

*3042 Silverberg Drive, Sidney, 308-254-2121; www.daysinn.com*
47 rooms. Pets accepted, some restrictions; fee. Complimentary continental breakfast. High-speed Internet access. Indoor pool, whirlpool. **$**

# SOUTH SIOUX CITY

This community is an extension of neighboring Sioux City, Iowa.
*Information: Visitors Bureau, 2700 Dakota Ave.,*
*402-494-1307, 800-793-6327; www.visitsouthsiouxcity.com*

## WHAT TO SEE AND DO
### PONCA STATE PARK

*R.R. 2, Ponca, 402-755-2284; www.ngpc.state.ne.us*

Approximately 1,400 acres. Panoramic views of the Missouri River Valley. Swimming pool, fishing, boating, hiking, horseback riding, cross-country skiing, picnicking, camping.

## HOTEL
### ★★MARINA INN CONFERENCE CENTER

*Fourth and B streets, South Sioux City, 402-494-4000, 800-798-7980;*
*www.marina-inn.com*

181 rooms. Pets accepted; fee. Restaurant, bar. Indoor pool, whirlpool. Airport transportation available. $

# YORK

This town originated as a stop on the Oregon Trail. It's now a thriving agricultural community.

*Information: York County Visitors Center, 116 S. Lincoln Ave.,*
*402-362-5531, 888-733-9675; www.yorkchamber.org*

## WHAT TO SEE AND DO
### ANNA BEMIS PALMER MUSEUM

*211 E. Seventh St., York, 402-363-2630*

Items and displays relating to the history of the city, York County and the state of Nebraska. Monday-Friday; closed holidays.

## HOTELS
### ★AMERICA'S BEST VALUE INN

*2426 S. Lincoln Ave., York, 402-362-5585, 800-452-3185; www.yorkpalmerinn.com*

41 rooms. High-speed Internet access. Outdoor Pool. $

### ★DAYS INN

*3710 S. Lincoln Ave., York, 402-362-6355; www.daysinn.com*

39 rooms. Complimentary continental breakfast. High-speed Internet access. Indoor pool, whirlpool. $

## RESTAURANT
### ★★★CHANCES R

*124 W. Fifth, York, 402-362-7755*

This restaurant, decorated with early 20th-century antiques, specializes in home-cooked classics. Expect to sample dishes such as crispy fried chicken and creamy mashed potatoes. American menu. Breakfast, lunch, dinner, late-night, Sunday brunch. Closed holidays. Bar. Children's menu. Valet parking. $$$

# NORTH DAKOTA

IN BISMARCK THERE IS A STATUARY GROUP, *PIONEER FAMILY*, AND BEHIND IT, GLEAMING white against the sky, towers the famous skyscraper capitol. One symbolizes the North Dakota of wagon trains and General Custer. The other symbolizes modern North Dakota—a place where a thousand oil wells have sprouted, dams harness erratic rivers and vast natural resources have been found.

This is a fascinating land of prairies, rich river valleys, small cities, huge ranches and vast stretches of wheat. Bordering Canada for 320 miles to the north, North Dakota shares straightline borders with Montana to the west and South Dakota to the south. The Red River of the North forms its eastern boundary with Minnesota. The Garrison Dam has changed much of the internal geography of the state's western region, converting the Missouri River, known as "Big Muddy," into a broad waterway with splendid recreation areas bordering the reservoir Lake Sakajawea. To the southwest stretch the Badlands in all their natural grandeur, and the open range about which Theodore Roosevelt wrote so eloquently in his *Ranch Life and the Hunting Trail.*

At various times, Spain, France and England claimed what is now North Dakota as part of their empires. French Canadian fur trappers were the first Europeans to explore the land. After the Louisiana Purchase, explorers Lewis and Clark crossed Dakota, establishing Fort Mandan. The Dakota Territory was organized on March 2, 1861, but major settlement of what later became North Dakota followed after the entry of the Northern Pacific Railroad in the early 1870s.

This is the state in which to trace 19th-century frontier history, to stand at the center of the continent, to see Native American dances and outdoor dramas or to watch the 10 million migratory waterfowl that soar across the sky each spring and fall.

## BISMARCK

On the east bank of the Missouri, near the geographic center of the state and within 150 miles of the geographic center of the continent, North Dakota's capitol flourished as a steamboat port called "the Crossing." As the terminus of the Northern Pacific Railway, Bismarck gained new importance and was named for the Chancellor of Germany to attract German capital for building transcontinental railroads. General Custer came to Bismarck to take command of the nearby newly constructed Fort Abraham Lincoln and in 1876 rode out to his fatal

★ **FUN FACTS**

Theodore Roosevelt National Park is considered one of the darkest spots in North America and the best place in the world to view the Northern Lights.

Entertainer Lawrence Welk was born in Strasburg, North Dakota.

Dakota is a Sioux word that means "ally."

# THE FREE-FLOWING MISSOURI RIVER

There's very little of the free-flowing Missouri River left in North Dakota—only one portion, from Garrison Dam to Bismarck, resembles the broad prairie river as seen by explorers Meriwether Lewis and William Clark. This route explores a section of Missouri River wetlands, allowing modern-day explorers the chance to see the cottonwood forests and wetlands that once stretched along the Missouri, before hydroelectric dams tamed the river.

From Mandan, travel north on Highway 25, which follows the Missouri's western banks. The route passes through farmland and then drops onto a broad, arid basin, with the green, cottonwood-fringed Missouri in the distance. If you don't mind traveling a few miles on gravel roads, turn off Highway 25 east toward the community of Price. Follow the road north along the banks of the river. A number of wildlife refuges string along the river—you may see wild turkeys, deer or bald eagles.

At Hensler, turn west on Highway 200A to visit Fort Clark State Historic Site. Fort Clark was built in 1830 by the American Fur Company as a trading post near a Mandan Indian earthlodge village. A second fort, Primeaus Post, was built on the site in the early 1850s and operated in competition with Fort Clark for most of that decade. Artists Karl Bodmer and George Catlin visited the site, as did German Prince Maximilian, John James Audubon and more than 50 steamboats per year. Many of Bodmer's paintings were of the people and village of Fort Clark.

Continue west along Highway 200A. At Stanton, follow County Highway 37 north to the Knife River Indian Village National Historic Site. One of the largest Hidatsa villages was located at the confluence of the Missouri and the Knife rivers, where this new interpretive center and earthlodge reconstruction are now found. More than 50 earthlodge remains suggest that Native Americans lived in this location for nearly 8,000 years. The circular depressions at the three village sites are up to 40 feet in diameter and are a silent testimony to the people that lived here.

Continue north to join Highway 200 and follow It across the Garrison Dam, the third-largest earth-filled dam in the United States. The dam backs up the Missouri River 175 miles to the west in 378,000-acre Lake Sakajawea. Continue to Highway 83, then head south, zipping past the coal strip mines at Underwood. At Washburn, leave the freeway and follow signs to the Fort Mandan Historic Site, where volunteers have reconstructed Lewis and Clark's log fort. The Lewis and Clark Expedition spent the winter of 1804-1805 here in a cottonwood blockade above the Missouri River. It was here that they met French-Canadian Toussaint Charbonneau, who would serve as their interpreter, and his young Shoshone wife, Sacagawea. This reconstruction of Fort Mandan is downstream from the original site, which has been swallowed by the river. The triangular fort is modest and small, considering that there were 40-odd members of the expedition living here. Also at the park are a visitor center, gift shop and picnic area along the river.

Return to Highway 83 and travel south for seven miles, then exit at Highway 1804 and follow this scenic route south along the free-flowing Missouri's eastern banks to Bismarck. Approximately 162 miles.

★
★
★
★
★

rendezvous with Sitting Bull. In 1883, Bismarck became the capital of the Dakota Territory, and in 1889, the seat of the new state.

*Information: Bismarck-Mandan Convention and Visitors Bureau, 1600 Burnt Boat Drive, 701-222-4308, 800-767-3555; www.bismarckmandancvb.com*

## WHAT TO SEE AND DO
### NORTH DAKOTA STATE CAPITOL
*600 E. Boulevard Ave., Bismarck, 701-328-2480; www.nd.gov/fac/index.html*

Constructed in 1933 on a $2 million budget after the original building burned in 1930, this state capitol building stands out from its traditionally domed peers. The 19-story Art Deco limestone tower is one of only four vertically oriented capitols in the United States (along with those in Nebraska, Louisiana and Florida). Beyond its distinctive exterior, the Skyscraper of the Prairies is capped with an observation deck, features lavish interiors fashioned from wood, stone and metal from all over the globe and has a cavernous Great Hall running to the legislative quarters. Tours are available on weekdays in the summer. Also on the grounds are the former Governors' Mansion, now restored and featuring historic displays, and the North Dakota Heritage Center, a regional history museum with an impressive collection of Plains Indian artifacts. Outdoors are two notable sculptures, one of Lewis and Clark guide Sacagawea, and another dubbed *The Pioneer Family* by Avard Fairbanks.

### WARD EARTHLODGE VILLAGE HISTORIC SITE
*4480 Fort Lincoln Road, Bismarck, 701-222-6455*

Mandan Indians once occupied this bluff above the Missouri River, living in dome-shaped homes built of logs and earth. By the time Lewis and Clark passed through the region, the village was deserted. Depressions remain where the houses once stood, and the site is now part of the city park system. Interpretive signs explain how the village was constructed and elements of Mandan cultural life. Spectacular views from the bluff. Daily dawn-dusk.

## SPECIAL EVENT
### UNITED TRIBES POWWOW
*3315 University Drive, Bismarck, 701-255-3285; www.unitedtribespowwow.com*

Among the most attended powwows in the United States, this annual event is one of the top cultural happenings in North Dakota. Some 1,500 Native American dancers and drummers, representing more than 70 tribes and clothed in traditional garb, perform at the Lone Star Arena at United Tribes Technical College. You'll find singing, dancing and drumming competitions, as well as a softball tournament, a parade, an intertribal summit, a pageant and plenty of food. Early September.

## HOTELS
### ★★BEST WESTERN RAMKOTA HOTEL
*800 S. Third St., Bismarck, 701-258-7700, 800-780-7234; www.bestwestern.com*

306 rooms. Pets accepted, some restrictions; fees. High-speed Internet access. Restaurant, bar. Fitness room. Indoor pool, children's pool, whirlpool. Airport transportation available. $

### ★EXPRESSWAY INN

*200 E. Bismarck Expressway, Bismarck, 701-222-2900, 800-456-6388;*
*www.expresswayinnandsuites.com*
163 rooms. Pets accepted; fee. Complimentary continental breakfast. Wireless Internet access. Fitness room. Outdoor pool, whirlpool. Airport transportation available. **$**

### ★FAIRFIELD INN

*135 Ivy Ave., Bismarck, 701-223-9293, 800-228-2800; www.fairfieldinn.com*
63 rooms. Complimentary continental breakfast. Wireless Internet access. Indoor pool, whirlpool. **$**

### ★★KELLY INN-BISMARCK

*1800 N. 12th St., Bismarck, 701-223-8001, 800-635-3559; www.kellyinns.com*
101 rooms. Pets accepted, some restrictions. High-speed Internet access. Restaurant, bar. Fitness room. Indoor pool, whirlpool. Airport transportation available. **$**

### ★★RADISSON HOTEL BISMARCK

*Sixth Street and Broadway Avenue, Bismarck, 701-255-6000, 800-333-3333;*
*www.radisson.com/bismarcknd_downtown*
215 rooms. Pets accepted. High-speed Internet access. Restaurant, bar. Fitness room. Indoor pool, whirlpool. Airport transportation available. Business center. **$**

### ★RAMADA LIMITED SUITES

*3808 E. Divide Ave., Bismarck, 701-221-3030, 800-295-3895; www.ramada.com*
66 rooms. Pets accepted; fee. Complimentary continental breakfast. Wireless Internet access. Fitness room. Indoor pool, whirlpool. **$**

## RESTAURANTS
### ★MERIWETHER'S

*1700 River Road, Bismarck, 701-258-0666*
American menu. Lunch, dinner, Sunday brunch. Bar. Children's menu. Casual attire. Outdoor seating. **$$**

### ★★PEACOCK ALLEY

*422 E. Main St., Bismarck, 701-255-7917; www.peacock-alley.com*
American, seafood menu. Lunch, dinner, brunch. Bar. Children's menu. Casual attire. **$$**

# DEVILS LAKE

Located near the shore of Devils Lake, this city offers some of the best fishing in North Dakota. The opening of the federal land office here in 1883 sparked the growth of the city.

*Information: Devils Lake Area Chamber of Commerce, Highway 2 E.,*
*701-662-4903, 800-233-8048; www.devilslakend.com*

**169**

**NORTH DAKOTA**

★
★
★
★
★

## WHAT TO SEE AND DO

### DEVILS LAKE

*Devils Lake, six miles south of town Highway 2 E., 701-662-4903, 800-233-8048;*
*www.devilslakend.com*

This lake gets its name from the Indian name Miniwaukan, which means "bad water." Bolstered by legends of drowned warriors, the name evolved into Devils Lake. Fishing, boating; hunting, golfing, biking, snowmobiling, picnicking, camping.

### FORT TOTTEN STATE HISTORIC SITE

*Highway 20, Devils Lake, 701-766-4441*

Built in 1867 to protect the overland route to Montana, this was the last outpost before 300 miles of wilderness. One of the best-preserved military forts west of the Mississippi; 16 original buildings. Pioneer Daughters Museum; interpretive center, commissary display; videotape program of the site's history. Summer dinner theater. Self-guided tours. Memorial Day-Labor Day, daily; rest of year by appointment.

## HOTELS

### ★FIRESIDE INN

*215 Highway 2 E., Devils Lake, 701-662-6760, 888-266-3948; www.comfortinn.com*

87 rooms. Pets accepted; fee. Complimentary continental breakfast. High-speed Internet access. Indoor pool, whirlpool. Business center. **$**

### ★★TOTTEN TRAIL HISTORIC INN

*Fort Totten State Historic Site, 701-766-4874; www.tottentrailinn.com*

10 rooms. Closed October-April. Complimentary full breakfast. **$**

# FARGO

Fargo, the largest city in North Dakota, was named for William G. Fargo of the Wells-Fargo Express Company. It's the hometown of baseball great Roger Maris, and a museum filled with his personal memorabilia is located in West Acres Mall.

With blackjack legal in North Dakota, Fargo has taken the lead in promoting its gaming tables. There are approximately 30 casinos in the city, making it a major tourist attraction for the three-state region including Minnesota and South Dakota. Charities and nonprofit organizations run the casinos and collect all profits above expenses. The 1996 dark comedy *Fargo* took its name from the city, gently poking fun at the residents' thick northern accents and Scandinavian heritage, but most of the movie actually takes place in Minnesota.

*Information: Fargo-Moorhead Convention and Visitors Bureau,*
*2001 44th St. Southwest, 701-282-3653, 800-235-7654; www.fargomoorhead.org*

## HOTELS

### ★AMERICINN

*1423 35th St. Southwest, Fargo, 701-234-9946, 800-634-3444;*
*www.americinnfargo.com*

61 rooms. Pets accepted; fees. Complimentary continental breakfast. Wireless Internet access. Fitness room. Indoor pool, whirlpool. Business center. **$**

## ★★BEST WESTERN FARGO DOUBLEWOOD INN

*3333 13th Ave. South, Fargo, 701-235-3333, 800-433-3235; www.bestwestern.com*

172 rooms. Pets accepted, some restrictions; fee. Restaurant, bar. Wireless Internet access. Indoor pool, whirlpool. Airport transportation available. Business center. Casino. **$**

## ★★BEST WESTERN KELLY INN

*1767 S. 44th St., 701-282-2143, 800-580-1234; www.bestwestern.com*

83 rooms. Complimentary continental breakfast. Internet. Restaurant, bar. Fitness room. Indoor pool, outdoor pool, children's pool, whirlpool. Business center. Casino. **$**

## ★COMFORT SUITES

*1415 35th St. South, Fargo, 701-237-5911, 800-228-5150; www.choicehotels.com*

66 rooms, all suites. Pets accepted. Complimentary continental breakfast. Wireless Internet access. Indoor pool, whirlpool. Business center. **$**

## ★COUNTRY INN & SUITES BY CARLSON

*3316 13th Ave., Fargo, 701-234-0565, 888-201-1746; www.countryinns.com*

99 rooms. Pets accepted, some restrictions; fee. Complimentary continental breakfast. Wireless Internet access. Fitness room. Indoor pool, whirlpool. Airport transportation available. Business center. **$**

## ★FAIRFIELD INN

*3902 Ninth Ave. Southwest, Fargo, 701-281-0494, 800-228-2800; www.fairfieldinn.com*

63 rooms. Complimentary continental breakfast. Wireless Internet access. Indoor pool, whirlpool. **$**

## ★HAMPTON INN

*3431 14th Ave. Southwest, Fargo, 701-235-5566, 800-426-7866; www.hamptoninn.com*

75 rooms. Complimentary continental breakfast. High-speed Internet access. Indoor pool, whirlpool. Business center. **$**

## ★★HOLIDAY INN

*3803 13th Ave. South, Fargo, 701-282-2700, 877-282-2700; www.holiday-inn.com*

315 rooms. Pets accepted, some restrictions. Two restaurants, bar. Fitness room. Indoor pool, children's pool, whirlpool. Airport transportation available. Business center. **$**

## ★HOLIDAY INN EXPRESS

*1040 40th St. South, Fargo, 701-282-2000, 800-465-4329; www.hiexpress.com*

77 rooms. Pets accepeted; fee. Complimentary continental breakfast. Internet access. Indoor pool, whirlpool. Airport transportation available. **$**

## ★KELLY INN-FARGO

*4207 13th Ave. Southwest, Fargo, 701-277-8821, 800-635-3559; www.kellyinnfargo.com*

59 rooms. Pets accepted, some restrictions. Complimentary continental breakfast. Wireless Internet access. Indoor pool, whirlpool. Business center. **$**

**171**

**NORTH DAKOTA**

★
★
★
★
★

### ★★RADISSON HOTEL FARGO

*201 Fifth St. N., Fargo, 701-232-7363, 800-333-3333; www.radisson.com/fargond*

151 rooms. Pets accepted, some restrictions; fee. Restaurant, bar. Internet access. Fitness room. Indoor pool, whirlpool. Airport transportation available. Business center. **$**

### ★SLEEP INN

*1921 44th St. S.W., Fargo, 701-281-8240, 800-424-6423;*
*www.sleepinnfargo.com*

61 rooms. Pets accepted, some restrictions. Complimentary continental breakfast. Wireless Internet access. Fitness room. Indoor pool, children's pool, whirlpool. Airport transportation available. Business center. **$**

## RESTAURANT
### ★★MEXICAN VILLAGE

*814 Main Ave., Fargo, 701-293-0120; www.mexicanvillagefm.com*

Mexican menu. Lunch, dinner. Closed holidays. Children's menu. Casual attire. **$**

# GRAND FORKS

Grand Forks stands at the point where the Red River of the North and Red Lake River form a fork. Socially, culturally and commercially the town is closely allied with its cousin city across the river, East Grand Forks, Minnesota. Originally a French fur trading post, Grand Forks later developed as a frontier river town. The arrival of the railroad and cultivation of nearby farmland brought about another change in its personality. The University of North Dakota plays a dominant role in the city's culture and economy. Grand Forks Air Force Base is 14 miles west on Highway 2.

*Information: Convention and Visitors Bureau, 4251 Gateway Drive,*
*701-746-0444, 800-866-4566; www.grandforkscvb.org*

## WHAT TO SEE AND DO
### GRAND FORKS COUNTY HISTORICAL SOCIETY

*2405 Belmont Road, Grand Forks, 701-775-2216; www.grandforkshistory.com*

This historical society maintains the Campbell House, the historic pioneer cabin of agricultural innovator Tom Campbell. Original log cabin portion dates from 1879. Also on the grounds are a log post office, one-room schoolhouse and Myra Carriage Museum, which houses a collection of late 19th- and early 20th-century artifacts from surrounding area. May-October, daily 1-5 p.m.

### TURTLE RIVER STATE PARK

*3084 Park Ave., Arvilla, 701-594-4445, 800-807-4723; www.parkrec.nd.gov*

Located in a green valley carved out by the gently winding Turtle River, this 784-acre park is a big recreational draw in the Grand Forks area. Because the river is stocked with rainbow trout, angling is a popular pursuit, and there are hiking and biking trails, as well as cross-country ski routes and a sledding hill. For overnighters, a dozen duplex rental cabins, with running water but without kitchens, and 125 campsites are available.

★
★ ★
★ ★
★
★

## UNIVERSITY OF NORTH DAKOTA

*Grand Forks, west end of University Avenue,*
*701-777-3304, 800-225-5863; www.und.edu*

The *Eternal Flame of Knowledge,* an immense steel-girded sphere, commemorates Old Main and past presidents. North Dakota Museum of Art; Chester Fritz Library houses artwork. Tours.

## HOTELS

### ★★BEST WESTERN TOWN HOUSE

*710 First Ave., North, Grand Forks, 701-746-5411, 800-867-9797;*
*www.bestwestern.com*

101 rooms. Pets accepted, some restrictions; fee. Restaurant, bar. Wireless Internet access. Indoor pool, whirlpool. Airport transportation available. Casino. **$**

### ★C'MON INN

*3051 32nd Ave., Grand Forks, 701-775-3320, 800-255-2323; www.cmoninn.com*
80 rooms. Complimentary continental breakfast. Internet access. Fitness room. Indoor pool, whirlpool. **$**

### ★COMFORT INN

*3251 30th Ave. South, Grand Forks, 701-775-7503, 800-424-6423;*
*www.comfortinn.com*

65 rooms. Pets accepted, some restrictions; fee. Complimentary continental breakfast. Wireless Internet access. Indoor pool, whirlpool. **$**

### ★FAIRFIELD INN

*3051 S. 34th St., Grand Forks, 701-775-7910, 800-228-2800;*
*www.fairfieldinn.com*

62 rooms. Complimentary continental breakfast. Internet access. Indoor pool, whirlpool. **$**

### ★★HOLIDAY INN

*1210 N. 43rd St., Grand Forks, 701-772-7131, 800-465-4329; www.holidayinn.com*
148 rooms. Wireless Internet access. Restaurant, bar. Fitness room. Indoor pool, children's pool, whirlpool. Airport transportation available. Casino. **$**

### ★LAKEVIEW INNS AND SUITES GRAND FORKS

*3350 S. 32nd Ave., Grand Forks, 701-775-5000, 877-355-3500;*
*www.lakeviewhotels.com*

86 rooms. Complimentary continental breakfast. Wireless Internet access. Indoor pool, whirlpool. **$**

### ★★RAMADA INN

*1205 N. 43rd St., Grand Forks, 701-775-3951, 888-298-2054; www.ramada.com*
100 rooms. Pets accepted, some restrictions. Restaurant, bar. Wireless Internet access. Fitness room. Indoor pool, children's pool, whirlpool. Airport transportation available. Business center. Casino. **$**

173

NORTH DAKOTA

★
★
★
★
★

# JAMESTOWN

Settlers and businessmen arrived after soldiers and railroad workers established Jamestown as a transportation center guarded by Fort Seward. When farmers discovered they could pay for their rich land with two years' worth of crops, the area developed as a prosperous agricultural town. The James River, the longest unnavigable river in the world, flows through the area. On the northeastern edge of town is Jamestown College, founded in 1883.

*Information: Jamestown Promotion and Tourism Center, 212 Third Ave. N.E., 701-252-4835, 800-222-4766; www.jamestownnd.com*

## WHAT TO SEE AND DO

### FRONTIER VILLAGE

*500 17th St., Southeast Jamestown, 701-252-8648 or 1-800-807-1511; www.buffalomuseum.com*

The big lure here is the "Worlds Largest Buffalo," a 60-ton concrete sculpture jutting out of the plains. The adjacent village is also a good place to get a glimpse of North Dakota's pioneer past. About a dozen historic structures were relocated here to spare them from the wrecking ball, including a one-room schoolhouse, a barbershop and a train depot. May-September, daily. Also onsite are the National Buffalo Museum, the home of White Cloud, an albino buffalo.

### WHITESTONE HILL BATTLEFIELD STATE HISTORIC SITE

*Kulm, 701-396-7731*

Probably triggered by the 1862 Sioux uprising in Minnesota, the September 1863 Battle of Whitestone Hill marked the beginning of a war between the U.S. Cavalry and the Plains Sioux that lasted for more than 20 years. Granite monument of bugler, graves of soldiers; small museum. Mid-May-mid-September, Thursday-Monday.

## HOTELS

### ★COMFORT INN

*811 S.W. 20th St., Jamestown, 701-252-7125; www.comfortinn.com*

52 rooms. Pets accepted. Complimentary continental breakfast. Wireless Internet access. Indoor pool, whirlpool. $

### ★★GLADSTONE INN AND SUITE

*111 Second St. Northeast, Jamestown, 701-252-0700, 866-748-4466; www.gladstoneinn.com*

100 rooms. Pets accepted; fee. Restaurant, bar. Fitness room. Indoor pool, whirlpool. $

### ★★QUALITY INN

*Highway 281 S., Jamestown, 701-252-3611, 800-726-7924*

120 rooms. Pets accepted; fee. Restaurant, bar. Indoor pool, whirlpool. $

# MANDAN

The Mandan tribe originally farmed this area, and today the agricultural tradition persists in the dairy and dry farms that surround the city. Lignite, a soft coal, is mined in this region. Mandan has been an important railroad city since tracks crossed the Missouri River the year the city was founded.

*Information: Bismarck-Mandan Convention and Visitors Bureau, 1600 Burnt Boat Drive, Bismarck, 701-222-4308, 800-767-3555; www.bismarckmandancvb.com*

## WHAT TO SEE AND DO
### CROSS RANCH NATURE PRESERVE
*The Nature Conservancy, 1401 River Road, Center, 701-794-8741*
This 6,000-acre nature preserve has mixed grass prairies, Missouri River floodplain forest and upland woody draws. Bison herd. Hiking and self-guided nature trails. Daily.

### FORT ABRAHAM LINCOLN STATE PARK
*4480 Fort Lincoln Road, Mandan, 701-667-6340; www.ndparks.com*
Historic site marks the fort which Custer commanded prior to his "last stand." Reconstructed fort buildings (tours, Memorial Day-Labor Day), and Mandan earthlodge

## THE LITTLE MISSOURI BADLANDS

Medora sits at the base of the dramatic Little Missouri Badlands, a deeply eroded gorge that exposes millions of years of sedimentary deposits in colorful horizontal striations. Medora itself is a fascinating historical town—Teddy Roosevelt lived near here in the 1880s, as did the flamboyant Marquis de Mores, a French nobleman who journeyed to the Dakota Territory to live out his cowboy fantasies. Before setting out to explore bluffs that rise behind the town, be sure to visit the Chateau de More, the luxurious frontier home built by the Marquis. When it was constructed in 1883, this 26-room mansion was the finest and most modern private home for hundreds of miles.

The Maah Daah Hey Trail is 100 miles long and connects the northern and southern sections of the Theodore Roosevelt National Park, passing through the Little Missouri National Grassland. The following hike covers four miles at the trail's southern extreme and explores the scenic badlands above Medora, passing through the fascinating and ruggedly beautiful badlands ecosystem. The area is home to prairie wildlife including pronghorn antelope, coyotes, white-tail deer, prairie dogs and rattlesnakes.

Begin at Sully Creek State Park, two miles south of Medora (the Maah Daah Hey Trail is also popular with mountain bikers, so you'll share the trail). The trail crosses the Little Missouri River, which is ankle-deep and easily waded in summer, and follows the river valley through stands of cottonwood, willow and silver sage. The path then begins to climb up the face of a badland mesa, eventually reaching a plateau. From a rocky escarpment, enjoy a magnificent overlook onto Medora and the Little Missouri River breaks. Continue north on the trail through prairie grassland to a side path, the Canyon Trail, which drops steeply down a rugged canyon wall to a prairie dog town. Follow the trail north, through a self-closing gate, to where the Canyon Trail rejoins the Maah Daah Hey. From here, hikers can return to Medora along a gravel road or continue north through more badlands landscape to the South Unit of the Theodore Roosevelt National Park headquarters.

175

★
★★
★★
★

village. Fishing, hiking, cross-country skiing, snowmobiling, picnicking, playground, concession, camping. Visitor center, amphitheater, museum, summer interpretive program.

## HOTEL

### ★★BEST WESTERN SEVEN SEAS INN & CONFERENCE CENTER

*2611 Old Red Trail, Mandan, 701-663-7401, 800-597-7327;*
*www.bestwestern.com*

122 rooms. Pets accepted. Restaurant, bar. Internet access. Indoor pool, whirlpool. Business center. $

# MEDORA

This village is a living museum of two of the most colorful characters of the badlands frontier—young, bespectacled Theodore Roosevelt and the hot-blooded, visionary Marquis de Mores. The Marquis, a wealthy Frenchman, established the town and named it for his wife, daughter of a New York banker. He built a packing plant

NORTH DAKOTA

★
★★
★★
★★
★

## THEODORE ROOSEVELT NATIONAL PARK

This national park is a monument to 26th president Theodore Roosevelt, who was the nation's champion of the conservation of natural resources. Roosevelt, who came to the badlands in September 1883 to hunt buffalo and other big game, became interested in the open-range cattle industry and purchased an interest in the Maltese Cross Ranch near Medora. He returned the next year and established another ranch, the Elkhorn, about 35 miles north of Medora. The demands of his political career and failures at raising cattle eventually forced him to abandon his ranching ventures.

This park preserves the magnificent badlands landscape as Roosevelt knew it. Wind and water have carved curiously sculptured formations, tablelands, buttes, canyons and rugged hills from a thick series of flat-lying sedimentary rocks. Thick, dark layers of lignite coal, which are sometimes fired by lightning and burn slowly for many years, are exposed in eroded hillsides. The fires often bake adjacent clay layers into a red, brick-like substance called scoria or clinker.

Elk and bison have been reintroduced and thrive here and can be easily seen throughout the park. There are several large prairie dog towns, and mule and whitetail deer are abundant. Wild horses can be seen in the South Unit, and the area is populated with hawks, falcons, eagles and other more common species.

The park is divided into three units. The South Unit is accessible from Interstate 94 (I-94) at Medora, where there is a visitor center (daily) and Roosevelt's Maltese Cross cabin. The Elkhorn Ranch Site on the Little Missouri River can be reached only by rough dirt roads, and visitors should check in with rangers at the Medora Visitor Center before venturing out (701-623-4466). The North Unit is accessible from US 85, near Watford City and has a visitor center. An additional visitor center is located at Painted Canyon Scenic Overlook on I-94 (April-October: daily). The park is open all year; visitor centers are closed on holidays.

Information: Park headquarters, 701-623-4466; www.nps.gov/thro

and icehouses, aiming to slaughter cattle on the range and ship them to metropolitan markets in refrigerated railroad cars. The plan fizzled, but not before the mustachioed Frenchman left his stamp on the community. Roosevelt came here in 1883 and won respect as part owner of the Maltese Cross and Elkhorn ranches and as organizer and first president of the Little Missouri Stockmen's Association.

*Information: Chamber of Commerce, 701-623-4910; www.medorand.com*

## WHAT TO SEE AND DO
### CHATEAU DE MORES STATE HISTORIC SITE
*612 E. Boulevard Ave., Bismarck, 701-623-4355*

This site commemorates the life of Antoine de Vallombrosa, the Marquis de Mores. The Marquis dabbled with a stagecoach line, an experiment with refrigerated railroad cars, and a beef packing plant. Remaining are the ruins of a packing plant, a 26-room, two-story frame mansion filled with French furnishings, a library, servants' quarters and relic room displaying the Marquis's saddles, guns, boots, coats and other possessions. An interpretive center is on the grounds. The site is not heated. Station-guided tours mid-May-mid-September, daily; rest of year by appointment.

## HOTEL
### ★AMERICINN MEDORA
*75 E. River Road South, Medora, 701-623-4800; www.americinn.com*

62 rooms. Pets accepted, some restrictions; fee. Complimentary continental breakfast. Indoor pool, whirlpool. $

# MINOT

Minot's advance from tepee and tarpaper to a supersonic-age city has been so vigorous that it calls itself the "Magic City." Where buffalo bones were once stacked by plainscombers stands a city rich from agriculture, lignite coal reserves, oil pools, industry and railroad yards on both sides of the Mouse River. Minot is the commercial center of a radius that sweeps into Canada. Minot State University is located here.

*Information: Convention and Visitors Bureau, 1020 S. Broadway,*
*701-857-8206, 800-264-2626; www.visitminot.org*

## WHAT TO SEE AND DO
### ROOSEVELT PARK AND ZOO
*1219 Burdick Expressway E., Minot, 701-857-4166; www.rpzoo.com*

Roosevelt Park and Zoo includes 90 acres of formal lawns and sunken gardens. On the grounds are a swimming pool, water slide and bathhouse. Lifeguards on duty. Late May-early September, daily.

### SCANDINAVIAN HERITAGE CENTER
*Broadway and 11th Ave., Minot, 701-852-9161; www.minotparkdistrict.org/scand.shtml*

A 230-year-old house from Sigdal, Norway; Danish windmill; flag display; statues of famous Scandinavians. Daily; Memorial Day-Labor Day, weekends.

**NORTH DAKOTA**

★
★
★
★
★

## HOTELS

### ★BEST WESTERN KELLY INN

*1510 26th Ave. S.W., Minot, 701-852-4300, 800-735-5868;*
*www.bestwesternminot.com*
100 rooms. Pets accepted, some restrictions. Complimentary continental breakfast.
High-speed Internet access. Bar. Indoor pool, whirlpool. **$**

### ★COMFORT INN

*1515 22nd Ave. S.W., Minot, 701-852-2201, 800-228-5150; www.comfortinn.com*
140 rooms. Pets accepted, some restrictions. Complimentary continental breakfast.
Indoor pool, whirlpool. **$**

### ★★HOLIDAY INN

*2200 Burdick Expressway E., Minot, 701-852-2504, 800-465-4329;*
*www.holiday-inn.com*
170 rooms. Pets accepted, some restrictions. Two restaurants, two bars. High-speed
Internet access. Fitness room. Indoor pool, whirlpool.

# VALLEY CITY

The railroad and the first settlers arrived here simultaneously to establish a community then known as Worthington. Later, as the seat of Barnes County, this town in the
deeply forested Sheyenne River Valley changed to its present name. The grain fields
and dairy farms of the surrounding area are the town's main industry.
*Information: Valley City Area Chamber of Commerce, 205 N.E. Second St.,*
*701-845-1892; www.hellovalley.com*

## WHAT TO SEE AND DO

### FORT RANSOM STATE PARK

*5981 Walt Hjelle Parkway, Fort Ransom, 701-973-4331, 800-807-4723;*
*www.ndparks.com*
This former frontier Army post has a historic farm that re-creates the life of early
homesteaders. The Sodbuster Days festival is held during the second weekends in
July and September. An arts and crafts festival is held during last weekend in
September. Downhill ski resort. Camping, picnic areas, hiking, cross-country skiing
and snowmobiling.

## HOTEL

### ★WAGON WHEELS INN

*455 Winter Show Road, Valley City, 701-845-5333; www.wagonwheelinn.com*
88 rooms. Indoor pool, whirlpool. **$**

## RESTAURANT

### ★DUTTON'S PARLOUR

*256 Central Ave. N., Valley City, 701-845-3390; www.valleygallery.com*
American menu. Breakfast, lunch. **$**

# WILLISTON

This city, which was first called Little Muddy, began as a small supply center for ranchers. As the area grew, farming and petroleum, discovered here in the early 1950s, had an impact on the local economy.

*Information: Convention & Visitors Bureau, 10 Main St., 701-774-9041, 800-615-9041; www.willistonndtourism.com*

## WHAT TO SEE AND DO

### FORT BUFORD STATE HISTORIC SITE
*15349 39th Lane N.W., Williston, 701-572-9034; www.nd.gov/hist/Buford/Buford.htm*

Established in 1866 near the merging point of the Missouri and Yellowstone rivers, Fort Buford served as the distribution point for government annuities to peaceful natives in the vicinity. During the war with the Sioux in the 1870s and 1880s, the post became a major supply depot for military field operations. The fort was the site of the surrender of Sitting Bull in 1881. Original features include a stone powder magazine, the post cemetery and a museum. Mid-May-mid-September, daily; rest of year by appointment.

### FORT UNION TRADING POST NATIONAL HISTORIC SITE
*15550 Highway 1804, Williston, 701-572-9083; www.nps.gov/fous*

The American Fur Company built this fort in 1829 at the junction of the Yellowstone and Missouri Rivers. During the next three decades, it was one of the most important trading depots on the Western frontier. In 1867, the government bought the fort, dismantled it and used the materials to build Fort Buford two miles away. Much of the fort has been reconstructed. A National Park Service visitor center is located in the Bourgeois House. Guided tours and interpretive programs are available in summer. Daily.

### LEWIS AND CLARK STATE PARK
*4904 119th Road N.W., Williston, 701-859-3071; www.ndparks.com-parks-lcsp.htm*

Situated on a northern bay in Lake Sakakawea—a man-made body of water created by damming the Missouri River—this state park is so named because the Lewis and Clark expedition camped nearby twice, on their 1805 westward journey in search of the fabled Northwest Passage and on the return trip east the next year. Today, the park is popular because of its marina, a jumping-off point for boaters and anglers. Of the fish lurking below, the most remarkable are immense paddlefish, prehistoric-looking beasts once thought to be extinct, and endangered pallid sturgeon, which grow up to six feet in length. A good trail system allows for hiking and cross-country skiing.

### LEWIS AND CLARK TRAIL MUSEUM
*Highway 85, Alexander, 701-828-3595*

Located on the first leg of the Corps of Discovery's westward route (south of Williston and the Missouri River in Alexander), this museum covers not only Lewis and Clark but also early homesteaders in North Dakota. The most notable exhibit is a scale model of Fort Mandan, where the party stayed during the winter of 1804-1805. Memorial Day-Labor Day, daily.

★
★
★
★
★

# OKLAHOMA

**PROBABLY EVERY STATE IS MISUNDERSTOOD IN ITS OWN WAY. BUT MAYBE OKLAHOMA HAS** a special claim. Is it the vast dusty terrain from which impoverished farmers fled during the Great Depression? Is it the good-ol'-boy land of "Okie from Muskogee" that Merle Haggard celebrated in song, or the romantic land of the stylized cowboy culture as sung about in the musical *Oklahoma!*? Is it Southern—bordered, as it is, by Arkansas on the east? Is it a northern annex of Texas? (The twang of the Lone Star state is certainly audible here.) Or does it belong to the West, with its neatly rectangular panhandle touching New Mexico and Colorado?

The area that was to become the state of Oklahoma was practically unknown to Americans at the time of the Louisiana Purchase of 1803. Believing those unsettled lands to be of little value, the government set them aside as "Indian Territory" in 1830, assigning a portion to each of the Five Civilized Tribes. Thousands of Creeks, Choctaws, Chickasaws, Seminoles and Cherokees were forced to leave the Southeastern U.S. and move to Oklahoma. About one-fourth of those forced west over this "Trail of Tears" died on the way of hunger, disease, cold and exhaustion. Today Oklahoma has the largest Native American population in the United States.

As the nation moved west, settlers squatted in the Indian Territory, wanting the land for development. On April 22, 1889, portions of the land were opened for settlement. In the next few years all unassigned Oklahoma land was opened by a series of six "runs." People who jumped the gun were called "Sooners," giving the state its nickname, the "Sooner State." Close to 17-million acres of land were settled in this way; the last lottery, a form of run, took place on August 16, 1901. Previously unsettled tracts became cities within eight hours.

Oklahoma produces millions of barrels of oil a year, and you might see churning derricks almost anywhere, including beside runways of the Oklahoma City airport. The state has vast expanses of lightly settled country—forests and green fields in the eastern part, ranchland and prairie in the drier west. Some people would be surprised to learn that Oklahoma has mountains, but in the southeastern corner of the state (Kiamichi County), there are seven ranges. Northeast Oklahoma has both rolling hills and flat prairies, along with several large lakes and plenty of state parks. The southwestern part of the state is true Great Plains and Chisholm Trail territory and has several major museums that explore the region's heritage and history, which started with the Kiowa, Comanche, Apache, the original inhabitants and then saw the impact of settlers and clashes between newcomers and natives. *www.ok.gov.*

**FUN FACTS**

More Native American tribes are headquartered in Oklahoma than in any other state.

The shopping cart was invented in Ardmore, Oklahoma.

Cimarron County is bordered by Oklahoma, Texas, New Mexico, Colorado and Kansas—more than any other county in the United States.

The word Oklahoma is a combination of two Choctaw words meaning "red man."

# ALTUS

In the spring of 1891, a flood on Bitter Creek forced a group of settlers to flee to higher ground, taking with them what possessions they could. Gathered together to escape destruction, they founded a town and called it Altus because one of them said the word meant "high ground." On the border between the high plains and the southland, Altus lies between winter wheat on the north and cotton on the south. Nearby Altus Air Force Base is the home of the 97th Air Mobility Wing.

*Information: Chamber of Commerce, 123 Commerce St., 580-482-0210; www.cityofaltus.org*

## WHAT TO SEE AND DO

### MUSEUM OF THE WESTERN PRAIRIE

*1100 Memorial Drive, Altus, 580-482-1044; www.okhistory.org/museums/westernprairie.html*

Exhibits depict all aspects of pioneer living in Southwestern Oklahoma. Tuesday-Saturday.

## SPECIAL EVENT

### GREAT PLAINS STAMPEDE RODEO

*Altus, Oklahoma, 580-482-0210; www.greatplainsstampederodeo.com*

A Professional Rodeo Cowboys Association-sanctioned rodeo; special events. Late August.

## HOTELS

### ★BEST WESTERN ALTUS

*2804 N. Main St., Altus, 580-482-9300, 888-537-1087; www.bestwestern.com*

100 rooms. Pets accepted, some restrictions; fee. Complimentary continental breakfast. High-speed Internet access. Fitness room. Indoor pool, outdoor pool. Business center. $

### ★★RAMADA INN

*2515 E. Broadway St., Altus, 580-477-3000; www.motel6.com*

20 rooms. Pets accepted; fee. Restaurant, bar. Indoor pool. $

# ALVA

Founded in 1893 as a land office for the largest land run in Oklahoma following the opening of the Cherokee strip, this small northwestern town is home to Northwestern Oklahoma State University.

*Information: Chamber of Commerce, 410 College Ave., 580-327-1647, 888-854-2262; www.alvaok.net*

## WHAT TO SEE AND DO

### ALABASTER CAVERNS

*Highway 50A, Freedom, 580-621-3381; www.wildlifedepartment.com*

On approximately 200 acres, Alabaster is said to be the largest known natural gypsum cavern in the world. Tours daily.

★
★
★
★
★

### GREAT SALT PLAINS
*Highway 38, Jet, 580-626-4731; www.greatsaltplains.com*
Approximately 840 acres with a 9,300-acre lake. Swimming, fishing, boating, nature trails, picnic area, playground, camping areas, cabins. Daily.

### LITTLE SAHARA
*101 Main St., Alva, 580-824-1471; www.waynoka.com*
Park with approximately 1,600 acres. Sand dunes. Picnicking, playground.

## HOTEL
### ★RANGER INN
*420 E. Oklahoma Blvd., Alva, 580-327-1981, 800-814-7402; www.rangerinnmotel.com*
41 rooms. Pets accepted, some restrictions. **$**

# ARDMORE
The Arbuckle Mountains are a few miles north of this Southern Oklahoma town. The community is close to Wichita and the Texas border.
*Information: Chamber of Commerce, 410 W. Main, 580-223-7765; www.ardmore.org*

## WHAT TO SEE AND DO
### GREATER SOUTHWEST HISTORICAL MUSEUM
*35 Sunset Drive, Ardmore, 580-226-3857; www.gshm.org.*
This museum details the history of the area, with displays of oil and agricultural machinery, military memorabilia and a re-creation of a pioneer community. Tuesday-Saturday 10 a.m.-5 p.m.; closed Sunday, Monday and holidays.

## HOTELS
### ★DAYS INN
*2614 W. Broadway St., Ardmore, 580-226-1761, 800-329-7466; www.daysinn.com*
47 rooms. Pets accepted; fee. Complimentary continental breakfast. Fitness room. **$**

### ★★HOLIDAY INN
*2705 W. Broadway Drive, Ardmore, 580-223-7130, 800-465-4329;*
*www.holiday-inn.com*
169 rooms. Pets accepted, some restrictions; fee. High-speed Internet access. Restaurant. Fitness room. Outdoor pool, children's pool. **$**

# ATOKA
This small South Oklahoma town was named for a leader of the Choctaw Nation. A small Civil War battle took place here in 1864.
*Information: Chamber of Commerce, 580-889-2410; www.atokacity.org*

## WHAT TO SEE AND DO
### BOGGY DEPOT STATE PARK
*475 South Park Lane, Atoka, 580-889-5625*
This park has approximately 420 acres with picnicking, playgrounds and camping areas. Daily.

## EXPLORING OKLAHOMA'S STATE PARKS

Begin your tour of Southeastern and Eastern Oklahoma at the small town of Broken Bow, located at the edge of the Ouachita National Forest. About six miles east of town on Highway 70 is the 1880s home of Choctaw Chief Jefferson Gardner. Nearby Beavers Bend State Park is one of the most gorgeous places in this part of the country. Lake Broken Bow, at 14,200 acres, offers park visitors 180 miles of pretty, wooded shoreline, as well as bass fishing, paddleboating, canoeing and swimming. The park is also adjacent to Mountain Fork River, popular for its trout fishing and canoe trips; on land, you can try horseback riding, miniature golf and golf on Cedar Creek Golf Course. Stay overnight here or continue on for an overnight at Lake Wister.

Continue north on scenic Highway 259 through the tree-covered Kiamichi Mountains and you'll enter the Ouachita National Forest. If you turn west on Oklahoma Highway 1, you'll be on the spectacular Talimena Scenic Drive, which makes a 54-mile reach between Talihina, Oklahoma and Mena, Arkansas. Have the camera ready to capture the vistas from various look-out spots on the sides of the road; look to the north to see the beautiful Winding Stair Mountains. At Talihina, go four miles southwest on Highway 271 to Talimena State Park, a prime spot for picnicking. Back on Highway 259, continue north and pick up Highway 59 north to Lake Wister State Park, a pretty, wooded spread of 33,428 acres that showcase 4,000-acre Lake Wister. Some of the park's 15 cabins have fireplaces. Less than three miles northeast of Highway 59 and Highway 270, Heavener Runestone State Park features gigantic stone tablets carved with runic alphabet characters. Nobody knows how it happened, but the markings are thought to have been made by Vikings around A.D. 1012.

Finish a driving tour at Tahlequah, capital city of the Cherokee Nation. Destinations here include the Cherokee Heritage Center and the restored 1889 Cherokee National Female Seminary, at Northeastern State University.

## HOTEL

### ★★BEST WESTERN ATOKA INN

*2101 S. Mississippi Ave., Atoka, 580-889-7381, 800-780-7234;*
*www.bestwestern.com*

54 rooms. Pets accepted, some restrictions; fee. Complimentary breakfast. High-speed Internet access. Restaurant. Outdoor pool. Airport transportation available. $

# BARTLESVILLE

The Bartlesville area is proud of its Western and Native American heritage, which involves three tribes—the Cherokee, Delaware and Osage. Oklahoma's first electricity was produced here in 1876 when Jacob Bartles, an early settler, hitched a dynamo to the Caney River. Oil, first tapped in the area in 1897, is the economic base of the city. Bartlesville has become internationally known for its distinguished, modern architecture, a building trend initiated by the H. C. Price family, which made its fortune in oil. The town boasts a number of both public and private buildings by Frank Lloyd Wright and Bruce Goff.

*Information: Bartlesville Area Chamber of Commerce, 201 S. Keeler, 918-336-8708, 800-364-8708; www.bartlesville.com*

## WHAT TO SEE AND DO
### FRANK PHILLIPS MANSION

*1107 S. Cherokee Ave., Bartlesville, 918-336-2491; www.frankphillipshome.org*

Built in 1909 by the founder of the Phillips Petroleum Company, this Neoclassical house has been restored to the 1930s period. The interior includes imported woods, marble, Oriental rugs and original furnishings. Listed on the National Register of Historic Places. Wednesday-Saturday 10 a.m.-5 p.m.; second Sunday of the month 1-5 p.m.; closed Thanksgiving.

### NELLIE JOHNSTONE OIL WELL

*Johnstone Park, 300 N. Cherokee, Bartlesville*

Replica of the first commercial oil well in the state. An 83-acre park with a low water dam on the Caney River. Fishing, picnicking, playgrounds, children's rides. Late May-Labor Day, daily; closed July Fourth. Park: daily.

### PRICE TOWER

*510 Dewey Ave., Bartlesville, 918-336-4949; www.pricetower.org*

Designed by Frank Lloyd Wright, this 221-foot office building was built for pipeline construction pioneer H. C. Price as headquarters for his company. The building design is based on a diamond module of 30/60-degree triangles. Although Wright designed many skyscrapers, Price Tower was his only tall building to be completed. Guided tours Tuesday-Saturday.

### TOM MIX MUSEUM

*721 N. Delaware, Dewey, 918-534-1555*

Exhibits and memorabilia of silent movie star Tom Mix, the first "King of the Cowboys." Displays of his cowboy gear; stills from his films. Tuesday-Sunday.

### WOOLAROC

*Highway 123, Bartlesville, 918-336-0307; www.woolaroc.org*

Complex covering 3,600 acres with wildlife preserve for herds of American bison, longhorn cattle, Scottish Highland cattle, elk, deer and other native wildlife. Paintings by Russell, Remington and other great Western artists are at the museum; exhibits on the development of America; artifacts of several Native American tribes, pioneers and cowboys. The Native American Heritage Center has multimedia shows, authentic Native American crafts, art displays and a nature trail (1 ½ miles). Picnic area. Late May-early September, Tuesday-Sunday; rest of month, Wednesday-Sunday 10 a.m.-5 p.m.

## HOTELS
### ★★BEST WESTERN WESTON INN

*222 S.E. Washington Blvd., Bartlesville, 918-335-7755, 800-780-7234; www.bestwestern.com*

109 rooms. Pets accepted; fee. Complimentary continental breakfast. High-speed Internet access. Restaurant. Outdoor pool. $

### ★★★INN AT PRICE TOWER

*510 Dewey Ave., Bartlesville, 918-336-1000, 877-424-2424; www.innatpricetower.com*

This contemporary hotel is located in the Frank Lloyd Wright-designed Price Tower. The tower suites, decorated in mid-century modern style, are two-story and offer views of the prairie. 19 rooms. Complimentary continental breakfast. Restaurant, bar. Business center. $$$

## RESTAURANTS

### ★MURPHY'S ORIGINAL STEAK HOUSE

*1625 S.W. Frank Phillips Blvd., Bartlesville, 918-336-4789*

Steak menu. Lunch, dinner. Closed Monday. $$

### ★★STERLING'S GRILLE

*2905 E. Frank Phillips Blvd., Bartlesville, 918-335-0707; www.sterlingsgrille.com*

Seafood, steak menu. Lunch Sunday-Friday, dinner. Bar. Children's menu. Outdoor seating. Three separate rooms with different motifs. $$

# BROKEN BOW

This Southeastern Oklahoma town is located near several state parks, including Broken Bow Lake. Timber and tourism are the area's main industries.

*Information: Chamber of Commerce, 113 W. Martin Luther King,*
*580-584-3393, 800-528-7337; www.brokenbowchamber.com*

## WHAT TO SEE AND DO

### BEAVERS BEND RESORT STATE PARK

*Highway 259A, Broken Bow, 580-494-6300; www.oklahomaparks.com*

This 3,522-acre mountainous area is crossed by the Mountain Fork River and includes the Broken Bow Reservoir. Swimming, bathhouse, fishing, boating, nature trail, picnic areas, playground, grocery, restaurant, camping, cabins. Nature center. Daily.

## HOTEL

### ★★THE CHARLES WESLEY MOTOR LODGE

*302 N. Park Drive, Broken Bow, 580-584-3303; www.charleswesleymotorlodge.com*

50 rooms. Pets accepted, some restrictions; fee. Restaurant. Outdoor pool. $

# CHICKASHA

Established to serve as a passenger and freight division point for the Rock Island and Pacific Railroad in 1892, this town site was on land originally given to the Choctaw in 1820. It became part of the Chickasaw Nation in 1834. It was incorporated in 1907 when the Oklahoma and Indian territories were joined to form the 46th state.

*Information: Chamber of Commerce, 221 W. Chickasha Ave.,*
*405-224-0787; www.chickasha-cc.com*

## WHAT TO SEE AND DO

### LAKE CHICKASHA

*Highway 62, Chickasha*

Swimming, waterskiing, fishing, hunting. Picnic areas. Camping.

★
★
★
★
★

## SPECIAL EVENTS
### FESTIVAL OF LIGHT
*Ninth Street, Chickasha, 405-224-9627; www.chickashafestivaloflight.com*
Lighted displays; 16-story Christmas tree; Crystal Bridge; shopping. Thanksgiving-New Years Eve 6-11 p.m.

### GRADY COUNTY FAIR
*828 W. Chickasha, Chickasha, 405-224-2216*
Third week in August.

## HOTEL
### ★★BEST WESTERN INN
*2101 S. Fourth St., Chickasha, 405-224-4890, 877-489-0647; www.bestwestern.com*
148 rooms. Pets accepted, some restrictions; fee. High-speed Internet access. Restaurant, bar. Indoor pool, whirlpool. Fitness center. $

# CLAREMORE

Claremore is most famous for being the birthplace of Will Rogers. He was actually born about halfway between this city and Oologah but claimed Claremore as his home because, he said, "nobody but an Indian could pronounce Oologah." Rogers County, of which Claremore is the seat, was named not for Will Rogers but for his father, Clem.

*Information: Claremore Area Chamber of Commerce, 419 W. Will Rogers Blvd., 918-341-2818; www.claremore.org*

## WHAT TO SEE AND DO
### LYNN RIGGS MEMORIAL
*121 N. Chickasaw Ave., Claremore*
Houses the author's personal belongings, sculpture of Riggs, original manuscripts and the original "surrey with the fringe on top" from *Oklahoma!* Monday-Friday.

### WILL ROGERS BIRTHPLACE AND DOG IRON RANCH
*9501 E. 380 Road, Oologah, 918-275-4201; www.willrogers.com*
Home where the actor and cowboy was born on November 4, 1879. Daily 8 a.m.-5 p.m.

### WILL ROGERS MEMORIAL
*1720 W. Will Rogers Blvd., Claremore, 918-341-0719, 800-324-9455; www.willrogers.com*
Mementos, murals, saddle collection, dioramas, theater, films, tapes and a research library are located here. Jo Davidson's statue of Rogers stands in the foyer. The memorial is on 20 acres once owned by the humorist. Garden with Rogers' tomb. Daily 8 a.m.-5 p.m.

## SPECIAL EVENT
### WILL ROGERS STAMPEDE PRCA RODEO
*Will Rogers Stampede Arena, Claremore, 918-798-3201; www.willrogersstampede.com*
Late June.

## HOTEL

### ★★WILL ROGERS INN CLAREMORE

*940 S. Lynn Riggs Blvd., Claremore, 918-341-4410, 800-644-9455;*
*www.magnusonhotels.com*
52 rooms. Pets accepted. Restaurant, bar. Outdoor pool. **$**

## RESTAURANT

### ★★HAMMETT HOUSE

*1616 W. Will Rogers Blvd., Claremore, 918-341-7333; www.hammetthouse.com*
American menu. Lunch, dinner. Closed Monday. Children's menu. **$$**

# DUNCAN

Once a cattle town on the old Chisholm Trail, Duncan has become an oil services and agricultural center. It was here that Erle P. Halliburton developed his oil well cementing business, which now operates all over the world.
*Information: Chamber of Commerce, 911 Walnut Ave.,*
*580-255-3644; www.duncanchamber.com*

## WHAT TO SEE AND DO

### CHISHOLM TRAIL MUSEUM

*1000 N Chisholm Trail Parkway, Duncan, 580-252-6692; www.onthechisholmtrail.com*
Interactive displays demonstrating the history of the Chisholm Trail. Monday-Saturday 10 a.m.-5 p.m., Sunday 1-5 p.m.. Closed major holidays.

### STEPHENS COUNTY HISTORICAL MUSEUM

*Fuqua Park, Highway 81 and Beech Avenue, Duncan, 580-252-0717*
Houses pioneer and Native American artifacts, antique toys, gem and lapidary display; Plains Indian exhibit. Tuesday, Thursday-Saturday. Closed holidays.

## HOTEL

### ★★HOLIDAY INN

*1015 N. Highway 81, Duncan, 580-252-1500; www.holiday-inn.com*
138 rooms. Pets accepted, some restrictions; fee. Wireless Internet access. Restaurant, bar. Indoor pool, children's pool. Fitness center. **$**

# DURANT

Long a farm and livestock-producing town in Oklahoma's Red River Valley, Durant has become a recreation center since the completion of Lake Texoma. Home of Southeastern Oklahoma State University, Durant has many mansions, magnolia trees and gardens.
*Information: Chamber of Commerce, 215 N. Fourth St.,*
*580-924-0848; www.durant.org*

## WHAT TO SEE AND DO

### FORT WASHITA

*Highway 199, Durant, 580-924-6502*
Originally built in 1842 to protect the Five Civilized Tribes from the Plains Indians; used during the Civil War as a Confederate supply depot; remains of 48 buildings are visible. Daily.

OKLAHOMA

★
★
★
★
★

### THREE VALLEY MUSEUM

*401 W. Main St., Durant, 580-920-1907*

Museum housed in the Choctaw Nation Headquarters building; contains turn-of-the-century artifacts, art and beadwork. Monday-Saturday, also by appointment; closed holidays.

## SPECIAL EVENT

### OKLAHOMA SHAKESPEAREAN FESTIVAL

*Southeastern Oklahoma State University, Durant, 580-924-0121; www.se.edu*

Musicals; children's show, teen cabaret; dinner theater. Late June-July.

## HOTELS

### ★★BEST WESTERN MARKITA INN

*2401 W. Main St., Durant, 580-924-7676, 800-780-7234; www.bestwestern.com*

62 rooms. Restaurant. High-speed Internet access. Outdoor pool, whirlpool. Airport transportation available. **$**

### ★COMFORT INN

*2112 W. Main St., Durant, 580-924-8881; www.choicehotels.com*

62 rooms. Pets accepted, some restrictions; fee. Complimentary continental breakfast. **$**

# ELK CITY

This was once a stopping point for cattlemen driving herds from Texas to railheads in Kansas. Centrally located on historic Route 66, Elk City lies near the center of the Anadarko Basin, where extensive natural gas exploration takes place.

*Information: Chamber of Commerce, 1016 Airport Industrial Road, 580-225-0207, 800-280-0207; www.elkcitychamber.com*

## WHAT TO SEE AND DO

### OLD TOWN MUSEUM

*2717 W. Third St., Elk City, 580-225-2207*

Turn-of-the-century house has Victorian furnishings, Native American artifacts, Beutler Brothers Rodeo memorabilia and more. Tuesday-Sunday.

## HOTEL

### ★★HOLIDAY INN

*101 Meadow Ridge, Elk City, 580-225-6637; www.holiday-inn.com*

151 rooms. Pets accepted, some restrictions. Complimentary full breakfast. High-speed Internet access. Restaurant, bar. Fitness room. Indoor pool, whirlpool, spa. **$**

## RESTAURANTS

### ★COUNTRY DOVE

*610 W. Third St., Elk City, 580-225-7028*

American menu. Lunch. Closed Sunday. **$**

### ★LUPE'S

*905 N. Main St., Elk City, 580-225-7109*

American, Mexican menu. Lunch Monday-Friday, dinner. Closed Sunday. Bar. Children's menu. **$$**

★
★
★
★
★

# ENID

Like many Oklahoma cities, Enid was born of a land rush. When the Cherokee Outlet (more popularly known as the Cherokee Strip) was opened to settlement on September 16, 1893, a tent city sprang up. It is now a prosperous community and a center for farm marketing and oil processing. Just south of town is Vance Air Force Base, a training base for jet aircraft pilots.

*Information: Chamber of Commerce, 210 Kenwood Blvd.,*
*580-237-2494, 800-299-2443; www.enidchamber.com*

## WHAT TO SEE AND DO
### HOMESTEADER'S SOD HOUSE
*Highway 8, Cleo Springs, 580-463-2441*
This two-room sod house built by Marshall McCully in 1894 is said to be the only original example of this type of structure still standing in Oklahoma. Period furnishings; farm machinery. Tuesday-Sunday.

### MUSEUM OF THE CHEROKEE STRIP
*4125 W. Glarriot, Enid, 580-237-1907*
Artifacts covering the Oklahoma history of the Plains Indians, the Land Run of 1893 and events from 1900-present. Tuesday-Saturday.

## SPECIAL EVENT
### CHEROKEE STRIP CELEBRATION
*111 W. Purdue Ave., Enid, 580-237-1907*
This city-wide festival commemorates the opening of the Cherokee Strip to settlers. Includes entertainment, parade, rodeo, arts and crafts, food. Mid-September.

## HOTELS
### ★★BEST WESTERN INN
*2818 S. Van Buren St., Enid, 580-242-7110, 800-378-6308; www.bestwestern.com*
99 rooms. Pets accepted; fee. High-speed Internet access. Restaurant, bar. Fitness room. Indoor pool, whirlpool. $

### ★★DAYS INN
*2901 S. Van Buren St., Enid, 580-237-6000, 800-329-7466; www.daysinn.com*
100 rooms. Pets accepted; fee. Complimentary breakfast. High-speed Internet access. Restaurant, bar. Fitness room. $

## RESTAURANT
### ★★SAGE ROOM
*1927 S. Van Buren St., Enid, 580-233-1212*
Seafood menu. Dinner. Closed Sunday. Children's menu. $$$

# GROVE

This tourism-fueled community is located in the Ozark foothills on Grand Lake. The town got its start as a trading center for French fur trappers and as a community for resettled Cherokees.

*Information: www.groveok.org*

## WHAT TO SEE AND DO
### CHEROKEE QUEEN I BOAT CRUISES
*11350 Highway 59 N., Grand Lake, 918-786-4272*
Narrated cruise on Grand Lake O' the Cherokees; entertainment, refreshments.

### HAR-BER VILLAGE
*4404 W. 20th St., Grove, 918-786-3488; www.har-bervillage.com*
Reconstructed old-time village with 90 buildings and shops typical of a pioneer town. March-November, Monday-Saturday 9 a.m.-6 p.m., Sunday 12:30-5 p.m.

### LENDONWOOD GARDENS
*1308 W. 13th St., Grove, 918-786-2938; www.lendonwood.com*
Houses one of the largest collections of chamaecyparis in the United States, plus rhododendrons, day lilies and azaleas. Gardens include the Display Garden, English Terrace Garden and Japanese Garden. Daily.

## HOTEL
### ★★SHANGRI-LA RESORT AND CONFERENCE CENTER
*57401 E. Highway 125 S., Afton, 918-257-4204, 800-331-4060; www.shangrilaok.com*
101 rooms. Restaurant, bar. Fitness room. Indoor pool, whirlpool. Tennis. $

# GUTHRIE

Guthrie was founded in just a few hours during the great land rush. Prior to the run, only a small-frame railroad station and a partially completed land registration office stood on the site. A few hours later, perhaps 20,000 inhabited the tent city on the prairie. Oklahoma's territorial and first state capital, Guthrie now has the most complete collection of restored Victorian architecture in the United States, with 1,400 acres of the city listed on the National Register of Historic Places. Included are 160 buildings in the central business district and the center of town, and numerous Victorian mansions. The town is being restored to the 1907-1910 era, including the expansive Guthrie Railroad Hotel and the former opera house, the Pollard Theatre. Some who have called Guthrie home at one time or another are Tom Mix, Lon Chaney, Will Rogers, Carry Nation and O. Henry.

*Information: Chamber of Commerce, 212 W. Oklahoma Ave.,*
*405-282-1947; www.guthrieok.com*

## WHAT TO SEE AND DO
### OKLAHOMA TERRITORIAL MUSEUM
*406 E. Oklahoma Ave., Guthrie, 405-282-1889; www.oklahomaterritorialmuseum.org*
Exhibits and displays of life in territorial Oklahoma during the turn of the century. Adjacent is the Carnegie Library, site of inaugurations of the last territorial and the first state governor. Tuesday-Saturday 9 a.m.-5 p.m.; closed Sunday, Monday, holidays and November and December.

### SCOTTISH RITE MASONIC TEMPLE
*900 E. Oklahoma Ave., Guthrie, 405-282-1281; www.guthrieok.com*
This multimillion-dollar Classical Revival building is said to be the largest structure used for Masonic purposes. The building contains the original state capitol, 13 artistic rooms and 200 stained-glass windows. Surrounding it is a 10-acre park. Monday-Friday 10 a.m. and 2 p.m.

### STATE CAPITAL PUBLISHING MUSEUM

*301 W. Harrison, Guthrie, 405-282-4123;*
*www.guthrieok.com*

Located in the four-story State Capital Publishing Company Building. Houses a collection of original furnishings, vintage letterpress equipment; exhibits featuring the history of the first newspaper in the Oklahoma Territory and period printing technology. Thursday-Saturday 9 a.m.-5 p.m.

## SPECIAL EVENT
### TERRITORIAL CHRISTMAS

*Guthrie, 405-282-1947; www.guthrieok.com*

Seven miles of lights outline architecture in the Historic District; streets are filled with persons clad in turn-of-the-century style clothes, horse-drawn vehicles; window displays echo 1890-1920 era. Friday after Thanksgiving-late December.

## HOTEL
### ★★BEST WESTERN TERRITORIAL INN

*2323 Territorial Trail, Guthrie, 405-282-8831, 800-780-7234;*
*www.bestwestern.com*

84 rooms. Pets accepted, some restrictions. Complimentary breakfast. High-speed Internet access. Restaurant, bar. Outdoor pool. **$**

## RESTAURANT
### ★STABLES CAFÉ

*223 N. Division, Guthrie, 405-282-0893; www.stablescafe.com*

American menu. Lunch, dinner. Closed holidays. Children's menu. **$$**

# IDABEL

The western portion of the Ouachita National Forest is located to the east of Idabel. Although predominantly evergreen, the deciduous growth—a mixture of oak, gum, maple, sycamore, dogwood and persimmon—makes the forest notable for its magnificent fall color.

*Information: Chamber of Commerce, 13 N. Central Ave., 580-286-3305*

**OKLAHOMA**

## WHAT TO SEE AND DO
### MUSEUM OF THE RED RIVER

*812 Lincoln Road, Idabel, 580-286-3616;*
*www.museumoftheredriver.org*

Interpretive exhibits of historic and prehistoric Native Americans; local archaeology; changing exhibits. Tuesday-Saturday 10 a.m.-5 p.m., Sunday 10 a.m.-5 p.m.

## HOTEL
### ★★QUALITY INN

*2800 N.W., Texas Ave., 580-286-6501; www.choicehotels.com*

99 rooms. Pets accepted; fee. Restaurant. **$**

m o b i l t r a v e l g u i d e . c o m

# KREBS

This community of 2,000 is known throughout the state for its Italian restaurants. The locally beloved Choc beer, first brewed at Pete's Place restaurant during prohibition, is made and sold here.

## RESTAURANTS

### ★★ISLE OF CAPRI

*150 S.W. Seventh St., Krebs, 918-423-3062;*
*www.isleofcapriofkrebs.com*

American, Italian menu. Lunch Monday-Thursday, dinner. Closed Sunday. Bar. Children's menu. $$

### ★★PETE'S PLACE

*120 S.W. Eighth St., Krebs, 918-423-2042; www.petes.org*

Italian menu. Dinner. Children's menu. $$

# LAWTON

Last of the many Oklahoma cities that sprang up overnight, Lawton had its land rush on August 6, 1901. It is now the state's third-largest city. Much of the city's prosperity is due to Fort Sill, established in 1869, and to the Goodyear Tire plant headquartered here, the world's largest. The Wichita Mountains provide a dramatic backdrop to the city.

*Information: Chamber of Commerce, 629 S.W. C Ave., 580-355-3541;*
*www.lawtonfortsillchamber.com*

★
★★
★★
★
★

## WHAT TO SEE AND DO

### FORT SILL MILITARY RESERVATION

*Highway 277, Lawton, 580-442-2521; www.army.mil*

A 94,268-acre army installation, U.S. Army Field Artillery Center and School. Geronimo, war leader of the Apaches, spent his final years here and is buried in the post's Apache cemetery. Daily.

### FORT SILL NATIONAL HISTORIC LANDMARK AND MUSEUM

*437 Quanah Road, Fort Sill, 580-442-5123; www.army.mil*

Forty-three buildings built of native stone during the 1870s, many of which are still being used for their original purpose. Monday-Saturday 8:30 a.m.-4:30 p.m.

### OLD POST CHAPEL

*N. Quanah Road, Fort Sill, Lawton, 580-442-5123; www.army.mil*

One of the oldest houses of worship still in use in the state. Monday-Saturday; services on Sunday.

### MUSEUM OF THE GREAT PLAINS

*Elmer Thomas Park, 601 Ferris Blvd., Lawton, 580-581-3460;*
*www.museumgreatplains.org*

Displays on Native Americans, fur trade, exploration, cattle industry and settlement of the area. Monday-Saturday 10 a.m.-5 p.m., Sunday 1-5 p.m.

### WICHITA MOUNTAINS WILDLIFE REFUGE

*32 Refuge Headquarters, Indiahoma, 580-429-3222*

This 59,060-acre refuge has 12 man-made lakes. Nonmotorized boating permitted on four lakes, trolling motors on three lakes; picnicking, camping only at Doris Campground; limited backcountry camping by reservation only. Quanah Parker Visitor Center, March-November, Friday-Sunday. Self-guided trails. Long-horn cattle, herds of buffalo, elk, deer and other wildlife can be viewed from several wildlife/scenic viewing areas. Daily.

## HOTELS
### ★QUALITY INN

*3110 N.W. Cache Road, Lawton, 580-353-3104; www.choicehotels.com*

95 rooms. Pets accepted; fee. Complimentary continental breakfast. Indoor pool, outdoor pool, whirlpool. $

### ★★RAMADA INN

*601 N. Second St., Lawton, 580-355-7155, 888-298-2054; www.ramada.com*

98 rooms. Pets accepted; fee. Restaurant, bar. $

## RESTAURANTS
### ★★FISHERMEN'S COVE

*Highway 49, Lawton, 580-529-2672; www.thefishermenscove.com*

Seafood menu. Lunch Sunday only, dinner. Closed Monday-Tuesday. Children's menu. $$

### ★★SALAS

*111 W. Lee Blvd., Lawton, 580-357-1600; www.salasrestaurant.com*

Mexican, American menu. Lunch, dinner. Closed Monday-Tuesday. $$

# MCALESTER

This town is named for James J. McAlester, who came to Indian Territory in 1870 armed with a geologist's notebook describing some coal deposits and a fine sense of commercial strategy. He set up a tent store where the heavily traveled Texas Road crossed the California Trail and later married a Native American woman, which made him a member of the Choctaw Nation with full rights. In 1911 he became lieutenant governor of the state.

*Information: McAlester Area Chamber of Commerce & Agriculture,*

*10 S. Third St., 918-423-2550; www.mcalester.org*

## WHAT TO SEE AND DO
### MCALESTER SCOTTISH RITE TEMPLE

*305 N. Second St., McAlester, 918-423-6360; www.mcalesterscottishrite.org*

Unusual copper dome containing multicolored lenses makes this a landmark when lighted. One of its most illustrious members was Will Rogers who took degrees in 1908. Tours, Monday-Friday 8 a.m.-5 p.m., by appointment. Closed holidays.

### ROBBER'S CAVE STATE PARK

*2300 Park Cabin Road, McAlester, 918-465-2565; www.oklahomaparks.com*

Approximately 8,200 acres including lakes, alpine forests and an outlaw cave. Swimming, bathhouse, fishing, boating; hiking and horseback riding trails, picnicking, playground, restaurant, grocery, camping, cabins. Amphitheater. Daily.

## HOTELS
### ★★BEST WESTERN INN OF MCALESTER
*1215 George Nigh Expressway, McAlester, 918-426-0115, 800-780-7234;*
*www.bestwestern.com*
61 rooms. Pets accepted; fee. Complimentary continental breakfast. High-speed Internet access. Restaurant. Outdoor pool. **$**

### ★★HIWAY INN
*1217 S. George Nigh Expressway, McAlester, 918-426-5050, 800-329-7466*
100 rooms. Pets accepted, some restrictions; fee. Restaurant, bar. Indoor pool, whirlpool. **$**

## RESTAURANT
### ★GIACOMO'S
*501 S. George Nigh Expressway, McAlester, 918-423-2662;*
*www.giacomositaliancuisine.com*
American, Italian menu. Lunch, dinner. Closed Sunday-Monday. Children's menu. **$$**

# MIAMI
Situated on the headwaters of Grand Lake, Miami has many recreational facilities.
*Information: Chamber of Commerce, 111 N. Main St.,*
*918-542-4481; www.miamiok.org*

## WHAT TO SEE AND DO
### COLEMAN THEATRE BEAUTIFUL
*103 N. Main St., Miami, 918-540-2425; www.colemantheatre.org*
Built as a vaudeville theater and movie palace in 1929, this structure features a Spanish Mission Revival exterior and Louis XV interior with gold-leaf trim and carved mahogany staircases. The original Wurlitzer pipe organ has been restored. Tours, Tuesday-Friday 10 a.m.-4 p.m., Saturday 10 a.m.-noon, also by appointment.

## HOTEL
### ★★BEST WESTERN INN OF MIAMI
*2225 E. Steve Owens Blvd., Miami, 918-542-6681, 877-884-5422;*
*www.bestwestern.com*
80 rooms. Pets accepted. High-speed Internet access. Restaurant, bar. Outdoor pool. Airport transportation available. **$**

# MUSKOGEE
Located near the confluence of the Verdigris, Grand and Arkansas rivers, Muskogee was a logical site for a trading center. Southward on the old Texas Road, over which families moved to Texas, and northward, over which cattle were driven to market, the town's location was commercially ideal. The railroad superseded the rivers in transportation importance, however, almost before the town was settled.

Today Muskogee is a diversified agricultural and industrial center, a town dotted with 32 small parks and the gateway to the eastern lakes area. The port of Muskogee is part of the McClellan-Kerr Arkansas River Navigation System, handling barges that go through the inland waterway system from Pittsburgh and Minneapolis to Houston and New Orleans.

The area's surroundings made it a logical location for the U.S. Union Agency for the Five Civilized Tribes (Cherokee, Chickasaw, Choctaw, Creek and Seminole). The agency is located in the Old Union Building.

*Information: Convention & Tourism Bureau, 425 Boston Ave., 918-684-6464, 888-687-6137; www.cityofmuskogee.com*

## WHAT TO SEE AND DO
### FIVE CIVILIZED TRIBES MUSEUM
*Honor Heights Park, 1101 Honor Heights Drive, Muskogee, 918-683-1701; www.fivetribes.org*
Art and artifacts of the Cherokees, Chickasaws, Choctaws, Creeks and Seminoles; displays relating to their history and culture. March-December, daily; rest of year, Tuesday-Saturday.

### FORT GIBSON HISTORIC SITE
*907 N. Garrison St., Fort Gibson, 918-478-4088; www.fortgibson.com*
Established as the state's first military post in 1824, the park includes 12 reconstructed or restored buildings on a 55-acre site; period rooms depict army life in the 1830s and 1870s. Fort Gibson National Cemetery is 1 ½ miles east. Mid-April-mid-October, Tuesday-Sunday 10 a.m.-5 p.m., rest of year, Thursday-Sunday 10 a.m.-5 p.m.

### HONOR HEIGHTS PARK
*North Honor Heights Drive Muskogee, 918-684-6302; www.muskogeeparks.com*
A 120-acre park with azalea, rose and chrysanthemum gardens; nature walks, lakes, waterfalls. Picnicking. Daily.

## HOTELS
### ★★AZALEA INN
*800 S. 32nd St., Muskogee, 918-682-4341*
142 rooms. Pets accepted; fee. Restaurant, bar. Fitness room. Indoor pool, whirlpool. $

### ★DAYS INN
*900 S. 32nd St., Muskogee, 918-683-3911, 800-329-7466; www.daysinn.com*
43 rooms. Pets accepted; fee. Complimentary continental breakfast. High-speed Internet access. Outdoor pool. $

## RESTAURANT
### ★OKIES
*219 S. 32nd St., Muskogee, 918-683-1056*
American menu. Lunch, dinner. Bar. Children's menu. $$

# NORMAN
Norman was founded on April 22, 1889, in the famous land rush known as the Oklahoma land run. The run opened what was once the Indian Territory to modern-day settlement.

A year later, the University of Oklahoma was founded. The city now offers numerous restaurants, museums, shopping areas, parks and hotels, as well as convention, conference and symposium sites. The University of Oklahoma, once mostly known as a football powerhouse, has been transformed into a respected academic and research institution.
*Information: Convention & Visitors Bureau, 224 W. Gray St.,*
*405-366-8095, 800-767-7260; www.visitnorman.com*

## WHAT TO SEE AND DO
### UNIVERSITY OF OKLAHOMA
*1000 Asp Ave., Norman, 405-325-1188, 800-234-6868; www.ou.edu*
This campus is home to 25,000 students and has more than 225 buildings. The University of Oklahoma Press is a distinguished publishing house. On campus are the Fred Jones Jr. Museum of Art (Tuesday-Sunday, 405-325-3272); Oklahoma Museum of Natural History (405-325-4712); Rupel Jones Theater (405-325-4101); University Research Park. (museums closed holidays) OU Visitor Center, Jacobson Hall, 550 Parrington Oval.

## SPECIALTY LODGINGS
### HOLMBERG HOUSE BED AND BREAKFAST
*766 Debarr Ave., Norman, 405-321-6221, 877-621-6221; www.holmberghouse.com*
Four rooms. Complimentary full breakfast. Built in 1914 by the first dean of the University of Oklahoma's College of Fine Arts. $

### MONTFORD INN BED AND BREAKFAST
*322 W. Tonhawa St., Norman, 405-321-2200, 800-321-8969; www.montfordinn.com*
Surrounded by gardens, this hotel is also near the college campus and many restaurants. 16 rooms. Complimentary full breakfast. Wireless Internet access. Whirlpool. $

## RESTAURANTS
### ★CAFÉ PLAID
*333 W. Boyd St., Norman, 405-360-2233; www.cafeplaid.com*
American, deli menu. Breakfast, lunch, brunch. Children's menu. Casual attire. $

### ★★★LEGEND'S
*1313 W. Lindsey St., Norman, 405-329-8888; www.legendsrestaurant.com*
Owner Joe Sparks has presided over this American-continental restaurant for 40 years. It's a favorite of university faculty. The intimate dining room is filled with original artwork and features a broad menu of pastas, steaks and daily seafood specials. American menu. Lunch, dinner, Sunday brunch. Bar. Outdoor seating. $$

### ★VISTA SPORTS GRILL
*111 N. Peters Ave., Norman, 405-447-0909; www.vistasportsgrill.com*
American menu. Lunch, dinner. Bar. Children's menu. Casual attire. $$

# OKLAHOMA CITY
What is now the site of Oklahoma's capital was barren prairie on the morning of April 22, 1889. Unassigned land was opened to settlement that day, and by nightfall the population numbered 10,000. No city was ever settled faster.

The city sits atop one of the nation's largest oil fields—there are even wells on the lawn of the Capitol. First discovered in 1928, the field was rapidly developed throughout the city. It still produces large quantities of high-gravity oil. Oil well equipment manufacturing became one of the city's major industries. Tinker Air Force Base is southeast of the city.

*Information: Convention & Visitors Bureau, 189 W. Sheridan, 405-297-8912, 800-225-5652; www.okccvb.org*

## WHAT TO SEE AND DO
### 45TH INFANTRY DIVISION MUSEUM

*2145 N.E. 36th St., Oklahoma City, 405-424-5313; www.45thdivisionmuseum.com.*
Exhibits showcase state military history from its beginnings in the early Oklahoma Territory through World War II and Korea to the present National Guard; Desert Storm exhibit; uniforms, vehicles, aircraft, artillery and an extensive military firearms collection with pieces dating from the American Revolution; memorabilia and original cartoons by Bill Mauldin. Tuesday-Friday 9 a.m.-4:15 p.m., Saturday 10 a.m.-4:15 p.m., Sunday 1-4:15 p.m.

### AQUATICUS

*2101 N.E. 50th, Oklahoma City, 405-424-3344*
This marine life science facility contains a comprehensive collection of aquatic life; shark tank; adaptations and habitat exhibits; underwater viewing. Daily.

### CIVIC CENTER MUSIC HALL

*201 N. Walker Ave., Oklahoma City, 405-297-2584; www.okcciviccenter.org*
Home of the Oklahoma City Philharmonic, Canterbury Choral Society, Ballet Oklahoma and Lyric Theatre of Oklahoma. Entertainment choices include Broadway shows and popular concerts.

### FRONTIER CITY

*11501 N.E. Expressway, Oklahoma City, 405-478-2412; www.frontiercity.com*
A 65-acre Western theme park; including more than 75 rides, shows and attractions; entertainment; shops, restaurants. Memorial Day-late August, daily; Easter-Memorial Day and late August-October, weekends only.

### GARDEN EXHIBITION BUILDING AND HORTICULTURE GARDENS

*3400 N.W. 36th St., Oklahoma City, 405-943-0827*
Azalea trails; butterfly garden; rose, peony and iris gardens; arboretum; the conservatory has one of the country's largest cactus and succulent collections.

### HARN HOMESTEAD AND 1889ERS MUSEUM

*1721 N. Lincoln Blvd., Oklahoma City, 405-235-4058; www.harnhomestead.com*
Historic homestead claimed in Land Run of 1889; 1904 farmhouse furnished with prestatehood objects. Three-story stone and cedar barn; one-room schoolhouse; working farm. Monday-Friday; closed holidays.

### INTERNATIONAL PHOTOGRAPHY HALL OF FAME AND MUSEUM

*2100 N.E. 52nd St., Oklahoma City, 405-424-4055; www.iphf.org*

Permanent and traveling exhibits; one of world's largest photographic murals. Monday-Friday 10 a.m.-5 p.m., Saturday 10 a.m.-6 p.m., Sunday 11 a.m.-6 p.m. Closed holidays.

### KIRKPATRICK SCIENCE AND AIR SPACE MUSEUM

*2100 N.E. 52nd St., Oklahoma City, 405-602-6664, 800-532-7652;*
*www.omniplex.org*

Includes a hands-on science museum, Air Space Museum, Kirkpatrick Galleries, gardens/greenhouse; Kirkpatrick Planetarium (shows change quarterly). Monday-Friday 9 a.m.-5 p.m., Saturday 9 a.m.-6 p.m., Sunday 11 a.m.-6 p.m.

### MYRIAD BOTANICAL GARDENS

*301 W. Reno Ave., Oklahoma City, 405-297-3995;*
*www.myriadgardens.com*

A 17-acre botanical garden in the heart of the city's redeveloping central business district. Features a lake, amphitheater, botanical gardens and seven-story Crystal Bridge Tropical Conservatory. Monday-Saturday 9 a.m.-6 p.m., Sunday noon-6 p.m.; closed holidays.

### NATIONAL COWBOY HALL OF FAME AND WESTERN HERITAGE CENTER

*1700 N.E. 63rd St., Oklahoma City, 405-478-2250;*
*www.nationalcowboymuseum.org*

**198**

Major art collections depict America's Western heritage; Rodeo Hall of Fame; landscaped gardens. Daily 9 a.m.-5 p.m.

### OKLAHOMA CITY MUSEUM OF ART

*415 Coach Drive, Oklahoma City, 405-236-3100; www.okcmoa.com*

Permanent collection of 16th- to 20th-century European and American paintings, prints, drawings, photographs, sculpture and decorative arts. Tuesday, Wednesday, Saturday 10 a.m.-5 p.m., Thursday and Sunday noon-5 p.m.; closed Monday, holidays.

### OKLAHOMA CITY NATIONAL MEMORIAL

*N.W. Fifth Street and North Robinson Avenue, Oklahoma City,*
*405-235-3313, 888-542-4673; www.oklahomacitynationalmemorial.org*

A series of monuments honor the men, women and children killed by a bomb at the Murrah Federal Building on April 19, 1995. The Gates of Time memorial represents the moment of the blast; the Field of Empty Chairs pays tribute to the 168 lives lost in the bombing. The Survivor Tree is an American elm tree that withstood the blast. Museum: Monday-Saturday 9 a.m.-6 p.m., Sunday afternoon 1-6 p.m. Also a reflecting pool, orchard and children's area. Daily.

### OKLAHOMA CITY ZOO

*2101 N.E. 50th St., Oklahoma City, 405-424-3344; www.okczoo.com*

This zoo is home to more than 2,000 animals representing 500 species. Daily 9 a.m.-6 p.m.; closed holidays.

## OKLAHOMA CITY THEN AND NOW

Single-day events have shaped both the past and present of this settlement in the American heartland. Oklahoma City was born on April 22, 1889, when the area known as the Unassigned Lands in Oklahoma Territory was opened for settlement. A cannon was fired at noon that day, signaling a rush of thousands of settlers who raced into the two million acres of land to make their claims on the plains.

Just over a century later, the city was the site of the April 19, 1995 bombing of the Alfred P. Murrah Federal Building by American terrorist Timothy McVeigh. Today, this event is memorialized at the Oklahoma City National Memorial. Begin at the Gates of Time, twin monuments that frame the moment of destruction: 9:02 a.m. The east gate represents 9:01 a.m. and the west gate 9:03 a.m. The Field of Empty Chairs consists of 168 bronze-and-stone chairs arranged in nine rows, representing the lives lost and the floor each victim was on at the time of the blast. Smaller chairs memorialize the 19 children killed. The area also includes an orchard and reflecting pool.

### OKLAHOMA FIREFIGHTERS MUSEUM

*2716 N.E. 50th St., Oklahoma City, 405-424-3440, 800-308-5336; www.osfa.info*
See antique fire equipment dating to 1736. Also, the first fire station in Oklahoma was reassembled here. Monday-Saturday 9 a.m.-4.30 p.m., Sunday 1-4.30 p.m.

### OKLAHOMA HISTORY CENTER

*2401 N. Laird Ave., Oklahoma City, 405-522-5248; www.okhistorycenter.org*
Located on 18 acres across from the capitol building, the History Center is a self-guided exploration of Oklahoma from past to present. Outside the museum, the Red River Journey offers visitors a walking tour of the Red River Valley. The grounds also include an outdoor oil field exhibit with drilling derricks, a portable derrick and machinery associated with Oklahoma oil explorations. Monday-Saturday 9 a.m.-5 p.m., Sunday noon-5 p.m.; closed holidays.

### OKLAHOMA NATIONAL STOCKYARDS

*2501 Exchange Ave., Oklahoma City, 405-235-8675; www.onsy.com*
One of the world's largest cattle markets, this stockyard features auctions of cattle, hogs and sheep. Monday-Tuesday.

### RED EARTH INDIAN CENTER

*2100 N.E. 52nd St., Oklahoma City, 405-427-5228; www.redearth.org*
Exhibits and educational programs encourage appreciation of Native American cultures. Daily Monday-Friday 9 a.m.-5 p.m., Saturday 9 a.m.-6 p.m., Sunday 11 a.m.-6 p.m.

### STATE CAPITOL

*2300 N. Lincoln Blvd., Oklahoma City, 405-521-3356; www.travelok.com*
Greco-Roman, Neoclassical building designed by S. A. Layton and Wemyss Smith. An oil well beneath the Capitol building reaches 1 ¼ miles underground. After

OKLAHOMA

★
★
★
★
★

pumping oil from 1941 to 1986, it is now preserved as a monument. The legislature meets annually for 78 days beginning on the first Monday in February. Tours daily.

## SPECIAL EVENTS

### BALLET OKLAHOMA
*7421 N. Classen Blvd., Oklahoma City, 405-843-9898; www.balletoklahoma.com*
Productions are staged October-April.

### FESTIVAL OF THE ARTS
*Downtown, Hudson Ave., Oklahoma City, 405-270-4848; www.artscouncilokc.com*
International foods, entertainment, children's learning and play area; craft market; artists from many states display their work. Six days in late April, Tuesday-Saturday 11 a.m.-9 p.m., Sunday 11 a.m.-6 p.m.

### INTERNATIONAL FINALS RODEO
*State Fair Arena Oklahoma City, 405-235-6540, 800-511-1552; www.iprarodeo.com*
The International Pro Rodeo Association's top 15 cowboys and cowgirls compete in seven events to determine world championships.

### OKLAHOMA CITY PHILHARMONIC ORCHESTRA
*Civic Center Music Hall, 201 N. Walker Ave., Oklahoma City, 405-297-2584; www.okcciviccenter.org*
Concerts are held weekly from mid-September-May.

★
★★
★★★
★★

### STATE FAIR OF OKLAHOMA
*333 Gordon Cooper Blvd., Oklahoma City, 405-948-6700; www.okstatefair.com*
Livestock, crafts, art exhibits; Native American ceremonial dances; carnival, parades. Arena and grandstand attractions.

## HOTELS

### ★BAYMONT INN OKLAHOMA CITY SOUTH
*8315 S. Interstate 35 Service Road, Oklahoma City, 405-631-8661, 877-229-6668; www.baymontinns.com*
122 rooms. Complimentary continental breakfast. Wireless Internet access. Outdoor pool. $

### ★★BEST WESTERN SADDLEBACK INN
*4300 S.W. Third St., Oklahoma City, 405-947-7000, 800-228-3903; www.bestwestern.com/saddlebackinn*
220 rooms. Pets accepted, some restrictions; fee. Complimentary full breakfast. Wireless Internet access. Restaurant, bar. Fitness room. Outdoor pool, whirlpool. Business center. $

### ★★COURTYARD OKLAHOMA CITY DOWNTOWN
*2 West Reno Ave., Oklahoma City, 405-232-2290, 800-217-9905; www.courtyard.com*
225 rooms. High-speed Internet access. Restaurant. Fitness room. Outdoor pool, whirlpool. Airport transportation available. Business center. $

## MUSIC TO BROADWAY'S EARS: *OKLAHOMA!*

Oklahoma is lucky to have one of the most popular Broadway musicals celebrating its name in the title. *Oklahoma!*, the first musical collaboration between Richard Rodgers and Oscar Hammerstein II, was different. It had a plot. The songs and dances emerged logically from the plot and the thoughts and emotions of the characters helped carry the storyline, which atypically for the time, had its share of dark moments and serious themes. The dancing was more folk-ballet style than kick-line. Even the rural setting of the play was unusual—most musicals were set in urban confines, with sophisticated, affluent characters, not farmhands.

When it opened on Broadway in 1943, critics thought *Oklahoma!* wouldn't make it to a second performance. Scouts who saw the show in out-of-town tryouts were said to deliver a verdict along the lines of "No girls, no gags, no chance." In the tryout stage, the show had a different title—*Away We Go!* Rogers and Hammerstein changed the title to *Oklahoma!* and added the exuberant song of the same name as the show's closing number. The rousing song thrilled the audience, which gave a standing ovation. The next day, the once-doubting critics could not find enough praise for the show, and *Oklahoma!* was on its to theatrical immortality. It set a record of more than 2,000 performances over five years at St. James Theatre and is still performed at theaters across the country.

### ★★★CROWNE PLAZA HOTEL

*2945 N.W. Expressway, Oklahoma City, 405-848-4811, 877-227-6963;*
*www.crowneplaza.com*

Located in the business district of Oklahoma City, this hotel offers easy access to city attractions. Granite bathrooms with closets, dark wood furniture and club chairs with ottomans are found in guest rooms. The Spa Select bedding package includes an amenity bag of lavender linen spray, an eye pillow and a CD of soothing music. 215 rooms. Pets accepted; fee. Wireless Internet access. Restaurant, bar. Fitness room. Outdoor pool, whirlpool. Business center. $

### ★★EMBASSY SUITES

*1815 S. Meridian Ave., Oklahoma City, 405-682-6000,*
*800-362-2779; www.embassysuites.com*

236 rooms, all suites. Pets accepted, some restrictions; fee. Complimentary full breakfast. Wireless Internet access. Restaurant, bar. Children's activity center. Fitness room. Indoor pool, whirlpool. Airport transportation available. Business center. $$

### ★GOVERNORS SUITES HOTEL

*2308 S. Meridian Ave., Oklahoma City, 405-682-5299,*
*888-819-7575; www.govsuitesokc.com*

50 rooms. Complimentary full breakfast. Wireless Internet access. Fitness room. Outdoor pool, whirlpool. Spa. Airport transportation available. $

### ★★HOLIDAY INN

*6200 N. Robinson Ave., Oklahoma City, 405-843-5558, 800-682-0049;*
*www.holiday-inn.com*

200 rooms. Pets accepted, some restrictions; fee. High-speed Internet access. Restaurant, bar. Fitness room. Indoor pool, whirlpool. Airport transportation available. Business center. **$**

### ★★★MARRIOTT WATERFORD

*6300 Waterford Blvd., Oklahoma City, 405-848-4782, 800-992-2009;*
*www.marriott.com*

Located in Oklahoma City's tony Waterford community, the hotel is 15 minutes from downtown and the airport. Enjoy a drink in the waterfront lounge or take a swim in the outdoor pool. Volleyball and squash facilities are also available. Rooms feature pillow-top mattresses and crisp white linens, and the granite bathrooms have jetted tubs and Bath & Body Works amenities. 197 rooms. Wireless Internet access. Restaurant, bar. Fitness room, spa. Outdoor pool, whirlpool. Business center. **$$**

### ★★★RENAISSANCE OKLAHOMA CITY CONVENTION CENTER HOTEL

*10 N. Broadway Ave., Oklahoma City, 405-228-8000, 800-468-3571;*
*www.renaissancehotels.com*

Located in downtown Oklahoma City at the corner of Broadway and Sheridan, the Renaissance Oklahoma City is a 15-story tower that is connected to the adjacent Cox Convention Center by a sky bridge. It's close to the restored Bricktown area, with its shops, restaurants, amusements and River Walk. A 13-story atrium dominates the center of the hotel and the lobby is filled with lush landscaping that includes koi ponds and a waterfall. 311 rooms. High-speed Internet access. Restaurant, bar. Fitness room, spa. Indoor pool, whirlpool. Airport transportation available. Business center. **$$**

### ★★★THE SHERATON OKLAHOMA CITY

*1 N. Broadway Ave., Oklahoma City, 405-235-2780, 800-285-2780; www.sheraton.com*
This downtown hotel is connected to the Cox Convention Center as well as many shops and businesses by an underground concourse. Contemporary styling is the theme, from the lobby with its leather sofas and modern art collection to the oversized guest rooms with long working desks with ergonomic chairs, black-and-white photographs and brown and black granite bathrooms. An outdoor pool, sun deck and fitness center are available, and pets are welcomed with bowls, treats and beds. 396 rooms. Pets accepted, some restrictions. Wireless Internet access. Restaurant, bar. Fitness room, spa. Outdoor pool. Business center. **$$**

## RESTAURANTS
### ★★ARIA GRILL

*1 N. Broadway Ave., Oklahoma City, 405-235-2780; www.sheraton.com*
American menu. Breakfast, lunch, dinner. Bar. Children's menu. Business casual attire. Valet parking. **$$$**

### ★★★BELLINI'S RISTORANTE & GRILL

*6305 Waterford Blvd., Oklahoma City, 405-848-1065; www.bellinis.net*
This casual restaurant has the ambience of an Italian piazza. Modern art hangs on the dark wood-paneled walls, and tables are set with black cloths. Everything from pizza

to steak, seafood to pasta dishes, are featured on the extensive menu. Offers a view of lakeside sunset. American menu, Italian menu. Lunch, dinner, Sunday brunch. Bar. Children's menu. Reservations recommended. Outdoor seating. $$

### ★BRICKTOWN BREWERY

*1 N. Oklahoma Ave., Oklahoma City, 405-232-2739; www.bricktownbrewery.com*
American menu. Lunch, dinner, late-night. Bar. Children's menu. Casual attire. $$

### ★★CAFÉ 501

*501 S. Boulevard St., Edmond, 405-359-1501; www.my501cafe.com*
International menu. Lunch, dinner. Children's menu. Saturday breakfast, Sunday brunch. $$

### ★★CASTLE FALLS

*820 N. MacArthur Blvd., Oklahoma City, 405-942-6133; www.castlefalls.com*
German menu. Dinner. Closed Monday-Wednesday, Sunday. Bar. Children's menu. Outdoor seating. $$

### ★★CATTLEMAN'S STEAKHOUSE

*1309 S. Agnew St., Oklahoma City, 405-236-0416;*
*www.cattlemensrestaurant.com*
Steak menu. Breakfast, lunch, dinner, late-night, brunch. Children's menu. Casual attire. $$

### ★★★THE COACH HOUSE

*6437 Avondale Drive, Oklahoma City, 405-842-1000; www.tch-ok.com*
The seasonally changing menu at this restaurant features local produce and meats, with rack of lamb as a signature dish. The cuisine is supported by an extensive wine list. Subdued lighting, double-linen table cloths, fine stemware and flatware, and copper chargers give the restaurant an elegant, formal feel. American menu. Lunch, dinner. Closed Sunday. Children's menu. Business casual attire. Reservations recommended. $$$

### ★COUNTY LINE

*1226 N.E. 63rd St., Oklahoma City, 405-478-4955; www.countyline.com*
Barbecue menu. Lunch, dinner. Bar. Children's menu. Casual attire. $$

### ★★DEEP FORK GRILL

*5418 N. Western Ave., Oklahoma City, 405-848-7678;*
*www.deepforkgrill.com*
Steak, seafood menu. Lunch, dinner, brunch. Bar. Children's menu. Business casual attire. Reservations recommended. Valet parking. $$

### ★GOPURAM TASTE OF INDIA

*4559 N.W. 23rd St., Oklahoma City, 405-948-7373;*
*www.gopuramtasteofindia.com*
Indian menu. Lunch, dinner. Children's menu. Casual attire. $$

**OKLAHOMA**

★
★
★
★
★

### ★★★JW'S STEAKHOUSE

*3233 N.W. Expressway, Oklahoma City, 405-842-6633; www.marriott.com*

This steakhouse in the Oklahoma City Marriott has dark wood paneling and red leather chairs and banquettes. Serving dinner only, JW's has the full steakhouse look and specializes in classics such as filet mignon and prime rib. Steak menu. Dinner, late-night. Children's menu. Business casual attire. Reservations recommended. Valet parking. $$$

### ★★KONA RANCH STEAKHOUSE

*2037 S. Meridian Ave., Oklahoma City, 405-681-1000; www.kona-ranch.com*

Steak menu. Lunch, dinner. Bar. Children's menu. Casual attire. $$

### ★★★LA BAGUETTE BISTRO

*7408 N. May Ave., Oklahoma City, 405-840-3047; www.labaguettebistro.com*

Just northwest of downtown, this bistro offers an authentic experience. The owners/ chefs hail from France and serve simple but authentic bistro fare (including baguette sandwiches) in an L-shaped dining room. French menu. Breakfast, lunch, dinner, brunch. Bar. Casual attire. $$

### ★★LAS PALOMAS

*2329 N. Meridian Ave., Oklahoma City, 405-949-9988*

Mexican menu. Lunch, dinner. Children's menu. Casual attire. $

### ★★SUSHI NEKO

*4318 N. Western Ave., Oklahoma City, 405-528-8862; www.sushineko.com*

Japanese menu. Lunch, dinner, late-night. Closed Sunday. Bar. Children's menu. Casual attire. Reservations recommended. Valet parking. Outdoor seating. $$

# OKMULGEE

The capital of the Creek Nation was established in 1868 and operates at the Creek Indian Complex. The Creeks gave the town its name, which means "bubbling water." Within Okmulgee County nearly five-million pounds of wild pecans are harvested annually. The city is the home of Oklahoma State University/Okmulgee, one of the country's largest residential-vocational training schools.

*Information: Chamber of Commerce, 112 N. Morton Ave.,*
*918-756-6172; www.tourokmulgee.com*

## WHAT TO SEE AND DO
### CREEK COUNCIL HOUSE MUSEUM

*106 W. 6th St., Okmulgee, 918-756-2324*

Museum houses a display of Creek tribal history. Tuesday-Saturday.

## HOTELS
### ★★BEST WESTERN OKMULGEE

*3499 N. Wood Drive, Okmulgee, 918-756-9200, 800-552-9201;*
*www.bestwestern.com*

50 rooms. Pets accepted; fee. Complimentary continental breakfast. High-speed Internet access. Restaurant, bar. Outdoor pool. $

### ★HENRYETTA INN AND DOME

*810 E. Trudgeon St., Henryetta, 918-652-2581, 800-515-3663*

85 rooms. Pets accepted, some restrictions; fee. Restaurant, bar. Fitness room. Indoor pool. $

# PERRY

Settled during the opening of the Cherokee Outlet, this town was once called Hell's Half-Acre. It's home to a Carnegie library, a public library built with money donated by Andrew Carnegie.

*Information: Chamber of Commerce, 300 Sixth St., 580-336-4684;*
*www.perrychamber.fullnet.net*

## WHAT TO SEE AND DO
### CHEROKEE STRIP MUSEUM

*2617 W. Fir Ave., Perry, 580-336-2405;*
*www.cherokee-strip-museum.org*

This museum includes a schoolhouse, pioneer artifacts and documents depicting the era of the 1893 land run. Tuesday-Friday 9 a.m.-5 p.m., Saturday 10 a.m.-4 p.m.; closed Sunday, Monday and state holidays.

## SPECIAL EVENT
### CHEROKEE STRIP CELEBRATION

*4125 W. Glarriot, Perry, 580-336-4684*

This festival commemorates the opening of the Cherokee Strip to settlers. Parade, entertainment, rodeo, contests, Noble County Fair. Mid-September.

## HOTEL
### ★★BEST WESTERN CHEROKEE STRIP MOTEL

*2903 Highway 77 W., Perry, 580-336-2218;*
*www.bestwestern.com*

88 rooms. Pets accepted, some restrictions; fee. Restaurant, bar. Indoor pool. $

# PONCA CITY

Ponca City was founded in a single day in the traditional Oklahoma land-rush manner. Although located in the Cherokee Strip, the town was named for the Ponca tribe. Ponca City is a modern industrial town surrounded by cattle and wheat country.

*Information: Ponca City Tourism, 580-763-8092, 866-763-8092;*
*www.poncacity.com*

## WHAT TO SEE AND DO
### KAW LAKE

*Highway 2, Ponca City, 580-762-5611; www.kawlake.com*

Located on the Arkansas River, the shoreline of this lake covers 168 miles. Water sports, fishing, boating, hunting. Recreation and camping areas located one mile off Highway 60. Daily.

★
★
★
★
★

### MARLAND MANSION ESTATE

*901 Monument Road, Ponca City, 580-767-0420;*
*www.marlandmansion.com*

A 55-room mansion built in 1928 by E. W. Marland, an oil baron, Oklahoma governor and philanthropist. Modeled after the Davanzati Palace in Florence, Italy, the estate features elaborate artwork and hand-painted ceilings. Tours. Daily 10 a.m.-5 p.m., Sunday 1-5 p.m.

### MARLAND'S GRAND HOME

*1000 E. Grand Ave., Ponca City, 580-767-0427; www.marlandgrandhome.com*

This structure houses an Indian Museum and a Daughters of the American Revolution Memorial Museum. Tuesday-Saturday 10 a.m.-5 p.m.

## HOTELS
### ★★HOLIDAY INN

*2809 N.14th St., Ponca City, 580-762-8311, 800-465-4329;*
*www.ihg.com*

138 rooms. Pets accepted, some restrictions. Restaurant, bar. Fitness room. Outdoor pool. $

# POTEAU

Rich in ancient history and pioneer heritage, Poteau is located in an area of timber and high hills. The nearby peak of Cavanal Hill provides a spectacular view of the entire Poteau River Valley. Poteau lies approximately 15 miles north of the Ouachita National Forest.

*Information: Chamber of Commerce, 201 S. Broadway St.,*
*918-647-9178; www.poteau-ok.com*

## WHAT TO SEE AND DO
### HEAVENER RUNESTONE

*Highway 59, Poteau, 918-653-2241; www.touroklahoma.com*

Scientists believe the Scandinavian cryptograph in eight runes carved into Poteau Mountain were inscribed by Vikings in A.D. 800. Other runes from the Scandinavian alphabet of the third through 10th centuries have been found engraved on several stones in the area. Daily.

### KERR MUSEUM

*23009 Kerr Manson Road, Poteau, 918-647-8221*

The home of former Senator Robert S. Kerr, this museum contains material detailing the history and development of eastern Oklahoma including natural history, pioneer, Choctaw and special exhibits. Tuesday-Sunday afternoons, also by appointment.

### SPIRO MOUND ARCHEOLOGICAL STATE PARK

*Spiro Mounds Road, Spiro, 918-962-2062; www.myspiro.com*

A 138-acre site with 12 earthen mounds dating from A.D. 600-1450. A reconstructed Native American house and excavated items are on display in the interpretive center. Summer, Tuesday-Sunday; winter, Wednesday-Saturday 9 a.m.-5 p.m., Sunday noon-5 p.m.

# ROMAN NOSE STATE PARK

*Information: www.oklahomaparks.com*

## WHAT TO SEE AND DO
### ROMAN NOSE STATE PARK

*Highway 8, Watonga. 580-623-7281; www.watonga.com*

Named after Chief Henry Roman Nose of the Cheyenne, this is a 750-acre area with a 55-acre, man-made lake stocked with bass, crappie, bluegill, rainbow trout and catfish. Facilities include a swimming pool, bathhouse, fishing, boating, paddleboats, golf, tennis, picnicking, playgrounds, concessions and a lodge.

## HOTEL
### ★★ROMAN NOSE RESORT

*Highway 8A, Watonga, 580-623-7281, 800-654-8240; www.oklahomaparks.com*

57 rooms. Pets accepted, some restrictions. Restaurant. Children's activity center. Outdoor pool. Tennis, Golf. $

# SEQUOYAH STATE PARK

*Information: www.oklahomaparks.com*

## WHAT TO SEE AND DO
### SEQUOYAH STATE PARK

*Highway 51, Tahlequah, 918-772-2046; www.oklahomaparks.com*

These approximately 2,800 acres in Oklahoma's Cookson Hills were once a bandits' hideout. The park is on Fort Gibson Reservoir, created by the dam of the same name. This 19,100-acre reservoir shifts its level less than most hydroelectric power lakes in Oklahoma and is stocked with bass, catfish and crappie.

## HOTELS
### ★INDIAN LODGE

*3370 State Highway 51, Wagoner, 918-485-3184; www.indianlodge.net*

25 rooms. Closed November-March. Outdoor pool. $

### ★★WESTERN HILLS GUEST RANCH

*19808 Park No.10, Wagoner, 918-772-2545, 800-368-1486; www.travelok.com*

18 rooms. Pets accepted, some restrictions. Restaurant, bar. Children's activity center. Outdoor pool, children's pool. Tennis. $

# SHAWNEE

The history of Shawnee is that of Oklahoma in miniature. In the center of the state, it stands on what was originally Sac and Fox land, which was also claimed at various times by Spain, France and England. It was opened by a land rush on September 22, 1891. Oil was struck in 1926. Shawnee is the home of Oklahoma Baptist University. Jim Thorpe, the great Native American athlete, and Dr. Brewster Higley, the physician who wrote, "Home on the Range," lived here. Astronaut Gordon Cooper was born and raised in Shawnee.

*Information: Chamber of Commerce, 131 N. Bell Ave.,*
*405-273-6092; www.shawneenet.com*

★
★
★
★
★

## WHAT TO SEE AND DO
### MABEE-GERRER MUSEUM OF ART
*1900 W. MacArthur Drive, Shawnee, 405-878-5300; www.mgmoa.org*
This art gallery features works by 19th- and 20th-century European and American artists as well as works from the Middle Ages and the Renaissance. Museum features artifacts of Egyptian, Babylonian, Grecian, Roman, Persian, Chinese, African and Polynesian civilizations as well as North, Central and South American native civilizations. Tuesday-Saturday 10 a.m.-5 p.m., Sunday 1-4 p.m.; closed Mondays, public holidays.

### SEMINOLE NATION MUSEUM
*524 S. Wewoka Ave., Wewoka, 405-257-5580; www.theseminolenationmuseum.org*
The museum traces the Seminoles' history from their removal from Florida via the Trail of Tears to the establishment of the capital in Oklahoma. Displays include a collection of Native American peace medals, replicas of a Chick (Florida Seminole house) and artifacts from the pioneer era through the oil boom days of the 1920s. Art gallery with Native American paintings and sculpture. Monday-Saturday 10 a.m.-5 p.m.; closed January.

## HOTEL
### SUPER 8 SHAWNEE
*4900 N. Harrison Blvd., Shawnee, 405-275-0089, 800-298-2054; www.ramada.com*
106 rooms. Pets accepted; fee. High-speed Internet acce. Restaurant, bar. Indoor pool. $

★
★
★
★
★

# STILLWATER
Stillwater was born overnight in the great land run of 1889. The settlement was less than a year old when, on Christmas Day 1890, the territorial legislature established Oklahoma State University (formerly Oklahoma A & M).
*Information: Convention & Visitors Bureau, 409 S. Main St.,*
*405-743-3697, 800-991-6717; www.come2stillwater.com*

## WHAT TO SEE AND DO
### LAKE CARL BLACKWELL
*11000 W. Highway 51C, Stillwater, 405-372-5157; www.lcb.okstate.edu*
A 19,364-acre recreation area operated by Oklahoma State University. Swimming, waterskiing, fishing, boating, sailing, hunting, picnic areas, campgrounds, cabins.

### OKLAHOMA STATE UNIVERSITY
*Washington Street and University Avenue, Stillwater, 405-744-9341;*
*www.osu.okstate.edu*
On a campus of 840 acres with an additional 4,774 acres of experimental university farms statewide, this university has more than 20,000 students. The Noble Research Center for Agriculture and Renewable Natural Resources, an education/research complex with an emphasis on the biological sciences is on campus. Buildings include Old Central, the oldest collegiate building in the state built in 1894 of pink brick, and attractive modified Georgian buildings of red brick with slate roofs.

## HOTELS

### ★★QUALITY INN

*2515 W. Sixth Ave., Stillwater, 405-372-0800; www.qualityinn.com*

139 rooms. Pets accepted. Complimentary continental breakfast. Restaurant, bar. Indoor pool, whirlpool. Fitness room. Business center. **$**

### ★★STILLWATER PLAZA

*600 E. McElroy Road., Stillwater, 405-377-7010, 800-353-6894;*
*www.bestwestern.com*

122 rooms. Pets accepted, some restrictions; fee. Wireless Internet access. Restaurant, bar. Fitness room. Indoor pool, whirlpool. Business center. **$**

# TAHLEQUAH

Tribal branches of the Cherokee met here in 1839 to sign a new constitution forming the Cherokee Nation. They had been driven by the U.S. Army from North Carolina, Alabama, Tennessee and Georgia over the Trail of Tears. The Cherokee were the only tribe with a constitution and a body of law written in their own language, using a written alphabet which had been created by Sequoyah. These talented people published the first newspaper in Indian Territory and in 1885 established the first commercial teleline in Oklahoma. The Southwestern Bell Telephone Company, to which it was later sold, established a monument to this remarkable enterprise on the Old Courthouse Square.

*Information: Tahlequah Area Chamber of Commerce, 123 E. Delaware St.,*
*918-456-3742, 800-456-4860; www.tahlequahok.com*

## WHAT TO SEE AND DO

### CHEROKEE HERITAGE CENTER

*21192 S. Keeler Drive, Tahlequah, 918-456-6007,*
*888-999-6007; www.cherokeeheritage.org*

A National Museum of Cherokee artifacts, this center features a reconstructed rural village. Monday-Saturday 10 a.m.-5 p.m., Sunday 1-5 p.m.

## SPECIAL EVENTS

### TRAIL OF TEARS

*Tsa-La-Gi Amphitheater, Tahlequah, 918-456-6007*

A professional cast presents a musical drama depicting the history of the Cherokee Tribe. Mid-June-Labor Day, Monday-Saturday evenings.

### CHEROKEE NATIONAL HOLIDAY

*Tahlequah, 918-456-0671; www.holiday.cherokee.org*

Celebration of Constitutional Convention. Championship cornstalk bow and arrow shoot, powwow. Labor Day weekend.

### ILLINOIS RIVER BALLOON FEST

*Tahlequah City Municipal Airport, Tahlequah, 918-456-3742; www.okballoonfest.com*

Balloon race, balloon glow, arts and crafts, carnival, skydiving exhibition, food. Mid-August.

**OKLAHOMA**

★
★
★
★
★

## HOTEL
### ★★TAHLEQUAH MOTOR LODGE
*2501 S. Muskogee Ave., Tahlequah, 918-456-2350, 800-480-8705*
53 rooms. Pets accepted. Complimentary full breakfast. Wireless Internet access. Restaurant. Indoor pool, whirlpool. **$**

# TENKILLER FERRY LAKE
*Information: www.oklahomafishingguides.com*

## WHAT TO SEE AND DO
### TENKILLER FERRY LAKE
*Highway 64, Tahlequah, 918-489-5643; www.laketenkiller.com*
The shores of this lake are lined with cliffs, rock bluffs and wooded slopes. The Tenkiller Ferry Dam on the Illinois River is 197 feet high and backs up the stream for 34 miles, creating more than 130 miles of shoreline. There are 12,900 acres of water surface. The lake has marinas, lodges and boat docks; the lower Illinois River is famous for its striped bass fishing.

## HOTEL
### ★★FIN & FEATHER RESORT
*RR 1, Gore, 918-487-5148; www.finandfeatherresort.com*
83 rooms. Closed October-Easter. Pets accepted, some restrictions; fee. Restaurant. Indoor pool with retractable roof, children's pool, whirlpool. Spa. Tennis. **$**

# TULSA

No oil derricks are visible to visitors, yet Tulsa is an important energy city. Oil and gas fields surround it, and the offices of energy companies are prevalent: more than 600 energy firms employ 30,000 people. This is the second-largest city in Oklahoma and its atmosphere is cosmopolitan.

With the completion of the Arkansas River Navigation System, Tulsa gained a water route to the Great Lakes and the Gulf of Mexico. The Port of Catoosa, three miles from the city and located on the Verdigris River, is at the headwaters of the waterway and is now America's westernmost inland water port.

*Information: Convention & Visitors Bureau, 616 S. Boston Ave.,*
*918-585-1201, 800-558-3311; www.visittulsa.com*

## WHAT TO SEE AND DO
### ARKANSAS RIVER HISTORICAL SOCIETY MUSEUM
*Tulsa Port of Catoosa, 5350 Cimarron Road, Catoosa,*
*918-266-2291; www.tulsaweb.com/port/museum.htm*
Located in the Port Authority Building, this museum has pictorial displays and operating models that trace the history of the 1,450-mile Arkansas River and McClellan-Kerr Navigation System. Monday-Friday 8 a.m.-4:30 p.m.

### BELL'S AMUSEMENT PARK
*3901 E. 21st St., Tulsa, 918-744-1991; www.teamled.com/bells/directions.htm*
Rides include a large wooden roller coaster, log ride, sky ride and bumper boats, plus two miniature golf courses and an arcade. June-August, daily; April-May and September, weekends.

OKLAHOMA

★
★★
★★
★

### BOSTON AVENUE UNITED METHODIST CHURCH

*1301 S. Boston Ave., Tulsa, 918-583-5181;*
*www.bostonavenue.org*

Designed and built in 1929 by Adah Robinson, this structure was the first large-scale Art Deco church. It features a 225-foot tower and many lesser towers decorated with bas-relief pioneer figures. The sanctuary is ornamented with Italian mosaic reredos. Tours after 11 a.m. Sunday service, during the week by appointment.

### CREEK COUNCIL OAK TREE

*18th Street and Cheyenne Avenue, Tulsa*

A landscaped plot housing the Council Oak, this tree stands as a memorial to the Lochapokas Creek tribe.

### GILCREASE MUSEUM

*1400 Gilcrease Museum Road, Tulsa, 918-596-2700; www.gilcrease.org*

Founded by Thomas Gilcrease, an oil man of Creek descent, this museum has a collection of Native American art and artifacts from 12,000 years ago to the present. The library houses about 90,000 items, including the earliest known letter sent to Europe from the New World. Tuesday-Sunday 10 a.m.-5 p.m.; closed Monday, Christmas Day.

### OXLEY NATURE CENTER

*6700 Mohawk Blvd., Tulsa, 918-669-6644; www.oxleynaturecenter.org*

This 800-acre wildlife sanctuary has numerous nature trails. Monday-Saturday 10 a.m.-4.30 p.m., Sunday noon-4.30 p.m.

### PHILBROOK MUSEUM OF ART

*2727 S. Rockford Road, Tulsa, 918-749-7941, 800-324-7941;*
*www.philbrook.org*

Exhibits include Italian Renaissance, 19th-century English, American and Native American paintings; Native American baskets and pottery; Chinese jade and decorative material; Southeast Asian tradeware; African sculpture. Housed in an Italian Renaissance Revival villa on 23 acres; formal and sculpture gardens. Tuesday-Sunday 10 a.m.-5 p.m., Thursday until 8 p.m.; closed holidays.

### SHERWIN MILLER MUSEUM OF JEWISH ART

*2021 E. 71st St., Tulsa, 918-492-1818; www.jewishmuseum.net*

The Southwest's largest collection of Judaica contains objects representative of Jewish history, art, ceremonial events and daily life from around the world. Monday-Friday 10 a.m.-5 p.m., Sunday 1-5 p.m.; closed Jewish holidays.

### THE TULSA ZOO

*6421 E. 36th St., Tulsa, 918-669-6600; www.tulsazoo.com*

More than 200 varieties of animals are housed within 68 acres of landscaped grounds. The zoo features Native American artifacts, geological specimens, dinosaur replicas, live plants and animals. Daily 9 a.m.-5 p.m.; closed third Friday in June and Christmas Day.

## UTICA SQUARE

*21st and Utica streets, Tulsa, 918-742-5531; www.uticasquare.com*

This upscale shopping district includes Saks Fifth Avenue, Coach and Williams-Sonoma. Set in a peaceful landscape that features manicured gardens, the area features many restaurants and cafés.

## SPECIAL EVENT
### DISCOVERYLAND! OUTDOOR THEATER

*19501 W. 41st St., Tulsa, 918-245-6552; discoverylandusa.com*

This theater presents Rodgers and Hammerstein's *Oklahoma!* in a 2,000-seat outdoor theater complex with a Western theme. Authentic Native American dancing, Western musical revue and barbecue dinner prior to performance. Mid-June-late August, Monday-Friday.

## HOTELS
### ★★BEST WESTERN TRADE WINDS CENTRAL INN

*3141 E. Skelly Drive, Tulsa, 918-749-5561, 800-780-7234; www.bestwestern.com*

164 rooms. Complimentary continental breakfast. Wireless Internet access. Restaurant, bar. Fitness room. Outdoor pool. Airport transportation available. Business center. $

### ★★★CROWNE PLAZA

*100 E. Second St., Tulsa, 918-582-9000, 800-227-6963; www.crowneplaza.com*

This hotel caters to business travelers with its central Tulsa location. A full-service spa, restaurant, lounge, business center, indoor and outdoor pools, fitness room, and conference facilities are among the services. 460 rooms. Pets accepted; fee. Wireless Internet access. Restaurant, bar. Fitness room, spa. Indoor pool, outdoor pool. Airport transportation available. Business center. $

### ★★DOUBLETREE HOTEL

*616 W. Seventh St., Tulsa, 918-587-8000, 800-222-8733;*
*www.doubletree.com*

417 rooms. Pets accepted; fee. Wireless Internet access. Restaurant, bar. Fitness room. Indoor pool, whirlpool. Airport transportation available. Business center. $

### ★★EMBASSY SUITES

*3332 S. 79th E. Ave., Tulsa, 918-622-4000, 800-362-2779;*
*www.embassysuites.com*

244 rooms, all suites. Pets accepted; fee. Complimentary full breakfast. Wireless Internet access. Restaurant, bar. Fitness room. Indoor pool, whirlpool. Airport transportation available. Business center. $

### ★HAMPTON INN

*3209 S. 79th E. Ave., Tulsa, 918-663-1000, 800-426-7866;*
*www.hamptoninn.com*

148 rooms. Pets accepted; fee. Complimentary continental breakfast. Wireless Internet access. Outdoor pool. Airport transportation available. Business center. $

### ★★★HILTON TULSA SOUTHERN HILLS

*7902 S. Lewis St., Tulsa, 918-492-5000, 800-774-1500; www.hilton.com*

Located in the Southern Hills area of Tulsa and across the street from Oral Roberts University, this hotel features spacious guest rooms with plush beds and Crabtree and Evelyn bath products. There's also complimentary wireless Internet access and a full fitness center. 282 rooms. Pets accepted, some restrictions; fee. Wireless Internet access. Restaurant, bar. Fitness center. Outdoor pool. Airport transportation available. Business center. $

### ★LA QUINTA INN

*6030 E. Skelly Drive, Tulsa, 918-665-2630, 800-447-0600; www.laquinta.com*

105 rooms. Pets accepted. Complimentary continental breakfast. Wireless Internet access. Fitness room. Outdoor pool. Business center. $

### ★★★MARRIOTT TULSA SOUTHERN HILLS

*1902 E. 71st St., Tulsa, 918-493-7000, 866-530-3760; www.marriott.com*

Rising 11 stories in two connected wings, the Marriott Tulsa Southern Hills offers well-appointed guest rooms with full amenities. It is located near golf courses, tennis facilities, the Tulsa Zoo and other area attractions. 383 rooms. Wireless Internet access. Restaurant, bar. Fitness room, spa. Indoor pool, whirlpool. Airport transportation available. Business center. $

### ★PRESIDENTIAL SUITES TULSA

*8338 E. 61 St. S., Tulsa, 918-254-0088, 888-627-1155;*
*www.presidentialsuitestulsa.com*

52 rooms. Pets accepted; fee. Complimentary full breakfast. Wireless Internet access. Bar. Outdoor pool. Spa. Airport transportation available. Business center. $

### ★★★RADISSON HOTEL TULSA

*10918 E. 41st St., Tulsa, 918-627-5000, 800-325-3535; www.radissontulsa.com*

This hotel features an indoor water park. Located in the heart of southeast Tulsa, near the Tulsa International Airport and the Philbrook Museum, the hotel has rooms that are comfortable and spacious. 325 rooms. Pets accepted, some restrictions. Wireless Internet access. Two restaurants, bar. Children's activity center. Fitness room. Indoor pool, outdoor pool, whirlpool. Airport transportation available. Business center. $

## RESTAURANTS

### ★BAXTER'S INTERURBAN GRILL

*717 S. Houston Ave., Tulsa, 918-585-3134; www.baxtersgrill.com*

American menu. Lunch, dinner. Closed Sunday; holidays. Bar. Children's menu. Business casual attire. Outdoor seating. $$

### ★★★BODEAN SEAFOOD

*3323 E. 51st St., Tulsa, 918-749-1407; www.bodean.net*

This popular restaurant serves creative seafood dishes—items are flown in twice daily—in a comfortable atmosphere that includes white linen-topped tables. A three-course prix fixe menu is available, and Tuesdays feature a four-course menu with three wines to match. Seafood menu. Lunch, dinner. Bar. Casual attire. $$

★
★
★
★
★

### ★★CAMERELLI'S

*1536 E. 15th St., Tulsa, 918-582-8900*

Italian menu. Lunch, dinner, brunch. Bar. Casual attire. Reservations recommended. **$$$**

### ★JAMIL'S

*2833 E. 51st St., Tulsa, 918-742-9097;*
*www.jamilsrestaurant.com*

Seafood, steak menu. Dinner, Lunch. Casual attire. **$$**

### ★METRO DINER

*3001 E. 11th St., Tulsa, 918-592-2616*

American menu. Breakfast, lunch, dinner. Children's menu. Casual attire. **$**

### ★★★POLO GRILL

*2038 Utica Square, Tulsa, 918-744-4280; www.pologrill.com*

The creative American cuisine served at this restaurant features French, Southern and Southwest influences. Signature dishes include oven-roasted tomato bisque, tender leaf spinach and strawberry salad, crispy grit cakes, grilled steaks and baked fudge. There is a nine-course prix fixe tasting menu and an extensive wine list. American menu. Lunch, dinner. Closed Sunday. Bar. Children's menu. Business casual attire. Reservations recommended. Outdoor seating. **$$$**

### ★RICARDOS

*5629 E. 41st St., Tulsa, 918-622-2668; www.ricardostulsa.com*

Mexican menu. Lunch, dinner. Closed Sunday. Children's menu. Casual attire. **$**

### ★★TI AMO ITALIAN RISTORANTE

*6024A S. Sheridan Road, Tulsa, 918-499-1919; www.tiamotulsa.com*

Italian menu. Lunch, dinner. Bar. Business casual attire. **$$**

### ★★★WARREN DUCK CLUB

*6110 S. Yale Ave., Tulsa, 918-495-1000;*
*www.doubletree.com*

This fine-dining restaurant is located inside the Doubletree Hotel. The menu features American classics such as grilled steaks, seafood and more. American menu. Breakfast, lunch, dinner, late-night. Bar. Children's menu. Valet parking. **$$$**

# WEATHERFORD

Weatherford is the home of Southwestern Oklahoma State University as well as *Gemini* and *Apollo* astronaut Thomas P. Stafford.

*Information: Chamber of Commerce, 522 W. Rainey Ave.,*
*580-772-7744, 800-725-7744; www.weatherfordchamber.com*

## WHAT TO SEE AND DO
### RED ROCK CANYON STATE PARK

*Highway 281, Weatherford, 405-542-6344; www.touroklahoma.com*

This park covers 310 acres and features a swimming pool and bathhouse. Hiking, picnicking and camping are also available. Daily.

### STAFFORD AIR AND SPACE CENTER

*Stafford Field, 3000 E. Logan Road, Weatherford, 580-772-5871;*
*www.staffordspacecenter.com*

This museum houses memorabilia of former astronaut Thomas Stafford, who flew on *Gemini VI* and *IX* as well as *Apollo X*. Monday-Saturday 9 a.m.-5 p.m., Sunday 1-5 p.m.

## HOTEL
### ★BEST WESTERN MARK MOTOR HOTEL

*525 E. Main St., Weatherford, 580-772-3325, 800-780-7234; www.bestwestern.com*

63 rooms. Complimentary full breakfast. High-speed Internet access. Outdoor pool. $

## RESTAURANT
### ★★T-BONE STEAK HOUSE

*1805 E. Main St., Weatherford, 580-772-6329; www.tbonesteakhouse.com*

Steak menu. Dinner. Bar. Children's menu. $$

# WOODWARD

A land run community, Woodward grew thanks to its location on the Great Western Cattle Trail. Temple Houston, son of Texas Republic President Sam Houston, lived and worked here as a lawyer and is buried in Elmwood Cemetary.

*Information: Chamber of Commerce, 1006 Oklahoma Ave., 580-256-7411,*
*800-364-5352; www.woodwardok.com*

## WHAT TO SEE AND DO

### HISTORIC FORT SUPPLY

*Highway 270, Woodward, 580-766-3767*

Established as a temporary cavalry supply camp in the late 1800s, the fort endured as a trail stop between Kansas, Texas and Oklahoma. Restored original buildings include the Powder Monkey's House and Teamsters Cabin, the Commanding Officer's Quarters and the Officer's Quarters. The Guard House is now a museum. Tours, Monday-Friday.

### PLAINS INDIANS & PIONEERS MUSEUM

*2009 Williams Ave., Woodward, 580-256-6136; www.pipm1.org*

Changing and permanent displays depict Native American culture and early life on the plains. Pioneer, cowboy and Native American artifacts and clothing; collection of personal belongings of Temple Houston, son of Sam Houston; exhibits from early-day banks; original building from historic Fort Supply; agriculture building; art center with changing exhibits. Tuesday-Saturday 10 a.m.-5 p.m.

## HOTEL
### ★★NORTHWEST INN

*Highway 270 and 1st Street, Woodward, 580-256-7600, 800-727-7606;*
*www.northwestinnok.com*

124 rooms. Pets accepted, some restrictions; fee. Wireless Internet access. Restaurant, bar. Indoor pool. $

**OKLAHOMA**

★
★
★
★
★

# SOUTH DAKOTA

THIS IS THE LAND OF THE PROUD AND MIGHTY SIOUX. IF YOUR ONLY PICTURE OF THIS TRIBE is from the 1990 film *Dances With Wolves*, a visit to South Dakota will reveal much about the fascinating history of this vast nation that ruled the plains, hunting buffalo by horseback. South Dakota Sioux are generally referred to as Lakota, Dakota or Nakota, and today there are more than 62,000 members of the tribes living in the state.

There are museums and monuments throughout the state where visitors can learn more about the Sioux, from the Crazy Horse Memorial and Indian Museum of North America in Custer, to the Cultural Heritage Center in the state capital of Pierre. Visit a powwow or tribal gathering with dancing and contests during the summer months in towns throughout the state. Or soak up the scenery with a drive along the Native American Scenic Byway, which stretches from Nebraska north through the center of South Dakota.

Beyond its rich Native American history, South Dakota is a quiet, sparsely filled space teeming with natural beauty. Each year, scores of tourists visit Badlands National Park, or trek a little further west to take a look at one of the country's most recognizable monuments, Mount Rushmore, a granite mountain carved with the visages of George Washington, Thomas Jefferson, Abraham Lincoln and Theodore Roosevelt.

South Dakota offers more than parks and presidential figures. It's one of the nation's richest archaeological dig sites. The largest and most complete *Tyrannosaurus rex* in the world, Sue (who now lives at Chicago's Field Museum) was discovered here, and mammoths, marine life and other creatures from the earth's past are found regularly. Join in an archeological dig during summer months with Rapid City's Archaeological Research Center, or any of the other organizations digging in the state. South Dakota tourism can provide tips on active digs.

Urbanites will find plenty to do in the state's big cities, from capital city Pierre in the center to Sioux Falls in the west.

Americana abounds in South Dakota, with roadside delights like the famously kitschy Corn Palace in Mitchell and more diners serving inexpensive, hearty meals and fantastic slices of fruit pie than any appetite can handle.

*Information: www.travelsd.com*

**FUN FACTS**

Mount Rushmore was supposed to depict the full torsos of the four presidents, not just their faces, but insufficient funds forced the carvings to stop.

Laura Ingalls Wilder's book *By the Shores of Silver Lake* is based on her childhood years in De Smet.

Dakota is a Sioux word meaning "ally."

Television news anchor Tom Brokaw is from Webster, South Dakota.

# ABERDEEN

The roots of Aberdeen's commerce are the three railroads that converge here, giving it the nickname "Hub City." Alexander Mitchell, a railroader of the 19th century, named the town for his Scottish birthplace. German-Russian immigrants arrived in 1884. Hamlin Garland, author of *Son of the Middle Border*, and L. Frank Baum, author of *The Wizard of Oz*, lived here.

*Information: Convention & Visitors Bureau, 10 Railroad Ave. S.W., 605-225-2414, 800-645-3851; www.aberdeencvb.com*

## HOTELS

### ★★BEST WESTERN RAMKOTA HOTEL

*1400 N.W. Eighth Ave., Aberdeen, 605-229-4040, 800-780-7234; www.ramkota.com*
154 rooms. Pets accepted. Restaurant, bar. High-speed Internet access. Fitness room. Indoor pool, whirlpool. Airport transportation available. Business center. $

### ★★RAMADA INN & CONVENTION CENTER

*2727 S.E. Sixth Ave., Aberdeen, 605-225-3600, 800-272-6232; www.ramada.com*
152 rooms. Pets accepted. Complimentary continental breakfast. High-speed Internet access. Restaurant, bar. Indoor pool, whirlpool. Airport transportation available. $

## TOURING THE BLACK HILLS

Magnificent forests, mountain scenery, ghost towns, Mount Rushmore National Memorial, Harney Peak (highest mountain east of the Rockies), Crazy Horse Memorial, swimming, horseback riding, rodeos, hiking, skiing, and the Black Hills Passion Play make up only a partial list of the attractions in this area. Memories of Calamity Jane, Wild Bill Hickock and Preacher Smith haunt the old Western towns. Bison, deer, elk, coyotes, mountain goats, bighorn sheep and smaller animals make this area home.

Black Hills National Forest includes 1,247,000 acres—nearly half of the Black Hills. The forest offers 28 campgrounds, 20 picnic grounds and one winter sports area. Two snowmobile trail systems, one in the Bear Lodge Mountains and the other in the northern Black Hills, offer 330 miles of some of the best snowmobiling in the nation. There are also 250 miles of hiking, bridle and mountain biking trails.

There is a whimsical story that explains the formation of the Black Hills. Paul Bunyan had a stove so large that boys with hams strapped to their feet skated on the top to grease it for the famous camp flapjacks. One day when the stove was red hot, Babe, Paul's favorite blue ox, swallowed it whole and took off. He died of a combination of indigestion and exhaustion. Paul, weeping so copiously his tears eroded the Badlands, built the Black Hills as a cairn over his old friend.

Geologists say that the Black Hills were formed by a great geologic uplift that pushed a mighty dome of ancient granite up under the sandstone and limestone layers. Water washed away these softer rocks, exposing the granite. This uplift was slow, and it may still be happening. Pactola Visitor Center, on Highway 385 at Pactola Reservoir west of Rapid City, has information and interpretive exhibits on Black Hills history, geology, and ecology. Memorial Day-Labor Day.
Information: www.blackhills.com

**SOUTH DAKOTA**

★
★★
★★
★

## RESTAURANT
### ★★FLAME RESTAURANT AND LOUNGE
*2 S. Main St., Aberdeen, 605-225-2082*
American menu. Lunch, dinner. Closed Sunday. Bar. Children's menu. Casual attire. **$$**

# BROOKINGS
Research done at South Dakota State University has helped make Brookings the agricultural capital of the state. It has developed diversified farming and manufacturing industries.

*Information: Chamber of Commerce-Convention & Visitor Bureau, 2308 E. Sixth St., 605-692-6125, 800-699-6125; www.brookingssd.com*

## HOTEL
### ★★DAYS INN BROOKINGS
*2500 E. Sixth St., Brookings, 605-692-9471, 877-831-1562; www.daysinn.com*
125 rooms. Pets accepted, some restrictions. Complimentary continental breakfast. Restaurant, bar. High-speed Internet access. Fitness room. Indoor pool, whirlpool. Airport transportation available. Business center. **$**

## RESTAURANT
### ★★THE RAM & O'HARE'S
*327 Main Ave., Brookings, 605-692-2485*
American menu. Lunch, dinner. Closed Sunday. Bar. Children's menu. Casual attire. **$$**

# CUSTER
This is where a prospector with Lieutenant Colonel Custer's expedition of 1874 discovered gold, prompting the gold rush of 1875-1876. Main Street was laid out in the 1880s, wide enough for wagons pulled by teams of oxen to make U-turns. Custer is the seat of Custer County, headquarters of the Black Hills National Forest and center of an area of great mineral wealth. Gold, quartz, beryl, mica and gypsum are some of the minerals that are mined here. Custer is a popular area for winter sports activities.

*Information: Custer County Chamber of Commerce, 615 Washington St., 605-673-2244, 800-992-9818; www.custersd.com*

## HOTELS
### ★BAVARIAN INN
*Highway 16 and 385 N., Custer, 605-673-2802, 800-657-4312; www.bavarianinnsd.com*
65 rooms. Pets accepted; fee. Complimentary continental breakfast. Indoor pool, outdoor pool, whirlpool. Closed December-February. **$**

### ★★STATE GAME LODGE
*Highway 16A, Custer, 605-255-4541, 800-658-3530; www.custerresorts.com*
68 rooms. Pets accepted, some restrictions; fee. Restaurant, bar. Closed October-April. **$**

### ★★SYLVAN LAKE RESORT
*24572 SD Highway 87 and Harney Peak, Custer, 605-574-2561, 800-658-3530; www.custerresorts.com*
33 rooms. Pets accepted, some restrictions; fee. Restaurant. Closed November-April. **$**

★
★
★
★
★

# CRAZY HORSE MEMORIAL

This large sculpture, still being carved from the granite of Thunderhead Mountain, was the life work of Korczak Ziolkowski (1908-1982), who briefly assisted Gutzon Borglum on Mount Rushmore. With funds gained solely from admission fees and contributions, Ziolkowski worked alone on the memorial, refusing federal and state funding. The sculptor's wife and several of their children are continuing the work.

Crazy Horse—the stalwart Sioux chief who helped defeat Custer and the United States Seventh Cavalry—is depicted astride a magnificent horse in this nine-story carving. When completed in the round, the mountain carving will be 563 feet high and 641 feet long—the largest sculpture in the world. To date, 8.4 million tons of granite have been blasted off the mountain. Audiovisual programs and displays show how the mountain is being carved.

The Indian Museum of North America is located here and has almost 20,000 artifacts in three wings. A Native American educational and cultural center opened in 1997. Memorial Day, Memorial Day-Native American Day (October 13), 7 a.m.-dusk; Winter 8 a.m.-5 p.m. Information: Avenue of the Chiefs, Crazy Horse, five miles north off Highway 16, 605-673-4681; www.crazyhorse.org

## SPECIALTY LODGING
### CUSTER MANSION BED AND BREAKFAST

*35 Centennial Drive, Custer, 605-673-3333, 877-519-4948; www.custermansionbb.com*
Six rooms. Complimentary full breakfast. $

## RESTAURANT
### ★ELK CANYON STEAKHOUSE

*511 Mount Rushmore Road, Custer, 605-673-4477*
Steak menu. Breakfast, lunch, dinner, brunch. Bar. Children's menu. Casual attire. $$

# CUSTER STATE PARK

This is one of the largest state parks in the United States—73,000 acres. A mountain recreation area and game refuge, the park has one of the largest publicly owned herds of bison in the country (more than 1,400), as well as Rocky Mountain bighorn sheep, mountain goats, burros, deer, elk and other wildlife. Four man-made lakes and three streams provide excellent fishing and swimming. Near the park is the site of the original gold strike of 1874 and a replica of the Gordon stockade, built by the first gold rush party in 1874.

The Peter Norbeck Visitor Center (May-October, daily) has information about the park and naturalist programs, which are offered daily (May-September). Paddleboats; horseback riding, hiking, bicycle rentals, Jeep rides, camping, hayrides, chuck wagon cookouts. The Black Hills Playhouse, in the heart of the park, is the scene of productions for 11 weeks (mid-June-late August, schedule varies; 605-255-4141). Information: Custer, five miles east on Highway 16A, 605-255-4515; www.custerstatepark.info

**SOUTH DAKOTA**

★
★
★
★
★

# DEADWOOD

This town is best known for gold and the famous Wild West characters such as Calamity Jane, Preacher Smith and Wild Bill Hickock who lived here. The main street runs through Deadwood Gulch. The rest of the town crawls up the steep canyon sides. A bust of Hickock by Korczak Ziolkowski—creator of the Crazy Horse Memorial—stands on Sherman Street. At the height of the 1876 gold rush, 25,000 people swarmed over the hillsides to dig gold. When gold was first struck at Deadwood, nearly the entire population of Custer rushed here. Predictably, at the height of a newer strike, nearly the entire population of Deadwood rushed to the town of Lead. Recently, legalized gambling has given Deadwood another boom.

*Information: Deadwood Area Chamber of Commerce and Visitors Bureau, 735 Main St., 605-578-1876, 800-999-1876; www.deadwood.org*

## WHAT TO SEE AND DO
### MOUNT MORIAH CEMETERY
*Deadwood, 605-578-2600*
Graves of Wild Bill Hickock, Calamity Jane, Preacher Smith, Seth Bullock and others.

### OLD STYLE SALOON #10
*657 Main St., Deadwood, 605-578-3346; www.saloon10.com*
Collection of Western artifacts, pictures, guns. This is the saloon in which Wild Bill Hickock was shot. Entertainment (four shows per day, Memorial Day-Labor Day), gambling, refreshments, restaurant. Daily; closed holidays.

## HOTEL
### ★★BULLOCK HOTEL & CASINO
*633 Main St., Deadwood, 605-578-1745, 800-336-1876; www.historicbullock.com*
28 rooms. Restaurant, bar. Internet access. Fitness room. Casino. **$**

## RESTAURANT
### ★★★JAKE'S ATOP THE MIDNIGHT STAR
*677 Main St., Deadwood, 605-578-1555, 800-999-6482; www.themidnightstar.com*
Located on the top floor of the Midnight Star Casino, this elegant dining room serves American favorites. Piano entertainment is provided five nights a week. American menu. Dinner. Bar. Children's menu. Casual attire. Reservations recommended. **$$**

# HILL CITY

Hill City is a beautiful mountain town in the heart of the Black Hills. The Black Hills Institute of Geological Research and a Ranger District office of the Black Hills National Forest are located here.

*Information: Chamber of Commerce, 324 Main St., 605-574-2368, 800-888-1798; www.hillcitysd.com*

## HOTEL
### ★★BEST WESTERN GOLDEN SPIKE INN & SUITES
*106 Main St., Hill City, 605-574-2577, 800-780-7234; www.hillcitysd.com*
87 rooms. Pets accepted; fee. Restaurant. Fitness room. Indoor pool, outdoor pool, whirlpool. Closed mid-November-mid-March. **$**

## RESTAURANT

### ★★ALPINE INN

*225 Main St., Hill City, 605-574-2749; www.alpineinnhillcity.com*
American, German menu. Lunch, dinner. Closed Sunday. Casual attire. **$**

# HOT SPRINGS

Hot Springs, the seat of Fall River County, is on the southeast edge of the Black Hills National Forest. Many local buildings are made of pink, red and buff sandstone. A Ranger District office of the Nebraska National Forest is located here.
*Information: Chamber of Commerce, 801 S. Sixth St.,*
*605-745-4140, 800-325-6991; www.hotsprings-sd.com*

## WHAT TO SEE AND DO

### HOT SPRINGS HISTORIC DISTRICT

*River Street, Hot Springs*
The presence of underground springs catalyzed the development of Hot Springs in the 1880s, with River Street being the epicenter of the boom. The district includes 130 buildings on more than 3,000 acres, including 39 impressive Richardsonian-Romanesque structures made of locally quarried sandstone. Several are occupied by spas fed by the springs, while others house eateries and art galleries.

### MAMMOTH SITE OF HOT SPRINGS

*Hot Springs, 605-745-6017; www.mammothsite.com*
Excavation of a remarkable concentration of mammoth skeletons; to date the remains of 51 mammoths, a camel and a giant short-faced bear have been unearthed. Daily.

# HURON

Huron, the seat of Beadle County, is also the administrative center for a number of federal and state agencies. Twelve city parks feature swimming, picnicking, golf, tennis and ballfields. Nearby De Smet is famous for being the home of author Laura Ingalls Wilder.
*Information: Huron Convention & Visitors Bureau, 15 Fourth St. S.W.,*
*605-352-0000, 800-487-6673; www.huronsd.com*

## WHAT TO SEE AND DO

### GLADYS PYLE HISTORIC HOME

*376 Idaho Ave. Southeast, Huron, 605-352-2528*
This Queen Anne-style house, built in 1894, was the residence of the first elected female U.S. senator. Daily, afternoons only.

### HUBERT H. HUMPHREY DRUGSTORE

*233 Dakota S., Huron, 605-352-4064;*
*www.huronsd.com/livinginhuron.htm*
Mid-1930s atmosphere; owned by the former senator and vice-president until his death; still owned by Humphrey family. Monday-Saturday.

★
★
★
★
★

## HOTEL
### ★★CROSSROADS HOTEL & CONVENTION CENTER
*100 Fourth St. S.W., Huron, 605-352-3204, 800-876-5858;*
*www.crossroadshotel.com*
100 rooms. Pets accepted, some restrictions; fee. Restaurant, bar. Indoor pool, whirlpool. Airport transportation available. **$**

# KEYSTONE
Sculptor Gutzon Borglum began drilling into the 6,200-foot Mount Rushmore in 1927. His carving took 14 years to complete and cost a mere $1 million, though it's now deemed priceless. Keystone is the entrance to Mount Rushmore and Custer State Park. A former mining town supplying miners for the Peerless, Hugo and the Holy Terror Gold Mine, it was also home to Carrie Ingalls (sister of Laura Ingalls Wilder) and the men who carved Mount Rushmore.
*Information: Chamber of Commerce, 605-666-4896, 800-456-3345;*
*www.keystonechamber.com*

## WHAT TO SEE AND DO
### BORGLUM HISTORICAL CENTER
*342 Winter St., Keystone, 605-666-4449, 800-888-4369*
Born in Idaho, Gutzon Borglum won acclaim for his early paintings and was sent by patrons to study in Paris. After he returned to the United States, his lifelike sculptures generated a buzz in the national arts community. Sculpting success led Borglum in 1916 to propose carving the likeness of Robert E. Lee into Stone Mountain in Georgia, a project that he left in 1925 after clashing with financiers. At the age of 60, he embarked on the work that immortalized his fame—carving presidents' faces on Mount Rushmore. Borglum died just before its completion and his son Lincoln finished the sculpture. The Borglum Historical Center tells the story of Gutzon's remarkable life, focusing on his Mount Rushmore days. The center's exhibits include a full-size replica of Lincoln's eye from the monument, assorted artworks by Borglum and a documentary about the Mount Rushmore project, narrated by former U.S. Senator (and South Dakotan) Tom Daschle. May, September, daily 9 a.m.-5 p.m.; June-August, daily 8 a.m.-6 p.m.

### RUSHMORE AERIAL TRAMWAY
*203 Cemetery Road, Keystone, 605-666-4478*
This 15-minute ride allows a view of the Black Hills and Mount Rushmore across the valley. May-mid-September, daily.

## HOTEL
### ★BEST WESTERN FOUR PRESIDENTS LODGE
*24075 Highway 16A, Keystone, 605-666-4472, 800-780-7234; www.bestwestern.com*
50 rooms. Pets accepted; fee. Closed November-March. Complimentary continental breakfast. High-speed Internet access. Fitness room. Indoor pool, whirlpool. Spa. **$**

# LEAD
The chain of gold mines that began in Custer and spread through the Black Hills to Deadwood ended in Lead. The discovery of gold here in 1876 eventually led to

SOUTH DAKOTA

★
★★
★★★
★★★★
★★★★★

the development of the Homestake Mine, one of the largest gold producers in this hemisphere. Lead is located on mountaintops with the Homestake Mine burrowing under the town.

*Information: Deadwood Area Chamber of Commerce and Visitors Bureau,*

*735 Historic Main St., Deadwood, 605-578-1876, 800-999-1876; www.lead.sd.us*

## HOTEL
### ★★GOLDEN HILLS RESORT
*900 Miners Ave., Lead, 605-584-1800, 888-465-3080*

100 rooms. Pets accepted, some restrictions; fee. Complimentary continental breakfast. Restaurant, bar. $

# MITCHELL

This is a tree-shaded town in the James River Valley, where agriculture is celebrated with a colorful nine-day festival each September at the famous Corn Palace, a popular tourist attraction.

*Information: Chamber of Commerce, 601 N. Main St.,*

*605-996-6223, 866-273-2676; www.cornpalace.org*

## WHAT TO SEE AND DO
### THE CORN PALACE
*601 N. Main St., Mitchell, 605-996-6223; www.cornpalace.org*

Mitchell dubs itself the Corn Capital of the World, a designation backed up by this one-of-a-kind community center. Each year since 1921, locals have decorated the exterior of the turreted, czarist Russia-style palace with different murals, but with a twist—the medium is not paint, but thousands of bushels of corn and other South Dakota grains. The initial intent of the place was to prove the fertility of the South Dakota soil, but it has since evolved into a roadside tourist attraction. The Corn Palace Festival, held annually in September, celebrates the annual fall harvest with concerts, a carnival midway and other festivities. After the harvest, pigeons devour the palace's second skin, leaving the grand façade blank and ready for redecoration the following spring. Daily 8 a.m.-5 p.m., until 9 p.m. in summer.

## HOTELS
### ★COMFORT INN
*2020 Highland Way, Mitchell, 605-990-2400; www.comfortinn.com*

72 rooms. Complimentary continental breakfast. High-speed Internet access. Indoor pool, whirlpool. Business center. Fitness room. $

### ★DAYS INN
*1506 S. Burr St., Mitchell, 605-996-6208; www.daysinn.com*

68 rooms. Pets accepted. Complimentary continental breakfast. Wireless Internet access. Indoor pool, children's pool, whirlpool. Business center. $

### ★★RAMADA INN
*1525 W. Havens St., Mitchell, 605-996-6501, 800-888-4702; www.ramada.com*

153 rooms. Pets accepted, some restrictions; fee. Restaurant, bar. Fitness room. Indoor pool, children's pool, whirlpool. Airport transportation available. $

SOUTH DAKOTA

★
★
★
★
★

## RESTAURANT

**★★CHEF LOUIE'S**

*601 E. Havens St., Mitchell, 605-996-7565*

Steak menu. Dinner. Closed Sunday. Bar. Children's menu. Casual attire. **$$**

# MOBRIDGE

The Milwaukee Railroad built a bridge across the Missouri River in 1906 at what was once the site of an Arikara and Sioux village. A telegraph operator used the contraction "Mobridge" to indicate his location. The name has remained the same. Today, Mobridge is centered in farm and ranch country and is still home for a large Native American population. Located on the Oahe Reservoir, Mobridge is noted for its superb fishing.

*Information: Chamber of Commerce, 103 Main St., 605-845-2387; www.mobridge.org*

## WHAT TO SEE AND DO

### SITTING BULL MONUMENT

*County 1806 off Highway 12, Mobridge*

Korczak Ziolkowski sculpted the bust for this monument to the legendary Lakota Sioux chief Sitting Bull. The burial ground on the hill affords a beautiful view of the Missouri River and surrounding country.

## HOTEL

### ★★BEST VALUE WRANGLER INN

*820 W. Grand Crossing, Mobridge, 605-845-3641, 888-884-3641;*
*www.wranglerinn.com*

60 rooms. High-speed Internet access. Restaurant, bar. Indoor pool, whirlpool. Business center. **$**

# PIERRE

Pierre is the capital of South Dakota, an honor for which it campaigned hard and won because of its central location—the geographic center of the state. The town grew thanks to cattle ranchers from the west, farmers from the east, local businesspeople and government officials.

*Information: Chamber of Commerce, 800 W. Dakota Ave., 605-224-7361,*
*800-962-2034; www.pierre.org*

## WHAT TO SEE AND DO

### CULTURAL HERITAGE CENTER

*900 Governors Drive, Pierre, 605-773-3458, www.history.org*

This historical museum north of the South Dakota State Capitol is home to collections of artifacts used by ranchers, miners and Native Americans. On display is the Verendrye Plate, buried by French brothers who explored this area in 1743 (making them the first Europeans to visit South Dakota), and more than 1,300 artifacts depicting the history of the Sioux tribes. Monday-Friday 9 a.m.-4:30 p.m., Saturday-Sunday 1-4:30 p.m.

### SOUTH DAKOTA DISCOVERY CENTER AND AQUARIUM

*805 W. Sioux Ave., Pierre, 605-224-8295; www.sd-discovery.com*

Visitors of all ages can encase themselves in a Body Bubble, explore a maze laden with displays about the lifestyles of wild animals or dismantle retired appliances at the

Take Apart Table. The modest aquarium houses fish native to South Dakota. Summer workshops allow kids to dig deeper into a science of their choosing. Daily until 5 p.m.; opening time varies by season.

## HOTELS

### ★★BEST WESTERN RAMKOTA HOTEL

*920 W. Sioux Ave., Pierre, 605-224-6877, 800-780-7234;*
*www.ramkotahotels.com*

151 rooms. Pets accepted. High-speed Internet access. Restaurant, bar. Fitness room. Indoor pool, outdoor pool, whirlpool. Airport transportation available. Business center. $

### ★DAYS INN

*520 W. Sioux Blvd., Pierre, 605-224-0411, 800-329-7466; www.daysinn.com*

79 rooms. Pets accepted. Complimentary breakfast. High-speed Internet access. Fitness room. $

## RESTAURANT

### ★★★LA MINESTRA

*106 E. Dakota Ave., Pierre, 605-224-8090; www.laminestra.com*

Set in Pierre's historic downtown in an 1896 building, the restaurant's dining room features original wainscoting and tin walls and ceilings. Upscale Italian fare is served here, including lobster tortellini and eggplant parmesan. Italian menu. Lunch Monday-Friday, dinner. Closed Sunday. Bar. Reservations not accepted. $$$

# RAPID CITY

In the last few decades, tourism has replaced gold mining as the main industry of Rapid City. Visitors come here to visit nearby Mount Rushmore or to learn about the many dinosaurs that once roamed the area (and even participate in dinosaur digs). Founded only two years after gold was discovered in the Black Hills, Rapid City is a boomtown that persevered. It is the seat of Pennington County, second-largest city in South Dakota, and home of Ellsworth Air Force Base.

*Information: Convention and Visitors Bureau, 444 Mount Rushmore Road N.,*
*605-343-1744, 800-487-3223; www.rapidcitycvb.com*

## WHAT TO SEE AND DO

### BLACK HILLS PETRIFIED FOREST

*8220 Elk Creek Road, Rapid City, 605-787-4560; www.elkresort.net*

Includes interpretive film on the Black Hills geology and petrifaction process; five-block walk-through area of logs ranging from 5-100 feet in length and up to 3-5 feet in diameter and stumps 3-5 feet in height. Self-guided tours. Rock, fossil and mineral museum; gift and rock-lapidary shops. Memorial Day-Labor Day, daily; weather permitting.

### DINOSAUR PARK

*940 Skyline Drive, Rapid City, www.dinosaurpark.net*

This park has life-size steel and cement models of the dinosaurs once numerous in the area. Daily 6 a.m.-10 p.m.

SOUTH DAKOTA

★
★★
★★
★★
★

### MUSEUM OF GEOLOGY

*O'Harra Memorial Building, 501 E. St. Joseph, Rapid City, 605-394-2467;*
*www.sdsmt.edu*

Exceptional display of minerals, fossils, gold samples and other geological material; first *Tyrannosaurus rex* skull found in South Dakota. Monday-Saturday, Sunday afternoons.

### THUNDERHEAD UNDERGROUND FALLS

*10940 W. Highway 44, Rapid City, 605-343-0081; www.thunderheadfalls.com*

This tunnel, which dates to 1878, is one of the oldest gold mining tunnels in the Black Hills area. Stalactites and gold-bearing granite formations. Falls are 600 feet inside the mine. May-October, daily during daylight hours.

## HOTELS

### ★★ALEX JOHNSON

*523 Sixth St., Rapid City, 605-342-1210, 800-888-2539; www.alexjohnson.com*

143 rooms. Pets accepted; fee. Restaurant, bar. High-speed Internet access. Airport transportation available. Business center. $

### ★AMERICINN RAPID CITY

*1632 Rapp St., Rapid City, 605-343-8424, 800-634-3444; www.americinn.com*

64 rooms. Pets accepted. High-speed Internet access. Fitness room. Indoor pool, whirlpool. Business center. $

### ★★BEST WESTERN RAMKOTA HOTEL

*2111 N. Lacrosse St., Rapid City, 605-343-8550, 800-780-7234; www.ramkota.com*

267 rooms. Pets accepted, some restrictions.Wireless Internet access. Restaurant, bar. Fitness room. Indoor pool, whirlpool. Airport transportation available. Business center. $

SOUTH DAKOTA

★
★
★
★
★

## MOUNT RUSHMORE NATIONAL MEMORIAL

The faces of four great American presidents—Washington, Jefferson, Lincoln and Theodore Roosevelt—are carved onto a 5,675-foot mountain in the Black Hills of South Dakota, as grand and enduring as the contributions of the men they represent. Senator Peter Norbeck was instrumental in the realization of the monument. The original plan called for the presidents to be sculpted to the waist. It was a controversial project when sculptor Gutzon Borglum began his work on the carving in 1927. With crews often numbering 30 workers, he continued through 14 years of crisis and heartbreak and had almost finished by March, 1941, when he died. Lincoln Borglum, his son, brought the project to a close in October of that year. Today, the memorial is host to almost 3 million visitors a year. An orientation center, administrative and information headquarters and a snack bar (daily) are on the grounds. Evening program followed by sculpture lighting and other interpretive programs; mid-May-mid-September, daily. Sculptor's studio museum. 2008/2009 operating hours: October-mid-May.

Information: Custer, 25 miles southwest of Rapid City off Highway 16A and Highway 244, 605-574-2523; www.nps.gov/moru

## BADLANDS NATIONAL PARK

This fantastic, painted landscape of steep canyons, spires and razor-edged ridges was made a national monument by President Franklin D. Roosevelt in 1939 and became a national park in 1978. Its stark and simple demonstration of geologic processes has an unusual beauty. Soft clays and sandstones deposited as sediments 26 to 37 million years ago by streams from the Black Hills created vast plains, which were inhabited by the saber-toothed cat, the rhinoceros-like brontothere, and ancestors of the present-day camel and horse. Their fossilized bones make the area an enormous prehistoric graveyard. Herds of bison roam the area again. Pronghorn antelope, mule deer, prairie dogs and Rocky Mountain bighorn sheep can also be seen.

The Ben Reifel Visitor Center, with exhibits and an audiovisual program, is open all year at Cedar Pass (daily). Evening programs and activities conducted by ranger-naturalists are offered during the summer. Camping is available at Cedar Pass and Sage Creek. The White River Visitor Center, 60 miles southwest of the Ben Reifel Visitor Center, features colorful displays on the history and culture of the Oglala Sioux.
Information: Highway 44, 605-433-5361; www.nps.gov/badl; Mid-August-October: 8 a.m.-5 p.m. November-spring: 8 a.m.-4 p.m.

### ★BEST WESTERN TOWN 'N COUNTRY

*2505 Mount Rushmore Road, Rapid City, 605-343-5383, 877-666-5383;*
*www.bestwestern.com*
99 rooms. Complimentary continental breakfast. High-speed Internet access. Outdoor pool, whirlpool. Airport transportation available. Business center. $

### ★DAYS INN

*1570 Rapp St., Rapid City, 605-348-8410, 800-329-7466; www.daysinn.com*
77 rooms. Complimentary continental breakfast. Fitness room. Indoor pool, whirlpool. Airport transportation available. $

### ★★HOLIDAY INN

*505 N. Fifth St., Rapid City, 605-348-4000, 800-465-4329; www.holidayinn.com*
205 rooms. Pets accepted; fee. High-speed Internet access. Restaurant, bar. Fitness room. Indoor pool, whirlpool. Airport transportation available. Business center. $

### ★★RAMADA INN

*1721 N. Lacrosse St., Rapid City, 605-342-1300; www.grandgatewayhotel.com*
139 rooms. Pets accepted; fee. Restaurant, bar. Fitness room. Indoor pool, whirlpool. Airport transportation available. Business center. $

## SPECIALTY LODGING

### ABEND HAUS COTTAGES & AUDRIE'S BED AND BREAKFAST

*23029 Thunderhead Falls Road, Rapid City, 605-342-7788; www.audriesbb.com*
10 rooms. No children allowed. Complimentary full breakfast. $

## RESTAURANTS

### ★FIREHOUSE BREWING CO.

*610 Main St., Rapid City, 605-348-1915; www.firehousebrewing.com*

American menu. Lunch, dinner. Bar. Children's menu. Casual attire. Outdoor seating. **$$**

### ★FLYING T. CHUCKWAGON SUPPER & SHOW

*8971 S. Highway 16, Rapid City, 605-342-1905; www.flyingt.com*

American menu. Dinner. Closed mid-September-late May. **$**

### ★★GREAT WALL

*315 E. North St., Rapid City, 605-348-1060; www.greatwalltogo.com*

Chinese menu. Lunch, dinner. Children's menu. Casual attire. **$$**

### ★★IMPERIAL

*702 E. North St., Rapid City, 605-394-8888*

Chinese menu. Lunch, dinner. Children's menu. Casual attire. **$$**

# SIOUX FALLS

At the falls of the Sioux River, this city has developed at a constant pace since it was reestablished in 1865 (after being abandoned in 1862 following threats of a Lakota attack). Cattle are shipped from a three-state area, slaughtered and packed here, then shipped east. Manufactured goods from the East are distributed throughout much of South Dakota from Sioux Falls.

Sioux Falls is the center for EROS (Earth Resources Observation Systems), an international center for space and aircraft photography of the Earth.

*Information: Chamber of Commerce and Convention and Visitors Bureau,*

*200 N. Phillips Ave., 605-336-1620, 800-333-2072; www.siouxfallscvb.com*

## WHAT TO SEE AND DO

### GREAT PLAINS ZOO

*805 S. Kiwanis Ave., Sioux Falls, 605-367-7003; www.gpzoo.org*

The centerpiece of Sherman Park, the Great Plains Zoo focuses on animals native to places outside of South Dakota: black rhinos, red pandas and Galapagos tortoises are among the 400 residents (representing 100 species in all). The zoo replicates a variety of ecosystems, including the Australian Outback and the banks of the Nile River, to give visitors a better understanding of how the animals live in the wild. A seasonal train takes riders on a behind-the-scenes look at the African Savannah exhibit, and summertime shows give kids a closer look at some of the animals. Daily; hours vary by season.

### OLD COURTHOUSE MUSEUM

*200 W. Sixth St., Sioux Falls, 605-367-4210; www.siouxlandmuseums.com*

Restored Richardsonian-Romanesque quartzite stone courthouse from 1890 contains exhibits of Siouxland history, special exhibits on local culture. Daily.

### PETTIGREW HOME AND MUSEUM

*131 N. Duluth Ave., Sioux Falls, 605-367-7097; www.siouxlandmuseums.com*

This restored Queen Anne house from 1889 is furnished to show the life of state's first senator. The house features galleries of Native American items and the cultural history of the Sioux. Daily.

★
★★
★★★
★★★★

## USS *SOUTH DAKOTA* BATTLESHIP MEMORIAL

*100, E. Sixth St., Sioux Falls, 605-367-7060; www.siouxfalls.org*

The *USS South Dakota* was the first ship to fire on Japanese enemies in World War II and played a role in every major Pacific battle between 1942 and 1945. Located in Sherman Park, the memorial pays honor to the crew that served on the *South Dakota* and has the same dimensions as the ship, which was sold by the Navy in 1962, and features many items that were once onboard. A small museum is also onsite. Daily Memorial Day-Labor Day.

# HOTELS

### ★AMERICINN

*3508 S. Gateway Blvd., Sioux Falls, 605-361-3538, 800-634-3444; www.americinn.com*

65 rooms. Complimentary continental breakfast. High-speed Internet access. Indoor pool, whirlpool. **$**

### ★BAYMONT INN

*3200 S. Meadow Ave., Sioux Falls, 605-362-0835, 877-229-6668; www.baymontinns.com*

78 rooms. Pets accepted, fee. Complimentary continental breakfast. Wireless Internet access. Indoor pool, whirlpool. Business center. Fitness center. **$**

### ★★BEST WESTERN RAMKOTA HOTEL

*3200 W. Maple St., Sioux Falls, 605-336-0650, 800-780-7234; www.ramkota.com*

226 rooms. Pets accepted, some restrictions. Restaurant, bar. Indoor, outdoor pool, whirlpool. Water park. Airport transportation available. **$**

### ★COMFORT INN

*3216 S. Carolyn Ave., Sioux Falls, 605-361-2822, 800-252-7466; www.comfortinn.com*

65 rooms. Pets accepted; fee. Complimentary continental breakfast. High-speed Internet access. Indoor pool, whirlpool.

### ★COMFORT SUITES

*3208 Carolyn Ave., Sioux Falls, 605-362-9711, 800-424-6423; www.comfortsuites.com*

60 rooms. Pets accepted; fee. Complimentary continental breakfast. Wireless Internet access. Indoor pool, whirlpool, Business center. Fitness center. **$**

### ★DAYS INN

*3401 Gateway Blvd., Sioux Falls, 605-361-9240; www.daysinn.com*

80 rooms. Pets accepted. Complimentary continental breakfast. High-speed Internet access. Fitness center. Airport transportation available. **$**

### ★★HOLIDAY INN

*100 W. Eighth St., Sioux Falls, 605-339-2000, 800-465-4329; www.holiday-inn.com*

299 rooms. Restaurant, bar. High-speed Internet access. Fitness room. Indoor pool, whirlpool. Airport transportation available. Business center. **$**

**SOUTH DAKOTA**

★
★
★
★
★

### ★KELLY INN - SIOUX FALLS

*3101 W. Russell, Sioux Falls, 605-338-6242, 800-635-3559;*
*www.kellyinnsiouxfalls.com*

43 rooms. Pets accepted. Complimentary continental breakfast. Wireless Internet access. Pool. Whirlpool. Airport transportation available. **$**

### ★★RAMADA INN AND SUITES AIRPORT

*1301 W. Russell St., Sioux Falls, 605-336-1020, 866-336-1020; www.ramada.com*

153 rooms. Pets accepted, some restrictions; fee. Restaurant, bar. High-speed Internet access. Fitness room. Indoor pool, whirlpool. Airport transportation available. Business center. **$**

### ★★★SHERATON SIOUX FALLS AND CONVENTION CENTER

*1211 N. West Ave., Sioux Falls, 605-331-0100, 800-325-3535;*
*www.starwoodhotels.com*

The Sioux Falls Convention Center is attached to this hotel by an indoor walkway, while the hotel itself offers 97,400 square feet of meeting space. Rooms cater to the business travelers with amenities such as oversized desks, data ports and voicemail, as well as plasma TVs and plush beds. The hotel has an indoor heated pool, whirlpool, sauna, fitness room and sun deck. The Falling Waters Grille offers a menu of traditional American fare for breakfast, lunch and dinner, while the Waters Edge Lounge is a popular stop for cocktails. 184 rooms. Pets accepted, some restrictions. Restaurant, bar. Wireless Internet access. Fitness room. Indoor pool, whirlpool. Airport transportation available. Business center. **$**

### RESTAURANT

### ★★★C.J. CALLAWAY'S

*500 E. 69th St., Sioux Falls, 605-334-8888; www.cjcallaways.com*

Overlooking Prairie Green Golf Course, this handsome, country-club-style restaurant offers creatively prepared regional fare. American menu. Dinner. Closed Sunday. Bar. Children's menu. Casual attire. Reservations recommended. Outdoor seating. **$$**

# SPEARFISH

The fertile valley in which Spearfish lies is at the mouth of Spearfish Canyon, famous for its scenery and fishing. A Ranger District office of the Black Hills National Forest is located here.

*Information: Chamber of Commerce, 106 W. Kansas, 605-642-2626, 800-626-8013;*
*www.spearfish.sd.us*

## WHAT TO SEE AND DO

### HIGH PLAINS WESTERN HERITAGE CENTER

*825 Heritage Drive, Spearfish, 605-642-9378; www.westernheritagecenter.com*

Covering pioneer life in the Dakotas, Montana, Wyoming and Nebraska, this history museum includes artwork, artifacts and snazzy custom saddles and Western furnishings. Among the exhibits is the original stagecoach that ran the Deadwood-to-Spearfish route and displays that cover mining, forestry and rodeo. Outside, there is a furnished log cabin, a one-room schoolhouse, a seasonal farm with small animals and pastures populated by bison and longhorn cattle year-round. Daily 9 a.m.-5 p.m.

## HOTELS
### ★BEST WESTERN BLACK HILLS LODGE
*540 E. Jackson Blvd., Spearfish, 605-642-7795, 800-780-7234;*
*www.bestwestern.com*
50 rooms. Pets accepted; fee. Complimentary continental breakfast. High-speed Internet access. Outdoor pool, two whirlpools. **$**

### ★FAIRFIELD INN
*2720 E. First Ave., Spearfish, 605-642-3500, 800-450-4442;*
*www.fairfieldinn.com*
57 rooms. Complimentary continental breakfast. Restaurants. High-speed Internet access. Indoor pool, whirlpool. **$**

### ★★HOLIDAY INN
*305 N. 27th St., Spearfish, 605-642-4683, 800-999-3541;*
*www.holidayinn.com*
145 rooms. Pets accepted; fee. Restaurant, bar. High-speed Internet access. Fitness room. Indoor pool, whirlpool. Airport transportation available. **$**

### ★★SPEARFISH CANYON RESORT
*10619 Roughlock Falls Road, Spearfish, 605-584-3435, 877-975-6343;*
*www.spfcanyon.com*
54 rooms. Pets accepted; fee. Bar. Whirlpool. **$**

# STURGIS

Originally a "bullwhackers" (wagon drivers) stop on the way to Fort Meade, this was once known as "Scooptown" because soldiers who came in were "scooped" (cleaned out) by characters such as Poker Alice, a famed cigar-smoking scoop expert. Now Sturgis is a busy Black Hills trade center.
*Information: Chamber of Commerce, 2040 Junction Ave., 605-347-2556;*
*www.sturgis-sd.org*

## WHAT TO SEE AND DO
### BEAR BUTTE STATE PARK
*North Highway 79, Sturgis, 605-347-5240;*
*www.state.sd.us-gfp-sdparks-bearbutt-bearbutt.htm*
Called Mato Paha (or Bear Mountain) by the Lakota people, the defining feature at this park is not actually a flat-topped butte, but a singular mountain (4,422 feet above sea level) rising from the plains. For generations, the mountain has been a spiritually significant site for the Lakota and Cheyenne people, and thousands of worshippers continue to visit the ceremonial area at its base every year. The 1.7-mile Summit Trail takes hikers on a steep path (gaining 1,253 feet) to the peak, where four states can be seen. The park also serves as the northern trailhead for the 111-mile Centennial Trail into the Black Hills. Bison roam free within the park's boundaries. The visitor center features displays on the area's ecology and history and there is a small campground and a lake with a boat ramp in the park. Visitor center, May-early September, daily 8 a.m.-6 p.m. Park, daily 8 a.m.-7 p.m.

SOUTH DAKOTA

★
★
★
★
★

## SPECIAL EVENT
### STURGIS RALLY
*Sturgis, 605-642-8166; www.sturgis-rally.com*

The biggest motorcycle rally in the country isn't just for bikers anymore—it attracts lawyers, doctors and virtually everybody else who's ever revved a bike. The inaugural rally was held by the local motorcycle club, the Jackpine Gypsies, in 1938, and was quite modest: nine racers riding in front of a small audience. The annual August event has since snowballed into an extravaganza that draws in a crowd of more than 450,000. (More than 100 marriage licenses have been issued to attending couples in recent years.) During the rally, five blocks of Sturgis' historic Main Street are open to motorcycle traffic only, creating a wild atmosphere of wall-to-wall bikes and people. The schedule includes motorcycle races and tours, and there are hundreds of vendors selling everything from leather of all descriptions to exotic foods. Hotels, campgrounds and restaurants in Sturgis book up months before the bikes roar into town. Mid-August.

## HOTEL
### ★DAYS INN
*2630 Lazelle St., Sturgis, 605-347-3027, 800-329-7466; www.daysinn.com*

53 rooms. Pets accepted, some restrictions; fee. Complimentary continental breakfast. Whirlpool. $

# VERMILLION

Vermillion, the seat of Clay County, was located below the bluffs of the Missouri River until the flood of 1881 changed the river's course, forcing residents to higher ground. Located in a portion of the state that was claimed twice by France and once by Spain before being sold to the United States, Vermillion now prides itself on its rich farmland, good industrial climate and the University of South Dakota, which is located here.

*Information: Chamber of Commerce, 906 E. Cherry St., 605-624-5571,*
*800-809-2071; www.vermillionchamber.com*

## WHAT TO SEE AND DO
### UNIVERSITY OF SOUTH DAKOTA
*414 E. Clark St., Vermillion, 605-677-5326, 877-269-6837; www.usd.edu*

On campus is the DakotaDome, a physical education, recreation and athletic facility with an air-supported roof. Art galleries and theaters are located in the Warren M. Lee Center for the Fine Arts and Coyote Student Center.

## HOTEL
### ★COMFORT INN
*701 W. Cherry St., Vermillion, 605-624-8333, 800-228-5150; www.choicehotels.com*

46 rooms. Pets accepted; fee. Complimentary continental breakfast. High-speed Internet access. Fitness room. Indoor pool, whirlpool. $

# WALL

Established as a station on the Chicago & North Western Railroad in 1907, Wall is a gateway to Badlands National Park. The town is a trading center for local farmers and ranchers and is noted for its pure water, which is brought up from wells 3,200 feet deep. A Ranger District office of the Nebraska National Forest is located here.

*Information: www.wall-badlands.com*

## WHAT TO SEE AND DO
### WALL DRUG STORE
*510 Main St., Wall, 605-279-2175; www.walldrug.com*

Ted and Dorothy Hustead bought the Wall Drug pharmacy in 1931 during the Great Depression. Business was lukewarm for five years until Ted put up signs around town advertising free ice water. It worked and business boomed. Now in the hands of a third Hustead generation, Wall Drug is a sprawling tourist outpost that attracts nearly 20,000 visitors on hot summer days, pouring some 5,000 glasses of ice cold water in the process. The signs remain integral and thousands are in existence along I-90, in European cities like Amsterdam and London, and even in local homes. All this advertising has helped the Husteads build an empire that includes not just a drugstore, but also a shopping mall and a 500-seat restaurant. Studies have shown that about three-quarters of I-90s traffic exits at Wall. Daily 6:30 a.m.-6 p.m.

## HOTEL
### ★DAYS INN
*210 10th Ave., Wall, 605-279-2000, 800-329-7466; www.daysinn.com*

32 rooms. Pets accepted, some restrictions; fee. Complimentary continental breakfast. High-speed Internet access. Fitness center. Whirlpool. **$**

## RESTAURANT
### ★WALL DRUG
*510 Main St., Wall, 605-279-2175; www.walldrug.com*

American menu. Breakfast, lunch, dinner. Children's menu. Casual attire. **$**

# WATERTOWN

Originally called Waterville, this settlement owed its boom to the railroads. Two large lakes, Kampeska and Pelican, are on the edges of town.

*Information: Convention & Visitors Bureau, 1200 33 St. S.E., 605-886-5814, 800-658-4505; www.watertownsd.com*

## WHAT TO SEE AND DO
### MELLETTE HOUSE
*421 Fifth Ave. N.W., Watertown, 605-886-4730; www.mellettehouse.org*

This house was built in 1883 by Arthur C. Mellette, the last territorial and the first state governor of South Dakota. Original Victorian furnishings, heirlooms, family portraits. May-September, Tuesday-Sunday afternoons.

### REDLIN ART CENTER
*1200 33rd St. S.E., Watertown, 605-882-3877; www.redlinart.com*

This center houses more than 100 of artist Terry Redlin's original oil paintings. Center also includes the only planetarium in the state, an amphitheater, gift shop and Glacial Lakes and Prairie Tourism Association. Daily; seasonal schedule.

## HOTEL

### ★★BEST WESTERN RAMKOTA HOTEL

*1901 S.W. Ninth Ave., Watertown, 605-886-8011, 800-780-7234;*
*www.watertown.ramkota.com*

101 rooms. Pets accepted, some restrictions. Restaurant, bar. High-speed Internet access. Indoor pool, whirlpool. Fitness center. Airport transportation available. **$**

## WIND CAVE NATIONAL PARK

Wind Cave, one of many caves in the ring of limestone surrounding the Black Hills, is a maze of subterranean passages known to extend more than 79 miles. It's named for the strong currents of wind that blow in and out of its entrance according to the atmospheric pressure. (When the pressure decreases, the wind blows outward; when it increases, wind blows in.) It was the rushing sound of air coming out of the entrance that led to its discovery in 1881. The cave and surrounding area became a national park in 1903.

The temperature inside Wind Cave is a constant 53 F. Various one- to two-hour guided tours (daily) and four-hour tours (June-mid-August, daily). Tours are moderately strenuous.

On the surface are prairie grasslands, forests and a wildlife preserve the home of bison, pronghorn elk, deer, prairie dogs and other animals. The Centennial Trail, a 111-mile, multiuse trail, takes visitors from one end of the Black Hills to the other. The trail begins here and ends at Bear Butte State Park. Visitor center (daily). Hours may vary throughout the year. Park (daily). 605-745-4600.

Information: Highway 385, Hot Springs, 605-745-4600; www.nps.gov/wica

★
★★★
★★
★

# INDEX

**235**

**INDEX**

★
★
★
★
★

★
★
★
★
★

**243**

**INDEX**

★
★
★
★
★

**245**

**INDEX**

★
★
★
★
★

★
★
★
★
★

nikko japanese steakhouse (Overland Park), *68*

Nodaway Valley Historical Museum (Clarinda), *23*

Nordic Fest (Decorah), *30*

Norfolk Country Inn (Norfolk), *153*

North Dakota State Capitol (Bismarck), *168*

Northwest Inn (Woodward), *215*

## O

O'Dowd's Little Dublin (Kansas City), *106*

Oglala National Grassland (Chadron), *143*

Ohana Steakhouse (West Des Moines), *36*

Okies (Muskogee), *195*

Oklahoma City Museum of Art (Oklahoma City), *198*

Oklahoma City National Memorial (Oklahoma City), *198*

Oklahoma City Philharmonic Orchestra (Oklahoma City), *200*

Oklahoma City Then and Now (Oklahoma City), *199*

Oklahoma City Zoo (Oklahoma City), *198*

Oklahoma Firefighters Museum (Oklahoma City), *199*

Oklahoma History Center (Oklahoma City), *199*

Oklahoma National Stockyards (Oklahoma City), *199*

Oklahoma Shakespearean Festival (Durant), *188*

Oklahoma State University (Stillwater), *208*

Oklahoma Territorial Museum (Guthrie), *190*

Okoboji Queen II (Arnolds Park), *48*

Okoboji Summer Theater (Okoboji), *48*

Old Brick House (Ste. Genevieve), *136*

Old Cathedral (St. Louis), *123*

Old Courthouse (St. Louis), *122*

Old Courthouse Museum (Sioux Falls), *229*

Old Cowtown Museum (Wichita), *74*

Old Creamery Theatre Company (Amana), *13*

Old Jail Museum (Iola), *61*

Old Market (Omaha), *159*

Old Post Chapel (Lawton), *192*

Old St. Vincent's Church (Cape Girardeau), *84*

Old Style Saloon #10 (Deadwood), *220*

Old Town Museum (Elk City), *188*

Old West Lawrence Historic District (Lawrence), *62*

Olde Broom Factory (Cedar Falls), *20*

Olive Tree (Wichita), *76*

Omaha Children's Museum (Omaha), *160*

Omaha's Old Market (Omaha), *159*

Omni Majestic Hotel (St. Louis), *127*

Ottumwa Park (Ottumwa), *49*

Overland Park Arboretum and Botanical Gardens (Overland Park), *66*

Overland Park Marriott (Overland Park), *67*

Ox Yoke Inn (Amana), *13*

Oxley Nature Center (Tulsa), *211*

## P

Palisades-Kepler State Park (Mount Vernon), *21*

Palmer House (Auburn), *140*

Panchovilla (Branson), *83*

Paramount Theatre (Cedar Rapids), *21*

Parker Carousel (Leavenworth), *63*

Parkway Hotel (St. Louis), *127*

Patee House Museum (St. Joseph), *118*

Paul Manno's (Chesterfield), *86*

Paulo & Bill (Shawnee), *70*

Pawnee Park (Columbus), *141*

Peacock Alley (Bismarck), *169*

Pear Tree Inn (Cape Girardeau), *84*

Pershing State Park (Chillicothe), *86*

Pete's Place (Krebs), *192*

Pettigrew Home and Museum (Sioux Falls), *229*

Pettis County Courthouse (Sedalia), *113*

Phelps House (Burlington), *17*

Philbrook Museum of Art (Tulsa), *211*

Phoenix Piano Bar & Grill (Kansas City), *107*

★
★
★
★
★

**250**

**INDEX**

★
★
★
★
★

**INDEX**

★
★
★
★
★

# NOTES

# NOTES

★
★
★
★
★